12/90

To Mom,

Merry Christmas!

We love you -

Bev, Terry, Michael & Daniel

D1572196

ERNEST HOLMES

His Life and Times

Books by Fenwicke L. Holmes

THE LAW OF MIND IN ACTION

BEING AND BECOMING

POEMS TO LIVE BY

THE FAITH THAT HEALS

KEY TO FINANCIAL FREEDOM

CALM YOURSELF

Coauthor with Ernest S. Holmes of

THE VOICE CELESTIAL *and with Masaharu*

Taniguchi of THE SCIENCE OF FAITH

ERNEST HOLMES

HIS LIFE AND TIMES

Fenwicke L. Holmes

ILLUSTRATED WITH PHOTOGRAPHS

DODD, MEAD & COMPANY

NEW YORK

Library of Congress Catalog Card Number: 70-96765

Printed in the United States of America

ISBN: 0-396-06054-4

Acknowledgments

When my brother, Ernest Holmes, became finally convinced that the writing of his biography in the not too distant future was inevitable, he commissioned me to write it. Wishing, as he said, to be presented exactly as he was—neither "deified" nor "vilified"—he assisted me personally with letters, direct conversations, and taped interviews before his death.

Despite this assistance and my intimate knowledge of the years in which we lived and worked together, an additional six years were spent in the research and study of his life and writings. I traveled to Hawaii to see my last living brother, Jerome, a retired clergyman and professor, to stimulate further memories of our boyhood. From our late brother William's family I secured the loan of an extremely helpful record he had made of our ancestry. I obtained personal interviews with Ernest's friends, old and new, as well as the invaluable cooperation of his fellow workers.

To all of them I tender my thanks for their assistance in making this book exactly what my brother wished it to be—an honest, authentic record of his life and spiritual unfoldment.

I regret that time, space, and the nature of this record preclude detailed individual mention of the wonderful work done by each and every one of Ernest's associates over the long years. Their contributions were of inestimable value, and I feel sure they will be detailed at a later date in a history of the Religious Science movement as a whole. But they are legion and, while Ernest Holmes himself would have wished each mentioned by name, with his love and gratitude, I have had to make the painful decision to stay with the central theme of my brother's personal growth and development in order, hopefully, to lead the reader without sidetrack or by-paths, down the clear road which Ernest himself traveled—a highway, in fact, which can bring each of us to fulfillment, creativity, joy, peace, and eternal life.

Special mention is due to Elaine St. Johns, the noted writer, for the contribution of taped interviews she had with Ernest in 1958, her recollections of his family life, and her rearrangement of some of my flowers of speech. She demonstrated the brilliance of brevity by eliminating one-third of my original manuscript. Let us all give thanks.

This is my own personal story of my brother as I saw it happen.

I have attempted to be completely objective but my intimate involvement in so much of my brother's life has made this most difficult and despite constant effort, most likely improbable. For this reason, this biography is not intended, nor represented to be an official chronicle of the United Church of Religious Science which is the culmination of his life work.

My special appreciation to the Board of Trustees for its faith in underwriting, to a great extent, my efforts in this project and to the Church staff for making available the historical files, records and library for my research, for their wise counsel and the endless hours devoted to answering my myriad questions, and for guiding my search through the source material.

—FENWICKE L. HOLMES

Contents

I

Ernest Is Born

A NEW AGE must wait upon some one to proclaim it, and no matter how great his future destiny and dignity, he must first be born as a baby. None of these thoughts were in the mind of the neighbor who had been routed out of bed at three o'clock to traverse the fields of snow and help bring a child into the world. I was four years older than he, and two brothers had already intervened—Guy, who was three, and Jerome, who was two. And there were four brothers older than I (another brother, Harry, had died).

My earliest recollection of Ernest is when I saw him at my mother's breast. I can still see my blue-eyed mother with her reddish-blond hair pinned in braids about her head. She had a whimsical way of smiling, which my brother Ernest inherited, and she wore that smile now as she looked at her son. Father seemed to be under some cloud and busied himself with putting another block of beechwood into the small iron stove in the corner of the bedroom. The temperature was at zero outside on that morning of the twenty-first day of January, 1887.

We boys had been sleeping in the low attic above the kitchen, where we were comfortable with the warmth from

3

the chimney and the feather beds atop the straw ticks that covered the ropes strung crosswise in the wooden frames.

We had worn our underwear to bed, but the floor was strewn with outer garments and shoes or moccasins kicked off from the feet of my oldest brother Walter, who was eleven, Luther, who was past nine, William, who was eight, and Charles, who was just past six.

We took a look at our new brother, but we were unimpressed and had only a vague wonder as to where he came from; neither Father nor Mother imagined that he would be any different from the rest of us, any more than we thought of ourselves as different from the neighbor farmer boys.

When we were old enough, we all had to pick up rocks in the fields, pick blackberries in the back pasture and strawberries among the daisies and buttercups. It was the hard, commonplace life of a Maine farm on the border of the Habitant country, where the Canucks, the Penobscot Indians and the semipioneer people of the region still raised large families so that they might fight nature in packs, survive the rigorous winters and harvest the rugged fields, always contending with the glacial stones that sprang out of the soil in spring faster than the sprouting of the seed.

This was the world into which my brother was born. They called him Ernest Shurtleff, taking the name from a popular young preacher who had a poetic temperament and later wrote the hymn, "Lead On, O King Eternal."

We made no protest when the midwife herded us and Father back into the kitchen, for we had heard the delightful ringing of sleigh bells. We ran to the window and each of us melted his own peekhole in the frosted pane to see who was going by. It was "Uncle Lon," and he was bound for Lincoln Village three miles away to sell eggs and butter.

My older brothers and I then began our favorite pastime of "looking at the pictures on the glass." They were there all right, etched in frost but clear and almost three-dimensional, the trees and ferns, the fox and bear, the moose and horse, men and women. Sometimes we breathed on the spot that we had cleared on the pane and so created some animals "all by ourselves."

In a few years Ernest would join us, but he would have more curiosity about the whole business. His intellectual inquiry began in infancy and it never let up. He wanted to know where our window-pane picture animals came from, was the weather hot or cold, where the animals lived and why they all turned pink and went away at sunset.

It was long, long afterward that he correlated these figures with the cosmic patterns of Hermes, Plotinus, and Swedenborg. Who could have believed that this curly-headed tot in the kitchen of a Maine farmhouse would someday proclaim that his breath had created infinitesimal representations of patterns held in the cosmic Mind.

Ours was a tiny farmhouse, which in after years was towed down the lane by a thrifty cousin and turned into a toolhouse and workshop. The rocky hillsides were called a farm, but Father looked upon it as a battleground, where the bushes from the back pasture made annual sorties against his ax and flame-throwing. Father was rather on the dreamy side of life, full of fun and imagination, but proud of his ability as a wrestler and able to throw any man in the neighborhood, in spite of his slight stature. His full name was William Nelson Holmes, and he had been born in Petitcodiac across the line in eastern Canada. His father traced his ancestry directly back to an English aristocrat, Sir William Ketchum, and we possessed a coat of arms of which we were half proud and wholly ashamed.

The Holmes family had migrated to America among the early colonists and settled first in Connecticut, where a town eventually grew up around them, which still bears the name Holmes and from which sprang some of the most noted names in American literature and jurisprudence. Some of the family later migrated to Massachusetts, Maine, New Brunswick, Iowa and Illinois. Grandfather Daniel Holmes married a Hoyt, and her mother was a Holstead, both of them important families in that part of the country. They had twelve children, of whom Father, born in 1846, was the seventh. And they lived well on the income of farming and a grist mill.

Father was the most scholarly among them, and it was planned that he have a complete education in some profession; but he ran away from home at the age of fourteen, and they did not know his whereabouts for many years. I never saw Grandmother Holmes, but I am told that she often stood at the garden gate waiting and grieving for him.

At the age of seventeen Father, under an assumed name, drifted into "The Neighborhood," a rural section of Lincoln, Maine. His was a lithe, eager and charming personality, and it soon dispelled the aloofness of the neighbors. For a while he worked on the farms and was able to save enough money to buy a hillside with a rundown house and two very good barns directly across the road from the Winborn Pinkham farm, where our mother, when a girl, had come to live with her mother and stepfather.

Father was a hard and intelligent worker without fear of innovation, and for several years he prospered. He originated a system of watering and feeding hens by means of chutes. By this method he was able to leave them all winter in the barn and come back in the spring to gather a washboiler full of eggs. The next year he planted yellow-eyed beans, sold the beans to the lumbermen and fed the pods to the pigs.

Meanwhile he had met mother, Anna Columbia Heath, and had fallen in love with her. In the history of faiths, Mother's name will someday be written beside those other mothers, Santa Monica and Susannah Wesley. Her faith in the immediate presence of God, her intellect, her originality and her administrative capacity were respected and admired among not only the common people of our boyhood but also the learned and prominent, and in social-service circles in the last third of the century of her life; for she lived almost one hundred years, and her activity was prodigious. It is impossible to unwind the thread that bound her closely to Ernest's life, and because he was so directly a child of her spirit it is necessary to give a brief story of her early life.

Mother's forebears were Scotch and English people who came into New England in the early seventeenth century. There is undoubted evidence that the Heath who came over on the *Mayflower* was one of her ancestors, but whether this is so or not, they came at an early date into the forbidding fastnesses of Sumner, Maine, where they became successful farmers. In the early nineteenth century James Heath, Sr. built a grist mill in the village of Oxford to grind his large crops of wheat and corn, and eventually it serviced the community. One of his sons inherited his name, and at the age of sixteen was sent to Bridgeton Academy, from which he was graduated four years later. He was typically Scotch in appearance, tall, ruggedly built, red-headed with pink-and-white complexion, and was said to be very handsome. Also, having inherited half his father's considerable fortune together with the mill, he was thought to be a "good catch" in the stream of matrimony. His courtship with Jeanette Ryerson was a nip-and-tuck affair, but he finally won the sprightly black-eyed miss with the sparkle in her eye, a sparkle that lasted for more than eighty years.

It dimmed for a time after the wedding, for Grandfather Heath became infected with the gold fever, and, having converted most of his holdings into ready cash, he set sail from Boston to the land of daydreams. He never arrived. No one knew what happened to him, but it was thought that someone on board ship had found out how much money he carried and had done away with him.

It was under these circumstances that Grandmother Heath gave birth on the first day of January, 1850, to a girl, whom they named Anna Columbia. Anna used to say of herself that she was not a pretty child, having a too-large nose, a too-big mouth, too-prominent cheekbones, with red-blond hair and blue eyes.

When Mother was six, she accompanied her Uncle Jacob (her father's brother) back to Lincoln, Maine, while her mother, the widowed Jeanette, stayed behind to run the mill. Those were the real horse-and-buggy days, and even with a pair of spanking bays it took nine days to cover the 365 miles.

As the weary journey came almost to an end they drove through the village itself. There were stores on each side of the unpaved street, each of them built on its own foundation level without regard to the others. Some of the porches were connected with each other by wooden walks, others by only a dirt path. The pedestrian had to step up or step down for the whole length of the street, and often into the mud. It remained unchanged throughout our boyhood. Both Ernest and I worked from time to time in one of these buildings, a hardware store owned by my brother Walter. Some of the money that financed Ernest's short adventure into the field of formal education in 1907 came from this very store.

The township of Lincoln was still pioneer, and farms were being cut out of the native forests, but there was a well-developed section called "The Neighborhood," about two and a half miles distant on the south side of town. It was here that various relatives had settled on the adjoining farms. En route they passed a great glacial deposit of shifting sand, to which Uncle Jacob referred by the Scottish name of *kame*. Here Anna's children would someday play "seashore" and watch for Viking ships and sometimes sail so far from the shores of reality as to miss the angry bell of the teacher in the little old red schoolhouse that stood nearby.

Uncle Jacob, who had been nearly voiceless during the journey, seemed suddenly to come to life. His tone was almost joyous as he pointed along the road.

"There up on the hill," he told little Anna, "home at last." And so they came to it, a great white house at the under side of the road in the midst of huge maples, and a sheep-cut lawn on which stood a watering trough gouged out of a solid log, with a long-handled pump beside it from which was drawn icy water even in the heat of summer.

Little Anna was welcomed by her relatives and began the

life of skill and industry that characterized her for almost a century. It was a matter of Scottish religion with the family that "Satan finds some mischief still for idle hands to do" and they forfended him by endless productive activity.

One task ran into another from early morning to bedtime. Little Anna became a helper to Sue in preparing vegetables, peeling apples, cooking and baking, washing dishes, sweeping and dusting, and seasonally in making cheeses and dipping candles. And always in the background there was knitting waiting to be done and the sewing of long strings of rags to be wound into a ball, ready for the loom that stood in the corner for winter weaving into rugs for the floor. Even at the age of six she was given her "stint" of one inch of knitting on mittens or stockings each morning, and another in the afternoon.

This is a part of the Ernest-story, for the home of his childhood was almost a duplicate of this, except that Mother added other activities to those already described.

When she was eleven her mother, Jeanette of the sparkling eyes, whom little Anna had not seen for almost six years, came to visit, and a great affection developed between mother and daughter. Jeanette sold the mill, moved to Lincoln and two years later married a young farmer named Winborn Pinkham, whose property was next to Heath's, on the south. Two children were born to them, Fred and Henry, who were part of Ernest's later life story. Anna, at the age of thirteen, went to live with her mother and helped take care of the two boys. After a year or two Anna came to the decision that life must have a greater purpose than this.

Accordingly, she determined to get an education at Mattanawcook Academy, a state-endowed institution in the village. Her mother was sympathetic, and young Anna was enrolled as a student in 1866 or 1867 and studied for six years or sallied forth into various neighborhoods as a teacher. It was here that she developed the art of speech and diction, learned the three R's and became the best speller in that part of Maine.

The years that followed were leading her by blind paths to a future that lay far beyond the horizon of imagination, through the meadows of education, up the steep inclines of married life, out across the western plains to California where she was to play an important part in Ernest's mature life. The earliest picture I have of her shows the upward tilt of her head, her broad brow, her strong nose and firm mouth, with a manner that was at once composed and forceful.

At night when her reddish-blond hair was unbound it reached clear to the floor. By day she braided it and wound it close about her head. She was of small stature, had strong muscles, and bore such a manner of confidence and firmness that no boy in her schools was unruly or bold with her more than once. He would suddenly find himself attacked from the rear, pulled to the floor and looking foolish to his school-mates. She imparted her love of learning not only to her pupils but to all whom she met. Her passion for mathematics was almost a love affair.

Her superintendent of schools was "Old Aaron Huntress" who would sometimes descend on the schoolroom like a bald eagle with a sprig of tobacco leaf in his mouth and harangue the children.

"I don't want you children to grow up with bad habits, no sir-ree." He would punctuate this with a streak of tobacco juice; it was a disgusting experience for Anna, who had been reared in an environment of cleanliness, but she said nothing at the time. Afterward, when his visit had been forgotten, she would assign studies in McGuffey's *Reader* or read aloud from Jeem's *Life of Washington* to emphasize the importance of good habits and religion.

This, then, was the young lady whom William Nelson Holmes met and immediately engaged in long conversations on farming. William was daring, experimental and had had good success with crop rotation, although he had no scientific knowledge of the chemistry of soils. She favored repeating crops yearly in fields where they had proved successful; how-ever, there was no heated difference between them. This held true throughout their long married life, partly, no doubt, owing to his adoration of her, which never failed in their sixty years together.

There was one difference, however, that stood between young William and Anna before any wedding day—the question of the assumed name. Anna disapproved and suggested that William write to his parents and use his legal name. He was satisfied with his present name, he told her, and she gently intimated that he keep it for himself, as she had no wish to share it. He was hurt, left The Neighborhood and went to the northern part of Pennsylvania, where he lived for some time with a married sister among the Dutch settlers and learned to speak, read and write their language.

He was an intellectual and easily mastered French, studying it by himself. Also, he acquired a knowledge of Latin and Greek roots so that he "wouldn't wear out the dictionary."

But back he came to The Neighborhood in Lincoln and to Anna, whose face he had carried in his mind like a treasured daguerreotype. He wrote his mother and father in Petitcodiac and told them his whereabouts and that he was hoping to visit home and bring a beautiful bride with him. Anna, really in love with him, was pleased with the influence she had exerted. They were married under his rightful name in November of 1875, twelve years before Ernest came into the world.

They journeyed to Canada to live with the Holmes clan, where it irked Anna to hear her husband, who was then twenty-eight years of age, called "Willie" by his family. A year later she knew a baby was coming and she wished to return to The Neighborhood. It was there that my oldest brother Walter was born. And it was there that my youngest brother, Ernest, was born—and with him the potential for the birth of an idea.

II

❧

The Holmes Family on the Move

LIFE IN LINCOLN, Maine, in the late 1880's was still a semi-pioneer existence, almost incredible to Anna's and William's great grandchildren of today; but it was very real to us, and it was a life of love and devotion as well. It is important to remember that Ernest Holmes, whose genius for living has inspired so many, was deeply rooted in the Maine soil, a product of the quiet, the grandeur, the challenge of The Neighborhood and our own fireside.

All nine of Anna's sons were born in the same diminutive house with the peaked roof and the long narrow ell. The building stood beside a small orchard of young apple trees; and north, by a hundred feet, there was a big weathered barn to store the hay cut from the small field. A lane bordered by stone walls ran to the dirt highway, below which was the Charles Pinkham farm.

Farther off, across the forest and lakes of the wilderness lying between us we could see Mount Katahdin, the highest peak in the state, snow-capped and looking frostily down upon the domain, where in later days summer visitors would come to build their cabins, fish the lakes for pickerel, perch and black bass or search out the elusive trout lurking in the still pools of mountain streams. Often Mount Katahdin stood

in sunlight as though aloof from it all. Sometimes when it
was raining Grandfather Pinkham would say, "I wisht I had
built my house over there—sunshine! Gaddum it!" Then he
would turn his grizzled head to make sure Mother hadn't
heard the forbidden words.

Our kitchen had the clean, inviting odor of burning birch
and maple, with the iron kettle puffing contentedly most of
the time or rattling its lid when the fire got hot beneath it,
the steam moistening the air and giving substance to the
frosted pictures of the window panes. Near the stove was a
cooking table with cupboards above it. But the sink, where
the spring water ran in through a leaden pipe, was in an al-
cove, and we could look out the window in winter and see
the great cake of ice where the water poured from the drain
and watch it steam and freeze again.

There were home-woven "hit-and-miss" rag rugs on the
kitchen floor, and the living room was entirely carpeted with
the same material, with a deep piling of oat straw that kept
out the winter chill. We children were allowed to sit on the
floor to play games, our toys being some rag dolls or hand-
carved wooden figures in imitation of horse-drawn sleds, domestic fowls and animals.

The older boys spent much time in the yard and barn,
feeding the chickens and livestock, bringing in the wood
from the great pile and arranging it in tiers along the shed
wall between the kitchen door and the cold and dreary closet
fifty feet down the line, like a terminal railroad station. Walter, Luther and William would stagger into the kitchen with
great armfuls and then sit down and reread any printed matter in the house.

At odd times in the evening the older boys got out the
homemade combs and carded the wool that Father had cut
from the sheep in the spring and Mother had washed in the
yellow soap she made with lye from ashes combined with
animal fat. Later in the night Mother would spin the wool
into yarn; she used the three-legged spinning wheel that always stood ready in one corner of the living room beside the

crude homemade loom. She never attempted to weave cloth, but in spare moments she worked at weaving rag rugs. Aunt Mary Buck used to help out on the rugs on the loom in her own home, but we boys had to tear up the cloth she brought us into narrow strips, sew the ends together and wind them on a ball ready for weaving.

After supper, while we were doing the dishes, Mother would sit before the open fire of the Franklin stove in a chair that had been made by cutting away half of the upper part of a barrel and stuffing the lower half with straw, covered by a cushion. She loved her barrel chair. It was there she would sit to nurse, dress and undress each one of her infants until he was a year old, after which the older boys had to do the work. She would place the infant in the heavy pineboard rocker, painted by the patina of time and sweaty little hands. If an older boy was sick, a rare occurrence, Mother would pull out the trundle bed and keep him beside her for the night. Otherwise he had to join the rest of us in the shivery room over the kitchen. Father went to bed when we did, but after we younger ones had climbed to our attic chamber, Mother simply resumed her activities—in some of which the older boys often shared—carding wool, spinning, winding yarn, sewing, making rugs, setting the house in order—ready to start before daybreak the next morning! And knitting, always knitting whenever her hands were free from other duties, never looking at her work except to "drop a heel" or "set a thumb"!

There were times, I know, when her thoughts were drawn away from us to the bigger world of which she had read and dreamed, for her mind was far wider than her environment. Then she would go to an unlighted room and look out at the stars. She knew many of them by name and they talked with her. "Your time will come, Anna. We have not forgotten you." She would turn her eyes away and gaze down the lane or across snowy fields to see the lights at the Pinkhams' or the Bucks'.

We knew nothing of her dreams then, but Willie or I

would often creep after her and ask, "What you lookin' at, Mother?"

"A dream was blowing across the moon."

"Where, where?" and we would stare out excitedly.

"It is gone by," she would say sadly.

We could see nothing but stars or the light from Aunt Ca'line Pinkham's house at the end of the lane.

It was down that lane we used to gallop on sunny summer mornings and race across the highway to the Pinkhams' farmhouse, there to smell Aunt Ca'line's kitchen. She smoked a clay pipe and the walls were saturated with the delightfully foul odor. Or we went into the spotlessly clean shed to watch the sparkling spring water bubble out of a lead pipe into a huge half-barrel. We were big-eyed with pride to learn that the spring was located on our own farm.

When there was nothing to eat at Aunt Ca'line's we knew the strawberry patches behind her house. Sometimes we ran below into the meadow. How sweet and clear was the water in the meandering brook with its banks covered with starflowers, daisies and buttercups! I can still see Ernest on his knees among them with his head tilted up from time to time, his mouth smeared with the red of the wild strawberries. Here we used to build a little dam, float our tiny birchbark canoes and play Indian. In our unclouded joy we could not have dreamed that we would live into an age where oceans would replace brooks, commandos would substitute for Indians, and a single blast would kill more people in a minute than had died in all the Indian Wars of America. How could we know? Nor could we know that this little boy Ernest, squatting here on his sturdy legs, would become a great figure in this new age and bring comfort to millions of people all over the world.

Just "down the road-a-piece" was the little red schoolhouse where every one of us, with the exception of Ernest, got his first start in formal education; and even Ernest tagged along, although there were no classes for him. He was the most inquisitive boy I ever knew and even at the age of five he was always asking "Why?" and Mother had nicknamed him "The Question Mark."

He listened in while the teacher drilled us in the three R's, spelling, American history and geography and pored over the geography book, begging us to read the poem printed above the picture of the globe; and he was soon quoting it from memory.

> O great big, beautiful, wonderful world
> With the wonderful waters around you curled,
> With the wonderful verdure upon your breast;
> World, you are beautifully dressed.

He loved poetry from the very first time he heard it. And Mother was always quoting verse to us. It was partly her own love for it and partly because it carried a moral lesson.

It remains unquestioned that she had a unique and original method of discipline. I never knew her to strike a child, and seldom punished him, because she had a better way. It might not work in this sophisticated age, but it worked with us. She had a whole repertoire of poems or stories with a meaning. Two, I remember most distinctly. One of them was the fascinating prose story of a boy by the name of Bennie Blubber, who cried every time he couldn't have what he wanted or whenever he was afraid something would happen to him. It wound up with his crying one night and his mother going into the bedroom to ask him why. "I'm crying because I don't know what I'll have to wear for pants in the morning the night after I've grown up to be a man."

Somehow it worked! The very name Bennie Blubber would snap a boy back into place like a lash. It saved time and patience when there were eight boys to be snapped!

I remember, too, the sentiment inspired by the tale of "Phoebe." How touching it was! How we grieved for Phoebe and how we admired the generous Little Miss who befriended her! Who could be greedy with his toys or jealous of his brother in face of the Little Miss?

Why, Phoebe, have you come so soon?
Where are your berries, child?
You surely didn't sell them all,
You had a basket piled.

No, Mother, as I climbed the fence
The nearest way to town,
My apron caught upon a stake
And so I tumbled down.

I scratched my arm and tore my dress
And I could not refrain
From bursting into bitter tears—
But not from bruise or pain.

And then I saw a pretty miss
Who chanced to pass me by;
She stopped and looking pitiful
She begged me not to cry.

The upshot of it was that Phoebe told the Little Miss that she couldn't go to Sunday school because she had no bonnet. Her father was poor, and there was a big family; but he had promised to buy her a gown if she picked berries enough to buy the bonnet. But now the berry season was over and she had spilled her basket. To which the Miss replied, "Here, here, take my bonnet!" But Phoebe at first refused on the ground that the girl's mother would be angry.

"My ma? No, never, she delights
All sorrow to beguile,
And 'tis the proudest joy she has
To see the wretched smile.

She taught me when I had enough
To give it to the poor
And never let a needy child
Go empty from the door. . . .

So then I took it, here it is,
For, Ma, what could I do—
And, Mother, I shall love that Miss
As long as I love you."

The whole tale oozed extravagant sentiment and the Little Miss was too heavily freighted with verbiage, but we all loved it. We enjoyed sentimentality, and almost wept. Ernest joined in even when he was too young to know exactly what it was about. But Mother knew! These lyrics gave a pure and undefiled example of generosity and goodwill that was a far better thing than "a bat on the head" when we needed discipline.

There were other stories, poems and even songs in a similar vein. Surely Ernest and I were still under this influence when, years later, we wrote so many sentiments for the greeting-card industry and several successful volumes of verse, including *The Voice Celestial*.*

Mother also had her own ideas about teaching, and she trained us in public speech when we were still in our infancy. At neighborhood gatherings in the old red schoolhouse, one or several of us could be heard declaiming, while Mother sat in the front row with her lips forming the words in case we stumbled.

It was in our own home, under Mother's guidance, that Jerome early showed the precocity that distinguished him through twenty years at school, where he was always known as "Jerry the Brain"—a title that followed him through fifty years of service as a missionary and linguist in Japan and the Hawaiian Islands. Jerome, a year older than Ernest, began reading *The Youth's Companion* at the age of three. I can see him clearly at the age of five down on his knees with the magazine spread out on a seat of a chair, reading aloud to the rest of us.

Along with learning, and equal to it, our parents believed in W-O-R-K. Father was up at three-thirty and worked a sixteen-hour day in the barn or fields. Often Mother dropped her own duties and went out to help him with planting seed, building the load when he was pitching hay, or climbing into

* Written by E. S. and F. L. Holmes, an epic poem covering the entire philosophy of the Science of Mind—325 pages; New York: Dodd, Mead and Company, 1960.

the loft to stack it. Sometimes she "spelled him" in flailing the beans on the barn floor. And then she would return to her housekeeping duties, cooking, washing, sewing and spinning. Her face was fixed and serious while preparing the children for bed or joining Father in the evening prayers, but when she was spinning, a light often glowed in her eyes. It was then I knew she was at her favorite pastime—thinking. I knew it because she once said to my brother William: "I can think clearly while doing any kind of work, but I can think even *better* when spinning. When I hear the whirring of the wheel and the buzzing of the spindle, it is music to me, and I can keep time to the rhythm as I move backward and forward. It stimulates my mind."

And Ernest, along with the rest of us, learned to help in the work. It is a New England habit that was to stand us in good stead.

The devotion of my father and mother to each other was one of the most reassuring things in our young lives. They loved each other, and I do not recall their ever having a quarrel. If they differed in opinion they talked it out by themselves.

We needed this sense of security in the rough life of a semipioneer farm. Times changed quickly on a small stone-strewed, bush-threatened Maine farm in those days, and we became the victims of Nature, which has driven so much of Maine back to the wilderness.

Our hardest times began the year that Father bought sheep in the fall and wintered them on the precious hay, for most of them failed to lamb and many of them died. In the spring the kitchen became a lamb nursery, where we tried to keep life in the frail little bodies with a baby's nursing bottle. Ernest was busy running back and forth between the house and barn across the wide yard, muddy in the spring thawing, and bringing in more mud than lamb. But his eyes sparkled with excitement. He chose one lamb for a pet and fed it tenderly, and became so attached to it that he was allowed to keep it all summer. I believe the first sorrow he ever had was when it was taken away in the fall. He knew where it was going as it was driven down the lane to the slaughter barn where his Uncle Fred conducted a thriving business, selling meat at wholesale in the village. Ernest wouldn't eat lamb for months afterward.

The following year Father bought calves to be fed and watered by Mother and us boys while he went away to work in the lumber camps. It was a cold winter; and for the only time in our remembrance the ground was frozen so deeply that the water wouldn't run through the lead pipe from the spring, and all of us had to pile out and bring in snow by the pailful and melt it on the kitchen stove. When the winter of hardship had passed, we had little to show for our efforts but a small herd of gaunt animals with long scraggly hair, who had eaten the profit out of the hayloft and sold for little.

At the end of ten years Father was through. The mortgage was foreclosed on the farm, and Father and Mother accepted fifty dollars in cash in lieu of legal costs and delays. So we went to live in an old rented house in the village and from there to first one and then another house that could be rented cheaply.

From that time, I remember, Mother was always cleaning, either to move out of one house to the next, or from one village to another. Father was working here, working there. Sometimes we followed—sometimes we stayed. But from the time we lost the farm until we settled in Bethel, Ernest never celebrated two birthdays in the same house.

We lived for a time in Transalpine, far from the old neighborhood and from the village. It was there that I broke my arm. And I shall never forget how Mother tied me to her own body to ease the jolting of the "pung" while we drove through winter drifts and across the ice of Mattanawcook Lake to the doctor who set the arm and applied the pine splints. Mother suffered with me and for me, I know, but she was a Spartan and a New Englander and never shed tears. Nor was she sentimental. She permitted one flitting kiss from

each of us when we went to bed but that was all. I think
Ernest as the youngest craved more, for in adult years he had
an unfulfilled hunger for affection that sometimes showed up
in a spontaneous embrace for all the world like a "kissing
cousin" or a Frenchman greeting a comrade. He loved everybody.

Love and "good luck" drew us back briefly into The Neighborhood again. Grandmother Pinkham had gone to the village to live, the farmhouse was vacant and the rent was free.
It was just the other side of Aunt Ca'line's place; up the road
and on the hill was the Buck farm, and between the two
houses, Uncle Lute and Aunt Gele had their small dairy and
egg farm. It was on this dairy farm that Ernest came to live
for a short period with our uncle and aunt some ten years
later.

But then one night Father came from the village; he and
Mother had a talk in the living room, and it was announced
that we were to move again.

Ernest left no time for silent astonishment.

"Where?" he asked.

Father had agreed to work in the lumber camps during the
winter, clear across the state in the great gap between Maine
and New Hampshire called Grafton Notch. And we would
join him there. We were excited, except for Mother, who
looked very sad. I could see that for once she had been crying; Walter was not to go with us. Our handsome, slender,
gentle, oldest brother Walter, sixteen now, would be sent to
the Weymouth lumber camps up on the Magalloway River
to take charge of the "wanigan" and keep books all winter
and on the drive in the spring. It was to be the first separation
of Mother's brood. He stood straight and proud, and reassured Mother with a kind of frightened tenderness.

Father left a few days later, riding with the lumberjacks on
the wagons heavily loaded with sleds and gear, stoves, kitchen
utensils and supplies. It would take two weeks to cover the
distance with the three wagons and six teams of heavy-footed
horses.

We followed afterward on the Grand Trunk Railroad. It took the better part of two days to make the trip; Mother and her seven sons jammed in between bags and bedding, baskets and packages of food, each of us hanging onto some small personal possession, and all of us grimy with the heavy coal smoke that streamed along the train like volcanic ash.

It was dusk on that October day when we finally drew into the station at Bethel, and blinked enough cinders from our eyes to climb down the steps and help load the "tote wagon," a big hayrack half filled with hay in front and loaded with camp supplies in the rear. We filled our lungs with the clean, cool air blowing down from the White Mountains, where Mount Washington, the highest peak in New England, was settling its nightcap at the close of the long day.

Our bundles and bags were soon thrown into the hayrack and we moved out over the frozen ground, bumping across the ruts cut by the day's traffic and pulled by four rough-coated horses with long streamers of frost billowing out from their panting nostrils. We stared ahead through the long, dangling legs of the driver perched on the seat above us, drew our clothing tighter at the neck or burrowed in the quilts Mother passed to us. At the end of three miles we stopped at an inn where there were beds but no food; but we soon dug out our own provisions, and Mother boiled potatoes, fried a "spider" full of salt pork and even baked some biscuits to be doused in pork gravy and molasses.

We were off again at five o'clock in the morning, often running beside the wagon to get warm, yelling back to Ernest to catch up or be left on the road. His short legs, bare below the knees, were unable to make the grade, so Luther and Charles grabbed him by the hands and swung him along at a pretty rate until they tumbled him into the wagon and shouted to Mother not to let him out again.

The springless wagon jolted the daylights out of us as we drove toward the Notch, passing small farms and lonely houses set among maple, oak and elm trees and always surrounded by stone fences like the great wall of China, hemming out the world.

We passed through a small settlement, skirted the edge of the Androscoggin River as it swept majestically away from us, and at length we were in the Notch itself, with its dark shade and frowning cliffs and Old Eyebrow staring down upon us. Wild animals sometimes sprang up and ran ahead of us, and flocks of partridges whirred away amidst the bushes. It was sublime, it was majestic, it was awful with its wild loneliness. I do not know what my mother was thinking as she sat upright robed in a particolored quilt. I wonder sometimes what was on her heart.

Was she recalling the simple sheltered days of her girlhood? Or the personal freedom of her young womanhood as schoolteacher? Was she aware of her great mental gifts, which were poured now into motherhood and consumed by its cares? Would it have raised her spirits had she been able to see into the future of the little boy who suddenly looked at her faraway eyes and flung himself into her arms in that abandonment to affection and sympathy which was native to him? I do not know.

We drove on through the primeval forests of spruce and pine, where Dan Clifford was building his lumber camps. We could see the smoke rising, no doubt from the kitchen fire where Father would even now be cooking a great meal for the lumberjacks. We came out on a large valley where Old Baldy, a huge granite mountain, stared down upon a farmhouse, abandoned and dilapidated. This was to be our home. Across the road was the ancient barn, too barren even for field mice but a playroom for us on stormy days. There was a meadow behind it and a sluggish, wandering stream, filled with brook trout that we learned to "fish out" with our homemade gear, where we could play in the lush grass during the short summer days; for the sun rose and set behind enclosing heights, and somber Old Baldy took on a short-lived halo and then returned to his silent meditations.

Mrs. Dan Clifford, who was there to receive us, took out

a large brass key and unlocked the door to the small entry-way. She pointed us to the left while she took the right side of the house. There was the typical odor of an abandoned house, as though the very memories of other days were de-caying in the dust of time.

We dropped our things in the kitchen and made haste for the woodshed, where we were happy to find three seats graded according to age. Then we built a fire for Mother. At dusk we went out to cut branches from the small fir trees that crept up to the kitchen door. These we laid on the floor in two small bedrooms, topping them with hay-stuffed mat-tresses and blankets so that we could sleep in warmth and comfort even on the coldest nights.

Our table was made of pine boards with crossed pieces of timber for legs, which were braced by narrow pieces running the full length, forming a V-shaped trough out of sight be-neath the broad oilcloth cover. We boys made use of the trough for amusement. Mrs. Clifford was a spiritualist, the first we had ever known, and often told us of seances in which she had heard strange rappings and voices. One of us would lie at full length on the trough just as the lamps were lighted in the early dusk and when Mrs. Clifford entered the room we "played ghost." Another brother would make mention of "spirits" and call upon them to "speak." The one who had been waiting patiently under the table would reply with rappings or a muffled voice. Mrs. Clifford rose to it like a pickerel being baited by salt pork. Finally Ernest put an end to our fun by lifting the edge of the oilcloth and asking, "Is that you, Fenny?"

That fall we went on with our schooling in the little red schoolhouse two miles down the road. Although I was "going on nine" I was more timid than Ernest when we came abreast of the Davis farmhouse, because there was a boy living there who was subject to fits. Ernest would watch him with grave interest, because Mrs. Clifford had said the boy was possessed by evil spirits—Ernest wanted to see if any of them came out.

When we arrived at school almost frozen that October

morning, we opened the door cautiously to spy out the ground. There was a great iron boxwood stove, and on a platform beyond was a desk with the teacher sitting behind it. At first we were reassured by his white beard streaked with yellow, until we heard his crackling voice.

"Come in, dang ya, and shet that door."

So we had to do it, creeping carefully toward the stove. Ernest was looking around curiously, but, like the rest of us, his eyes came to focus on the old man sitting there with his shrewd little eyes fixed upon this new brood who had come to double his attendance. He had long, thinning gray hair that ran down into his beard, and there were thick bristles completely circling his neck.

He made us take our seats with the four girls and three boys and ordered us to get out our books and "larn." He never *asked* us to recite but gave orders like a sergeant, which he may have been in the Civil War some thirty years before. "Get up out of the seat and read. Stand straight or I'll help ya in my feeble way; we don't want to have to use laudanum about it, either." He never laid hand, ruler, nor a strap on any of us brothers, although he nearly walloped the life out of a great hulk of a farmboy who was stupid, strong but nonresistant. We were good youngsters and learned rapidly, because there were no grades to hamper our speed. It seems strange in retrospect that we learned so much from a senile old man, whose speech was full of Yankee colloquialisms, blurred consonants and nasal vowels, but he actually knew what was in the textbooks; and we came to welcome his abrupt order, "Shet up and set daown."

Ernest had already learned to read. I suppose it would be truer to say that he could remember hearing something read and could repeat it almost verbatim, an ability that he retained through his long and learned life, not only from his own reading but from the speech of others. And so, although he was not yet six and not a regular pupil, he listened—and learned—along with the rest of us.

*   *   *

In Grafton the daylight hours are short in the fall, and dusk would be descending before we passed through the young spruce and fir trees that seemed to run down from the forest to meet us on the highway—and there was one spot of primeval trees. Ernest used to make me nervous by inquiring about "the wild man of the woods," and hoping we would run into him. There really was such a man, who was occasionally glimpsed running through the forests, but he never bothered us, except that sometimes at night we could see his face pressed against the curtainless window. The tales about him were authenticated later, for he was caught with no garment but a vest and taken to a state institution. Ernest used to jabber about him, and I suppose he wanted to know "why." He must have thought it through, for once he said, "If he lost his mind in the woods, Mother, how can he find it again if they don't let him loose?"

Mother used to say that the famous Holmes humor wasn't Holmes at all, it was Ryerson, from her side of the family. Be that as it may, Father was inventively imaginative and charmingly whimsical. Stories he told over a half-century ago to the lumberjacks in camp and on the river drives found their way out, and I have heard them from time to time. These stories were fabricated to tell to the Canucks and the other lumberjacks to while away the hours after dinner. After eating a regular diet of pork, beans sweetened with molasses and baked in the ground and topped with more molasses and vinegar, garnished with brown bread and washed down with tea or coffee, there was still a dull time until they crawled into their bunks; and during this between-period Father told wildly fantastic tales and imaginative stories, such as "The Sunk Soose," "The Ding-Maul" and "The Invisible Eye." "The Sunk Soose has feet but no body, and you can see its tracks in the snow in early morning, but you never see it—or 'them.' They are hunting for something. Who knows what? Tracks run right up to the camp door but they don't go in, unless it's a skunk; and in that case, of course, it isn't a sunk.

If you should ever so much as *think* you see a sunk, you should say your prayers and stop drinking."

Father personalized all the sounds of the forest and kept the men in such a state that some of them would not go back to their own camps alone at night. You could hear voices without mouths, see animals with only one eye. "The whole woods is full of eyes gleaming in the lantern light, but they all come in pairs. If you see only one eye, look again, that is called second sight. If it's still there, run for your life."

These men liked to whittle wooden chains for us children, and it was fun to watch them turn a square piece of birch two inches in diameter and three feet long into strong links of a chain. If they were doing it for us on a Sunday, then Father would read the Bible to them and talk a little, not piously but actually reversing their fears and telling them that even if there were bad animals and bad men, they had no need to fear anything except their own conscience. Then he would sit by the table and write out sermons for his own edification. We still have a full volume of them written in his fine hand on lined note paper and bound in brown oil-cloth cut from an old table cover.

The thing I remember best about Father, apart from the one whipping he ever gave me, was something he said in his late years. It had to do with the fact that during all the years when his children were growing up, he had found it necessary to work in other parts of the state where he could earn a better wage in order to support us and send us to school. "I got by with my loneliness by looking forward to my dreams at night. I would go to bed and dream of Mother and the family."

He was a quiet-spoken man and appeared subdued in the presence of Mother, but it was because of his great respect for her; and I think it was also a kind of atonement for the number of children she had borne him.

He had had little schooling, but, like Ernest, was a genuinely self-educated man. As I have said, he seldom read anything that was not printed in the French language, and I recall his pleasure when I brought back a lot of literature from Paris in 1930. Nothing would have pleased him more than to have read Ernest's textbook, *The Science of Mind,* translated into the French by Auguste J. Berg, former interpreter for the United Nations; but it came too late, for at the age of eighty-six he fell victim to his own exuberance. He was running uphill on Ernest's estate in Palms, and Ernest asked why.

"I wanted to test my wind," Father said. Later on he loaded a wheelbarrow with the trunk of a palm tree and pushed it up the same hill. But the strain proved too much for him. Humorous to the last, he died with the one regret that he couldn't leave a fortune to each member of the family instead of just brains. Until then the family had remained without a death for fifty-five years!

When Ernest was six we left Grafton Notch and moved to Newry Corners, into an old house set on a hillside above the country road. Father was off to a new job, and Mother worked incessantly with her cleaning, cooking, knitting, carding and spinning. Ghandi would have been proud of us, for we were a compact and self-sufficient family.

In the fall Mother sent us out to pick apples for the neighbors and ourselves, and then in the long afternoons we peeled, cored, quartered and strung them like beads on a string, so that they could be hung up to dry. In winter these dried apple pieces were soaked in water and cooked into sauce or an occasional pie. The cellar was an appetizing sight with its barrels of apples, beets, turnips and potatoes. Fresh apples kept only for a short time into the winter. We were given one apiece each day while they lasted; after that each of us was allowed half a rutabaga turnip on Sunday afternoon. The turnip was cold and firm and when cut in halves could be easily scraped with the end of a kitchen knife, making delectable juicy flakes that a boy could swish around in his mouth like candy.

Once in a great while we had a molasses candy pull. But

nothing equaled the "sugaring-off" parties in the spring. These were held in the schoolhouse, and the whole neighborhood took part. Sap from sugar-maple trees, caught in a bucket from their bleeding sides, had already been boiled down to a syrup. On the night of the party a huge flat pan was set on the long box stove and the syrup boiled to a gumlike thickness. Each of the neighbors brought his own milk-pan and filled it with snow from the yard and ladled out the syrup onto the surface. It turned into delicious mouthfuls of chewy sweetness, and we ate to our heart's desire and our stomach's discontent. Some of us ate pickles between bites to take away the sweet taste and renew our appetites.

Life was interesting enough, for we were country folk and knew how to slide on the snow, catch the brook trout, and we all enjoyed "going berrying" for blueberries, blackberries and raspberries. Even the peddling butcher provided a moment's entertainment. He drove his horse down the country road, banging a pan to attract customers. He had half a beef ready for cutting up; the liver, heart, and stomach cleaned for tripe. Good cuts of beef were worth six or eight cents a pound, but Mother bought boiling beef or a little mutton when the butcher had it. Liver and hearts were almost worthless, and the butcher usually made her a present of them "for the sake of the kids." I recall that once he gave Ernest a cow's horn that my brother used in playing Daniel Boone.

It was close to a pioneer life, but we didn't know how primitive it was, nor did we feel the biting chill of winter as we sat beside the kitchen fire in the evening, watching Mother knit or popping corn on the hot stove lid. Mother usually told us stories and sometimes discussed our school work. We never thought of taking home a school book in those days. Our active minds could read and absorb everything the books told us while we were in the schoolroom.

Ernest at six tried to take part in everything. Walter, back with us after his winter job, and Luther, both now in their teens, had nothing in common with him except for their intellectual curiosity. They borrowed a few books here and there and were inveterate bookworms without possessing that unitive or philosophic quality that develops a philosophy of life and that distinguished Ernest throughout life.

At Newry Corners, Ernest, like Mary's lamb, still followed us to school and asked questions that sometimes surprised the teacher. I think she liked him for his inquisitive face, and I remember seeing her put her arm around him at one time, but he pulled away like a weaned colt. I am not sure we were all as pleased with him; it was hard for us to live with those everlasting questions—to which we brothers did not have the answers either. But a year later, when we left Newry Corners, we settled into a new way of life, and Ernest's questions got better—and worse.

III

∾

Bound for Bethel

BETHEL, MAINE, was to be our first town.

Until we moved there we were a family of eight sturdy country boys accustomed only to the farm, the lumber camps and hard, rough work. But Bethel was not a country village. It was one of the oldest towns in the state, with a tradition of culture far above the average of Maine in those days. Pretty and tree-fringed, it was still a business center for a big section of the countryside, with a railroad station, summer hotels and an academy that extended education four years beyond grammar school.

It was in this town that Ernest Shurtleff Holmes was to really grow up. He was seven when the family moved there and fifteen when we left. Here he received his first exposure to a culture wider than the fields and woods, our own fireside, the country school or the village church. And it was here that he obtained his first—and last—formal scholastic education, asked some of his best questions and had his first encounter with Protestant denominationalism.

There were three churches in Bethel: the Methodist, the Congregationalist and the Universalist. Mother wanted us to attend the Congregationalist—and that, of course, was that.

We didn't even know that we were Bethel-bound on that

September morning of 1894 when we dumped our rude be-
longings into the hayrack and headed for Swan's Corner,
where we were to stay for a while, three miles from the center
of Bethel. Mother had her plans to enrich the family income
by taking boarders from the mill just across the road. But she
didn't lose sight of the fact that we were "within reach of the
church." And despite the three miles of dusty road and three
longer dusty miles back again, for the first few Sundays the
trek was a major adventure.

We began to get ready for it on Saturday. We had only
one pair of pants apiece—knee-length until you reached the
age of fifteen—and each of us had to do his own cleaning and
pressing with an iron hot from the kitchen stove. Then as
soon as supper was over on Saturday, we filled the washboiler
and other utensils and heated water on the kitchen stove.
The tub Mother used for washing clothes was now converted
into a bathtub and set in the middle of the kitchen floor; the
stove and steam kept the room warm even on the coldest of
nights. We soaped and soaked sitting in the tub with our
knees drawn up under our chins. Then we got into our night-
shirts and climbed into cold beds.

Meanwhile Mother had been cleaning and cooking all day.
She did no cooking on Sunday as that was the Lord's day and
the way she had been brought up to do by her Uncle Jacob.
But on Sunday morning she was up early and routed us out
to get ready for Sunday school and church. All the sons took
pride in looking as neat and clean as possible—and to make
sure our hair would look smooth we put a teaspoonful of
sugar into a saucer of water and combed it with this original
"stay-comb." It would stay that way until we started for home
after church. Mother was dressed in skirt and waist, and her
beautiful hair was braided and pinned like a crown around
her head. She was a striking figure walking easily and with a
matriarchal dignity as she led her brood of eight boys to the
House of God.

It used to be said laughingly that the deacons met us at
the door with flyswatters because of the sugar on our hair.

But no one actually laughed at us, not even the "son of the richest lady in town," which was quite as well for him. We were, after all, a generous contribution to a small congregation; and we all sat quietly, and most of us listened well.

One Sunday, when the adventure had worn a little we complained to Mother that it was too long a walk to church, and she in her wisdom let us stay home. So we took an excursion into the woods. We got back tired, hungry and dirty just as night came on. Mother said nothing, but we went to church thereafter.

The church had been built in 1847, and the pews had high straight backs and cushioned seats. Our family occcupied two of them, and the ushers shut the swinging doors softly and with great dignity "to prevent the devil from getting in and our getting out," Guy used to say, with his usual style of rolling a wicked eye. Ernest tinkered with the hymnbook and often acted spellbound. I wondered why, and discovered two reasons: one, he was counting the pages of the minister's manuscript as they were turned over; second, he was trying to peer through the partly closed curtains that screened the boy who was pumping the organ—and wondering if he would ever get his chance at it. Later on, he did get his chance, for shortly we moved to Bethel to live.

The sawmill was closed, and Mother was ready to transfer her brood to better surroundings and better schools; and it was because of our fine church attendance that good fortune came to us, for a woman with eight clean sons could not pass unnoticed, especially as we knew more about the Bible than any other children in the Sunday school.

The village dowager, an ambitious, proud and wealthy woman, lived at the top of Main Street and looked down on her village with a patronizing eye. Her husband was a physician who chose to live in this Maine town, although he could have enjoyed successful practice in Cleveland, Ohio, from where most of his patients came. He was one of the earliest psychiatrists in America, and in later years I visited a vast Philadelphia hospital where an entire floor was named for him. He employed hypnosis and suggestion as well as drugs and exercise, and when I was eighteen he taught me the art of hypnosis. It was to these two people we owed our good fortune at that time.

They had purchased an old house near their estate in order to protect the entrance from undesirable neighbors. They thought it a fine idea for us to live there, and we thought so too. There were about ten rooms, and for the first time in our lives we slept with only two to the room. We had need of the space now, for Mother always had an extra boy in the house whom she was helping to get some schooling.

We soon found, too, that the church deacon, Dr. Tuell, who was the dentist and a prominent citizen, had taken us under his wing. As it turned out, he proved to be a relative of Mother's. He visited us often and looked after our dental needs without cost. He looked upon us as good examples of Congregationalism and Sunday school scholarship.

And he looked upon Mother for what she was—a gallant woman whose small frame housed that great faith in the immediate presence of God and who, despite the rigors of her life, had daringly developed her intellect and clung to her independence of thought and originality.

It was in the wider culture of Bethel that Mother began to come into her own wider expression . . . but she had been long preparing for it. She and Father together in the backwoods had continually sought for expanding awareness, and their sons as well as their neighbors had benefited from it.

Reading was always the favorite pasttime in our family, although up to the time Ernest was nine years of age we had only three books, except for one book that Mother and Father kept hidden for many years. *The Story of the Bible* was our childhood favorite. It had some illustrations, and we loved to look at the flying angels, especially Elijah en route to Heaven in a chariot. There was also the King James Bible itself and a book of verse. I recall an illustrated poem:

Fire, Fire, Fire, let's build it higher,
Give it a poke to send up the smoke.

Mother had other mental stimulants. One of them was *The Secret Book,* which moved as she moved and which she and Father read at night or when storms prevented outdoor work. It was Henry Drummond's *Natural Law in the Spiritual World.* It had come to them way back on the farm in Lincoln as part of a subscription to a Chautauqua Correspondence Course. What a boon to the intellectually curious of our day was this really outstanding institution of Chautauqua! Probably no one else in Lincoln was a subscriber. But Father and Mother studied the course eagerly and intelligently, read the books loaned to them through the mails, discussed the subjects and argued over them between themselves, answered the questions successfully and obtained the coveted reward of a "Certificate of Efficiency." They felt both daring and secretive; it gave them not only further education but also ambition for their children. In particular Mother gained a liberal religious point of view.

Part of our education lay in Mother, part in the Bible from which she read aloud every evening. I have never known anybody who took her religion more sincerely, while at the same time as a matter of course. She never prayed anxiously or alarmingly. She kept her anxieties to herself, and I know they were often great throughout most of our boyhood. But God was taken openly into her confidence, and we went to bed without doubt that He and Mother would take care of us while we slept.

In later years Ernest used to comment on the fact that he himself had not been reared in an atmosphere of religious fear. No one talked of a devil, and no one was afraid of future punishment. We were, in fact, serene and safe, and the family prayers, which anticipated our bedtime, gave us full assurance that God would protect us in the night, especially as each of us repeated to himself:

> Now I lay me down to sleep
> I pray the Lord my soul to keep;
> If I should die before I wake
> Take me to heaven for Jesus' sake.

Father, too, became ingrained in a theological liberalism and joined Mother in the determination to save their children from the dualism of good and evil then propounded by so many ministers.

There were terrifying aspects to this dualism in which God and the devil were in conflict over the souls of men. With lurid word pictures of hell fire and damnation, many theologians of the day sought to frighten souls into heaven. Hell, according to the theology of an earlier period (middle of the nineteenth century), was paved with the bodies of unbaptized infants, and God's judgments were so arbitrary that He at times damned a soul for His own glory. Eternal damnation in the unquenchable fires of hell was the lot of the unregenerate and the unbaptized, while a watchful devil supervised his hordes at their fiendish task.

I remember what was called *The Child's Hymnal,* a small volume bound in cloth. One of the hymns warned children to obey their teachers and parents or

> Ravens will pick out their eyes
> And eagles eat the same.

In an adult hymnal, without the music, was a hymn for both children and adults:

> Lord, what a wicked wretch was I
> To mourn and murmur and repine,
> Because the wicked sit on high—
> In robes of wealth and honor shine;
> But, Oh, their end! Their wretched end,
> Thy sanctuary taught me so!
> On slippery rocks they take their stand
> While fiery billows roll below.

But both Father and Mother sought to counteract this teaching in their own way. I remember one Sunday morning while we were still in Lincoln, Father, with some of us children, left Mother at home and drove the two and a half miles to church.

The subject of "worms" seemed to be uppermost in the preacher's mind that day, and he opened with the hymn that asks oratorically, "Would He devote His sacred head to such a worm as I?" Glancing at his congregation and pointing at each in turn, men and women, deacons and sinners, and even including himself, he declared that all were worms doomed to decay in the dust from which they had sprung. He offered little hope for anyone.

On the way home Father stopped the horse and let him nibble grass by the roadside while he turned and spoke to us.

"Don't be scared, boys, about worms of the dust. Reverend Ernest Shurtleff wouldn't say you are worms. You are not worms, and it's a big lie. Jesus said, 'Ye are gods,' and you are like God if you keep that way. Man was made by God. Any other story is a lie."

Never before had I seen Father really angry, for he was almost docile when Mother was around. But now his face was tense, his voice was loud, as he repeated fiercely, "It's a lie, a lie, a darned big lie." Then, as though the subject were settled for all time, he clucked at the horse, "Geddy-up," and we drove home.

He told Mother about it and in our hearing, too. I didn't know then, but I believe now that he took a kind of pride in the theological knowledge that enabled him to give the lie to the minister. Mother agreed with him, but she softened his vehemence by saying, "A man could tell a lie without actually being a liar—" She stopped quickly when she noticed our interest. "Don't try it," she said.

Ernest Shurtleff, the young preacher after whom their son Ernest was named, had been a great source of stimulation and cheer to my mother in Lincoln when her ninth son was born.

The clergyman often had come wheeling into the farmyard

on his bicycle with its six-foot wheel, the only one we ever saw for many years. Soon he and Mother would be deep in conversation and argument. They both benefited from it. Half fearfully, he adopted some of the points of view that later appeared in diluted form in some of his discourses. He afterward became well known as an author, writing for *The Youth's Companion, The Saturday Evening Post,* and other periodicals, with a strong philosophical and metaphysical slant. The last we heard from or about him was as a minister in Paris, where he lived for a number of years.

But for Mother in Bethel, six years after Reverend Shurt-leff disappeared from her life, history was repeating, and another minister, a Reverend Farley, often came knocking on her door.

No doubt he called on us at first in the interest of the church and Sunday school, but he found something he hadn't expected, a well-educated woman, up-to-date in her reading and with a more advanced point of view than any parishioner in town. He argued and debated with her, and some of her ideas were reflected in the Sunday sermons that followed. So far as I am aware only her sons William and Walter knew this at the time, because Mother kept it to herself. "She had a Mona Lisa smile, though, when I told her," William said, "and she warned us not to talk about it."

Ernest was very friendly toward everybody and wanted them to be happy. At this period he had no particular pal. He liked to be with us, and he enjoyed the company of older people. And as always, he was asking questions, wanting to know how it happened and why. Even the preacher came under his scrutiny. "How does he know?" he asked Mother. "Did God talk to him?" And when the preacher prayed, he wondered why God required so much information.

Despite his probing questions and his deep interest in spiritual matters, my brother Ernest was never, from the day of his birth until he left this plane, in any way pious in a church sense.

I recall that in Bethel his interest in the boy who was pumping the church organ continued, at times, to outweigh his interest in the sermon. Later when Jerome and I held this honorable assignment successively he was even more interested, and shared our exultation when we came into our annual wages of five dollars for the year.

Eventually it was Ernest's turn to succeed us, and he learned as we had before him to prize the job for another reason; we could read books instead of listening to the sermon.

Sometimes one or the other of us got so excited by the story that we forgot the organ, and Miss Laura Hall, the organist, had to bang the foot pedal to get our attention and set us to pumping. Miss Hall was a fine musician, and once when asked what she considered the most difficult piece of church music to play, she said, "The foot pedal, loud enough to wake Ernest and so soft the congregation won't hear it."

While he certainly could not be called pious, Ernest had a mystical temperament; although he would never admit it until the last few years of his life. As a boy he had a way of personalizing the trees in the forest and held a kind of communion with them. This sense was sharpened by an experience when he was ten years old. The organist, Miss Hall, who was also a skillful painter, one day took Ernest with her while she sketched some trees in the woods on the hillside. First she went up to a white birch, embraced it and began to talk to it. It did not seem strange to him; he knew she was talking to "a living something" and felt that it understood.

He learned from silent communion with nature—and he went on trying to learn from his fellowman. But mostly, despite his questions, he had to figure things for himself.

After Reverend Farley departed to other flocks we had a preacher who was a graduate of Bates College; and he was really good in his way, but he had no terminal facilities when it came to prayer. We timed him one Sunday; he prayed for exactly twenty-three minutes. He seemed to think it necessary to bring the Lord up-to-date on current events and some private affairs and kept reminding Him that He had made some unfulfilled promises. Ernest was so bored he tried to sleep but finally amused himself with drawing mental sketches of the natural scenery through which the preacher dragged the tribes of Israel. On the way home he told us that the children of Israel got drowned in the Red Sea. We asked him where he got that nonsense. "Why, the preacher left them half way across and went back to get the Egyptians. The next thing you know—wham! They was swallowed up!" He knew better, but he demanded a more logical sequence.

We had a Sunday school teacher whose piety was respected but whose theology was aged in the wood. The Pharisees had nothing on her when it came to Sabbath rest. She was against any pleasure on Sunday and was terribly upset, therefore, when she learned what Ernest planned to do after Sunday school. He intended to join the rest of us in going into the woods to gather arbutus, those palely pink mayflowers with which we filled the small tissue-paper or birch-bark baskets that we constructed to hang on the door of our best girl on May Day. The teacher told him that it was a very wicked thing he was about to do. "Even the ass," she said desperately, "knows enough to lie down on Sunday. Promise me you won't go."

So Ernest promised, to please her. He didn't want her to suffer for him. But after he got home, he had an argument with himself. It was his first personal and direct experience with theology. He had read the New Testament enough to know what Jesus had said about the Sabbath, and the word *ass* intrigued him. He finally decided that if you could pry an ass out of the ditch on Sunday you might as well go a little farther into the woods and look for more! There was a ditch down in the lower pasture that ought to be scouted for foundered asses, and it ran right into the woods. So he went. He regretted the whole episode later, not because he had broken his word but because he was ashamed of having given it, and it made an impact on him that lasted a lifetime. He was vary wary of promises and seldom made them. He would come to agreements and keep them, but he almost hated the word *promise*. " 'Hell is paved with good intentions,' " he quoted, "but half of them are broken promises."

Ernest was learning from experience. But he was still full of questions.

IV

Education — Formal and Informal

IT WAS NOW that Ernest entered into a new experience—
formal education. In Bethel the younger boys, including
Ernest, went to a proper grammar school, where Jerome and
I got jobs as janitors, sweeping the classrooms and stoking
the huge furnaces with maple and birch cordwood four feet
in length.

There was no public high school in town, but much to
Mother's satisfaction the older boys were admitted to a private school that was called Gould's Academy. Now that it is
rich and famous it is known as Gould Academy. At that time
there was only one weather-worn, two-story frame building
while today there is a college-sized campus and three million
dollars' worth of buildings. Meager as the accommodations
then were, the tuition cost seven dollars a term, with three
terms a year, and I was held back a couple of years because
we had no money to pay for it.

We boys paired off naturally. Jerome and I were great pals;
Walter paired with Luther, and they proved good students
and athletes; William and Charles did everything together
and made high grades; Guy cut school most of the time and
lived on a farm where he broke horses to saddle, riding the
wild mustangs brought on from a western range. In later life

Ernest and Guy were very close until the latter's death. Ernest was left to find his own companionship, but he told me that he never felt lonely on that account. I think we even bored him as we sat around the Mazda lamp and studied Greek and Latin.

He did not like school in spite of his intellectual curiosity. It was too confining, and it seemed a waste of time to recite what you already knew—he wanted to get on with it. He preferred reading the Bible at home to studying history at school and read a great deal of it.

By this time Ernest was reading books and magazines avidly like the rest of the family. We were not bookworms but prodigious readers. We read everything in the well-stocked Bethel library—fiction, biography and poetry. Mother was known in town as "the mother of those children who are always toting books." We devoured the Horatio Alger success stories, such as *Forging to the Front;* the *Rollo Books* of travel, like *Rollo in England;* and the *Oliver Optic Stories of the Old West.* Hunting and Indian stories were of our period and also tales like *Out on the Pampas.* All of James Fenimore Cooper's *Leatherstocking Tales* brought the Indians right into our house, although written fifty years before. We had lived in the woods and on the lakes and streams, and we knew something of the life of the wild at firsthand. The Mark Twain stories were favorites with us. We knew he was Samuel Clemens but we liked his nickname better. He was still living and writing or passing through his last agonizing years; his Mississippi River tales, *Huckleberry Finn,* and his *Innocents Abroad* were a source of excitement and mirth for everyone in the family.

Ernest liked books of mythology with such stories as Caligula's feeding his horse on golden grain, and sometimes he would join Jerome in buying twenty-five-cent books that were as exciting to them as the "comics" are to the children of today. They once chipped in and bought *Peck's Bad Boy.* Mother discovered it hidden under a cushion and picked it up with tongs and put it in the fire in the kitchen stove, thus arousing such curiosity among us boys that all of us chipped in to buy another copy.

Ernest was already trying to find answers in print to some of his big questions, reading James Russell Lowell, Henry Wadsworth Longfellow, and both the prose and poetry of Oliver Wendell Holmes. He often played "Authors" with us in the evening, and titles like *The Autocrat of the Breakfast Table, Elsie Venner,* and so on, would intrigue his interest; and he would go to the library and pick up copies of them on his way home from school the next day.

Despite his obvious lack of love for the processes of formal education, I never recall that he needed help with his schoolbooks. He loved beautiful things, and he drank with an unquenchable thirst from the books of a wider knowledge. He read good translations of *The Iliad* and *The Odyssey,* and *The Last Days of Pompeii.* He particularly liked Longfellow's *Evangeline,* intrigued more by the poetry than the girl's search for the lost lover. In after years he learned *Hiawatha* by heart and used it as part of his entertainment programs on the dramatic platform. The influence on him is shown in his rendition of "The Song of the Seraphim," which he contributed to our epic, *The Voice Celestial.*

Books were an escape as well as an education for all of us from the world of work to the world of adventure and intrigue, as dramatic as boys experience today from the movies, radio and television. And Ernest read—and read. But with less homework to do than the rest of us and not too much interest in school, he was definitely restless when, five nights a week we older ones sat around the large table in the living room with the flame of the big lamp burning white in its Mazda mantle and studied our lessons for two or more hours. There was little talking while we translated our Greek and Latin, learned our English lessons, with Mother helping us when we ran into difficulty with our mathematics. Our industry was rewarded in that proud moment in school at examination time when we were the only ones who had an average of 90 percent or more and were excused from the tests. I can still savor the moment when we walked out in triumph.

It was an outward triumph, for which our youngest brother developed very little taste, yet if his great learning was acquired in later years outside the classroom, I believe these schooldays set a pattern of method of acquisition, everything being preceded by "Why?" as though the effect must be involved in the cause. In later life I once heard him say, "If you can ask an intelligent question, you know the answer to it." And how he used this faculty in learning from college professors in private conversation and lessons I shall relate later on.

I do not think we brothers considered his questions invariably intelligent back there in Bethel, particularly if we did not know the answers ourselves or if he asked them while physically jumping around during our evening study period.

Our answers, I recall, were usually, "Shut up, will you *please!*" And if he didn't "please," Mother had only to say a word and he pleased immediately.

We had work to do outside of school hours, sometimes around the house or garden, frequently for a neighbor, cleaning up or cutting lawns, chore-boy jobs, summer hotel (I, myself, worked in one every summer as bellboy and table waiter) or janitor work; and Mother allowed us to keep part of what we earned.

Ernest early developed a talent for art collections, a taste that followed him down the years; his home in Los Angeles was as full of treasures, mostly oriental, as a museum, but beautifully arranged for natural living. Some of these priceless pieces overflowed later into the Religious Science buildings. In Bethel, before he was out of short pants, he was collecting swords, pictures, prints, antique furniture, all acquired by hard-earned savings from chores, errand running, organ pumping and a shrewd capacity for "Yankee trading."

Another talent that was to follow Ernest with rich rewards

through the years began developing in Bethel. He had started "speaking pieces" at the age of six, and he enjoyed it!

Since the town's chief entertainment was the "church social," with an occasional operetta done by the local talent, the church was always putting on little plays, readings or some kind of musical program. Ernest's first piece went something like this:

> You'd scarce expect one of my age
> To speak in public on the stage,
> And if I chance to fall below
> Demosthenes and Cicero,
> Don't view me with a critic's eye
> But pass my imperfections by.

He fascinated everybody, and we were all proud of him. His boy's voice was as clear as the strong rich voice that delighted millions in the past half-century.

There were activities in Bethel for the whole family. Gould's Academy had a forward-looking sports program in which we participated. Some of us played tennis, and Walter and Luther were members of the football squad. They played in a pasture, and all the other brothers yelled for them from the sidelines.

None of us was musical, although we enjoyed the church singing and amateur operas put on by local talent. Bethel was the home town of William Rogers Chapman, who conducted the Knickerbocker Chorus in New York. He and his talented wife were founders of the famous Maine Festival of Music, which developed amateur talent all over the state and eventually built many auditoriums to house it. Rehearsals for the State Festival were held in a local hall for months in advance of the big event and, because Dr. Tuell's wife was the leading soprano, all of us were introduced into music of a superior quality.

Occasionally we were all invited to a town dance, where we picked up a small amount of rhythm in the waltz, two-step and polka. Ernest drifted around and through such events, partly attentive, partly absorptive and partly inquisitive. Whether at a dance or festival, he seemed always to have some abstract inquiry, seldom critical, never offensive, but "downright prying" to us. "How high was the tower in which the wildly unhappy soprano was imprisoned?" . . . "What was the name of the musical instrument the lover played on?" . . . "Why did they choose fat women with light voices and thin men with heavy voices for the leading parts?" Always with that little puzzling grin that was impossible to interpret. His eyes lit up in a way to reinforce this grin and the eyes, together with a whimsicality inherited from Mother and Father, were to charm millions of listeners during his professional life.

In later years in public addresses he frequently would swing away from the stream of deep logic that he had been following with a humorous comment, which in turn suggested an anecdote or poem, and sometimes he would illustrate the illustration, as though he had changed his theme. But when he swung back to the main topic, the delighted listener was unaware of his having made the excursion. Ernest never lost his way, although I have heard him groan a little when reading some of the transcriptions. "I got it all in," he said to me once, "but I was all in when I got it." Owing to the extreme editing of printed texts, this characteristic in the original has been unnoted and unappreciated. Whether or not it is "good form" does not matter, nor did it concern him. Like any great orator, he knew his power with an audience and conducted their emotions like the leader in an orchestra "from grave to gay, from lively to severe."

And he always gave his listeners a feeling of logical sequence that would bring them in confidence and triumph to a conclusion. Even in his early questioning he seemed to know a better answer than most of the ones given him. He was a true philosopher, beginning in childhood to practice the art of determining effects from the given causes.

In later years he used to say that philosophy is geometrical, "You are always given one angle, the context will usually provide the second and you can compute the third. This is the secret of the Trinity." He would smile one of those enigmatical smiles and add, "Everybody has an angle. Pity I didn't study higher mathematics!" But he early became an adept in the field of syllogistic argument, and few were his equals in either inductive or deductive reasoning; yet he deplored public debate as an instrument of propaganda. Woe to those who inveigled him into it, for he often entrapped them in their own arguments, compelling them to concede the opposite of their earlier contentions.

Friday evening was a big evening for all of us boys. We were permitted to go visiting until nine o'clock or, better still, to have company. It was a big evening for Mother, too. As our stay in the town lengthened and Father was earning good wages, we moved into a more modern house, clothing was more plentiful and on Friday evening Mother had leisure to "receive" callers. Not only Reverend Farley or his successors, and our staunch friend, Dr. Tuell, but other members of the community dropped in. There were many educated and well-traveled people in our midst, among them two judges who held benches in Portland but whose families lived in the home town. We saw them from time to time, and a frequent visitor was Frank C. Hanscom, our principal at Gould's Academy.

Mr. Hanscom was a tall, handsome, mustached man, who held his head a little to one side and was popular with the better students who walked around the campus with the same tilt of the head. Although he had no college degree himself, he employed college men for his faculty, and no high school in the state sent better prepared students to Colby, Bates and Bowdoin. He was, in fact, a college in himself, inspired by love of knowledge and the ability to impart it. He belonged to the generation of mighty men who taught the fundamentals of education—reading, writing, spelling, mathematics and Latin, which underlay classical education. He spent his entire life at Gould's and proved his point against the attempted invasion of "progressive education," being given honorary degrees by colleges and building up a famous institution with every facility for learning.

All of our callers enjoyed talking to Mother, and all of us boys including young Ernest enjoyed listening. There was great excitement on the company nights when we all played games, mostly "Authors" or "Whist." At first we played "Whist" by using a pack of cards called "Rook," because the church frowned on "the cards with the wicked backs." As a matter of fact, this once famous game of Rook was designed to be played exactly like "Whist"—later to be called contract bridge—but with different insignia. This was one of the few cases of being able to eat your cake and keep it. Eventually it was decided to "be just a little wicked" and use an ordinary deck of cards.

But perhaps the most exciting thing that happened in the young life of each of the brothers, our biggest single thrill, was the birthday on which he became fifteen years old. Until that day a Holmes was merely a boy—and easy to identify as such. He wore pants that came just below the knees and from there on down he either went bare or wore hand-knit wool socks and laced shoes. At fifteen he became a man. He could "go into long pants"!

On our arrival at Swan's Corner, Walter, then eighteen, and Luther, then sixteen, had already achieved this sartorial eminence. Soon after we moved into Bethel, William and Charles made the great leap. It was my turn next to don breeches; then Guy graduated officially, although in his case it was hard to believe he had been in knee pants on that local farm breaking wild mustangs.

A year later, the year Ernest entered his teens, Jerome "became a man," leaving Ernest the sole heir to seven pairs of knee pants besides his own. Anna Columbia Holmes had come to town with a brood of "two men and six boys"—six

years later her brood consisted of "seven men" and one re-
luctant "boy"—Ernest.

Ernest was not out of countenance about his status—he was
ever of a cheerful and equitable disposition—but as the new
century rolled round and he passed his thirteenth birthday,
he became somewhat in a hurry to catch up to those long
pants.

The fullness of time had not yet arrived for Ernest—neither
physically, mentally nor spiritually; there was no hint, nothing in his personality or character at that time to suggest his
future as an enlightened spiritual leader. He had not heard
then nor did he later recognize any "call" that he would
admit—no voices, no visions, no sudden illumination. He was
always to insist that the understanding that he developed was
the result of natural growth using a law and faculties and a
power indwelling every man. There was nothing supernatural, occult or esoteric about it.

Since this involves basic principles in the teaching of
Ernest Holmes, it would be important to my brother as well
as historically accurate to emphasize that he was a vital, normal, thoroughly happy schoolboy with a bright, inquiring
mind, a sound body, a great sense of mischief and fun, and
he was without a care in the world except for those rare times
when Mother was sick. Then the whole house was still and
tense, and we went about doing the housework with sober
faces. Each of us had his assigned task, two with the bedrooms, two with the sweeping and two with the dishes, while
one did the cooking. All of us could cook, because Father
and Mother were both experts. But Mother had an iron will,
and after the nervous beat of her heart had been replaced
by its natural rhythm she was up and about once more.

But for the other days of his boyhood, Ernest read and
played and swam and fished, worked and learned without any
plans or any concern for the future. If he had anything on his
mind as he rounded the bend into his teens, it was his desire
to get into long trousers and his increasing, unanswerable,
insatiable questionings.

About the first there was nothing to do but spend two more years a-growing.

About the second he could—and did—go right on asking; but now he took himself and his questions on a family tour.

V

A Teen-Age Question Mark

Ernest Goes to School

IT WAS IN January of 1902 that Ernest finally "went into long pants," and it was truly as though the curtain rose on a new act in his life. For it was in that same year that our family left Bethel.

It is hard to lay aside the conscious memory of a small and intimate world in which you lived and which you loved so much.

Those had been happy, busy, family years; and I have told their history in so much detail because they were the years of Ernest's "growing up" as well as the last in which we would all be living together.

Ernest was now fifteen, and from that time on he earned his own living. He was on his way to that independence and initiative that would someday culminate in a new message to the world.

In the spring of 1902 we had a letter from Uncle Henry. He had bought the farm on which we were born and had intended to run it by himself. But he was suffering from rheumatism and found it hard enough to take care of the livery stable. So he wrote to find out if we would like to buy the farm from him. Charles and William were all for it. They had been working at odd jobs the past year after their grad-

uation from Gould's, and Charles thought all they had to do
on a farm like that was "to bottom chairs and it would pay
for itself." So they rushed off to Lincoln and the odd little
farmhouse three miles from the village.

Mother knew the hardships of a remote and primitive
farmhouse, but she had pioneer blood in her veins and did
not hesitate to go along with her sons; besides, she wanted to
be near Father, who was already in Lincoln, located on the
edge of the village in a rough woodsman's camp. He had just
come in from the "drive" on the Penobscot River where the
logs had been floated down from the winter's cutting away
back in the mountains. They were safely nestled now in the
arms of a great "boom" of chained logs that held them safe
from floating away in the spring floods, and Father was settling the camp for the summer beside the great saw and pulp
mill that employed a hundred Polish immigrants. He had
taken over the camp as a boardinghouse and was running it
independently of the company. The men slept in rough
bunks and came into the cook's camp only for meals. After
a winter on baked beans and brown bread, they were raven-
ous as wolves for the great steaks and stews. At that time beef
could be bought at five cents a pound, and there was so much
profit that Father was enjoying a good income for the first
time in his life. And so it was that Mother and six of her
"young men" returned to Lincoln—and Father.

Jerome and I stayed on in Bethel and finished our prepara-
tory school education at Gould's Academy, where the name
Holmes is a tradition to this day. But when we graduated we
went "home" to the farm.

The house in which we were all born hadn't been odd to
me as a little boy, but now I noted that whoever had constructed it must have had ambitious designs beyond the reach
of his pocketbook. He had evidently built the long, low
one-story "ell" part of the building first and then, finding the
expense too great, had cut the cost in half on the two-story
front by sawing it right across the middle. It was an archi-

tectural monstrosity, and Guy, taking one look at it, said, "The front and back and both sides look like 'ell."

Ernest had returned to Lincoln with Mother and the boys and remained there for a while but lived with Aunt Louisa. She was one of the eleven sisters and brothers in Father's family, most of whom had moved from Canada to the States. She was a Ballantine now and had a large family of her own, but she had an enormous house, and they were well-to-do farmers. They raised all kinds of vegetables as well as hay and cattle and were the only people in Lincoln who produced large crops of carrots to feed the stock.

Although the whole family was religious and read the Bible every day, they still hadn't found the answers to half the questions Ernest asked. The questions had been getting more pointed the past year. He had spent part of the previous year with Aunt Carrie Steeves, another sister of Father's, who lived in Boston. She and her family were Baptists, and Ernest had gone to church with them and had been filled with wonder and unsolved questions. Aunt Carrie hadn't minded his questions, being assured, I suppose, that they didn't matter so long as she didn't answer them anyway. She had too big a family to take care of and work enough for two women. She was easygoing and was untroubled with metaphysical theories while immersed in physical realities. Ernest retained the unanswered questions and propounded them to Aunt Louisa.

"What is it you want to know, really?" she asked.

"Everything, I guess," he answered.

"Well, I haven't gone that far," she said, "and I think you've gone too far."

But all he wanted to know was the answer to "what" and "why" and "how" and to resolve some doubts about "where." The questions were all about life and religion, and he really didn't know himself what he was after—he was just wondering. There was no one to confirm or deny his conjectures. We were not regular church members in Lincoln, and the ministry was weak on philosophy and long on theology of its kind. I think this is one of the chief reasons why Ernest developed an independent philosophy of life on his own account.

He sought knowledge from every source and turned it over in his mind, accepting and rejecting at will. He never had any use for authority as such and always claimed that if he had to have a hell he would make his own.

"Not that I believe in one," he said many times. "If there was one, God would have to have a hand in it, and if He did have a hand in it, He wouldn't be God, He would be the devil."

Strange talk for a boy in his early teens and by no means a finished philosophy, but keen! Mother wondered sometimes, but she kept her own counsel. She herself had never believed in a devil and she saw no reason to argue either for or against him.

After a spell Ernest left Aunt Louisa's to work for Father at the boarding camp down by the pulp mill. He was what was called a "cookie," a kind of busboy, waiter and assistant cook. I remember him dimly in that capacity. He was very strong, had a finely proportioned body with well-muscled arms and legs and was undeniably handsome with his intelligent face and wavy reddish-brown hair, and that slight inquisitive slant of the mouth that distinguished him through life. Above all, he was wholesome without craving for excitement. He already had the practical mind that ultimately enabled him to organize and finance a great institution. I first observed it at the boarding camp. Father was paying him ten dollars a week, high wages in those days, and he made an equal amount on the side. He bought himself a washing machine and turned out clean clothes for the men at five cents a garment.

Later on Ernest moved to the farm, where he worked for a little more than a year. Father had bought the place from William and Charles, because they were not designed for farmers. They went off to teach school; William eventually became the superintendent of a system of forty schools in

Connecticut and Charles was a teacher and Boy Scout leader all his life, mostly in Massachusetts.

Father planted potatoes and raised some of the finest crops in the state. They were called the Penobscot potatoes and had a ready market in Boston. Walter, who had been teaching school, turned to the hardware business and in addition bought or leased specially built barns to store not only Father's crop but all the potatoes he could buy in the countryside. Ernest helped with the planting and the hay crops. He also assisted in the milking, since Father also carried on a milk route for a number of years; however, Ernest seldom delivered. He didn't like farming and said cow's tails left an unpleasant taste in his mouth and you couldn't get away from it without going away. He attended public high school for a few months, but he didn't like that either.

I was not strong enough to farm and got a job as a cook in the lumber woods that fall of 1902. We pitched camp in among ancient spruce and pine trees, and my "cookie" dug a hole in the ground and burned hard wood over it to make live coals. Then we filled an iron kettle with parboiled beans and pork, flavored with molasses and mustard and buried it overnight in the coals—New England "ground-baked beans." The pastry baking was done in a "shed oven." It soon proved that I was miscast as a cook, and the big boss gave me five dollars and sent me home.

I found a letter from my Greek teacher at Gould's, urging me to go to Colby College. He could arrange my tuition on the basis of my scholarship and find a job for me. So I decided to go.

I worked my way through the first two years of college by cooking in a lunchroom, shoveling snow and carrying coal; the last two years, with some assistance from Father, I earned my living by tutoring. Jerome went off to Bates College the next year, and we both came home with A.B. degrees and Phi Beta Kappa keys. Ernest, too, went his way onward and upward. And, of course, I never lost contact with what he was doing.

But I was actually to see little of my brother for the next nine years except in the summer.

The year following my graduation in 1906, I was seriously ill from overwork and from an operation for appendicitis. For five weeks that summer I had a tent pitched on the shore of Mattanawcook Lake in Lincoln. Friends from the village came to see me or fish with me. There were four interconnecting lakes teeming with white perch, bass and pickerel, and we used a canoe to reach any chosen spot. Father bought a large sailboat and for years afterward we sailed in any weather or fished for perch with hook and angle worms. Mother was an eager angler and often caught a great bucketful of fish and served New England fish chowder to as many as twenty or thirty relatives and guests at a time.

Ernest came up in the summer and Father was so pleased with our camp life that he built us a summer cottage on the lake. Walter bought a motor boat and canoe, relatives built a cottage beside us and altogether we had a great time. Our evenings were as exciting as the days. We had a good-sized attic in the cottage, which we kept filled with cast-off garments and what we called "stage properties," and we played charades. Largely, it was a guessing contest on words. I recall a simple charade played by Mother. When we came into the room, she was wearing a gray dress and eating a cookie. That was the whole charade. We finally guessed it, but I think Mother gave a laughing clue or two. The word was *"ingratiate."* She had a love for words such as I have seldom observed. She could spell any word in the English language.

I know that Ernest inherited the love of words from her but doubt that I can say as much for his spelling. This gift of words enabled him to express abstract principles in concrete, understandable language.

I do not know whether it was ambition or the Holmes tradition that urged him toward a final try at formal education, but in the fall of the year 1904, he and a friend from the pulp mill had set out for Gould's Academy in Bethel. Our oldest brother, Walter, having met with success in his hardware business, where Ernest had been working for a time, lent him a couple of hundred dollars, and with his own savings Ernest felt competent to tackle education. He enrolled and began studies in English, Latin and mathematics, but his head and his heart wouldn't work in unison. The only time they worked as a team was when he was pondering life, reading and communing with nature. He used to skip classes at Gould's, hire a horse and carriage from the livery stable and ride off alone into the blue haze beyond the Bethel hills. He was not as lonely there as he was in the schoolroom. He loved the quiet woods and revisited the spot where Miss Hall, the artist-organist, had introduced him to the listening trees.

He reveled in poetry, and many a poet like Wordsworth visited him there and affirmed that

> . . . . I have felt
> A presence that disturbs me with the joy
> Of elevated thoughts; . . . .
> A motion and a spirit, that impels
> All thinking things, all objects of all thought
> And rolls through all things.

He sometimes harmonized his feelings with the Psalmist and wondered if the prophets bothered themselves with a formal education. This would introduce bigger problems, and he would have an imaginary tangle with the preachers he had heard. They seemed to think God had dictated the Bible, and Ernest could not accept that. The authors were nature lovers, he thought, and they set their strength against social and political evils and not against an imaginary devil. The preachers, on the other hand, got their information second hand and used the Bible for proofs of hell and damnation. One of them had recently given a lecture at the Congregational church on "The Devil in Black and White," and he was partly right, Ernest thought, because he said that if you scratched through the whitewash you might find the devil underneath. But it wasn't a devil, it was just plain *you*.

So, having had a talk with the trees and himself, with an occasional aside to God, Ernest would drive home in the lavender twilight and go to his bedroom and read the Bible and other books. Bolstered by pillows he would lie for a long time in reflection; for "the thoughts of youth are long, long thoughts." Only he went beyond adolescent fancies into a world of wonder and abstract reflection. Again he asked himself, "Who am I?" "What am I?" "Why am I here?" "Who is God?" It was a prophetic forecast of the inquiries that would one day expand into the philosophy of religion that made him famous. He tasted the sweet elixir of original thinking but felt a little uneasy when he arrived at the belief that he "could will against God if he wanted to," although he wasn't sure if he could get away with it.

Somewhat to his relief he found that Mrs. Barker, the woman with whom he boarded, was a kindred soul and dared to do her own thinking without help of the clergy. She was a positive-minded and feisty old lady some eighty years of age, wife of the town clerk. Ernest had one day overheard a short conversation between her and a man who had come to the door to see her husband.

"Is the old man at home?" the man had asked.

"There are no old people living here," was her answer.

When she was taken desperately ill, Dr. Tuell, in his endless rounds to comfort the sick and needy, called on her.

"Does my doctor think I'm going to live?" she asked.

"No."

"Do the neighbors think I'm going to die?"

"Yes."

"Then I won't," she said firmly, and she didn't.

Ernest's admiration of her independence of spirit gave support to his belief that a life of independent thinking and living was not based upon conventional education. He detested the confinement of the schoolroom and the dead letter of Latin. He decided to leave Gould's and look for learning in the world of the living.

"Why should I study Latin and Greek when I don't have

an English vocabulary big enough to translate them?" he asked himself, although in later years, when he told me about it, he admitted it was poor logic.

At any rate, he persuaded himself to go out into the world and not to return to Lincoln. Where would he go for answers to those endless questions churning within him? He recalled his visit with Aunt Carrie and her family in Boston three years before, and he remembered the public library there—it would be a good place to go.

So it was that he left the safe world of his childhood and went out into a teeming metropolis. The year was 1905. Ernest was eighteen years old.

VI

⌒𝓏⌒

Backdrop of World Events (1880-1905) Ernest Moves to Boston—Is Baptized

To UNDERSTAND Ernest Holmes, it is necessary to pause and look at the world-consciousness into which he was born and the shape that it was taking. Here was no mystic dreamer, no detached contemplative; here was a man who was to meet, vitally and positively, through spiritual means, the challenges of his time.

How far events had penetrated the world-soul during the first two decades of my brother's life I do not know; I do know that already during his first eighteen or twenty years the seeds of world change and world discord were being sown which would bear fruit in exactly those years when Ernest became a leader spearheading a revolutionary spiritual concept.

Certain it is, however, that neither world nor national events had penetrated very far into the back country where we were born. During our stay in Bethel we did share the national indignation over the sinking of the battleship *Maine;* we did whittle wooden swords and charge San Juan Hill in imitation of Teddy Roosevelt; I remember that we stopped a croquet game to go over to our picket fence and receive from an excited neighbor the horrifying news of President McKinley's assassination. But the actual significance of events resulting from the Spanish-American War, the succession to the presidency of Theodore Roosevelt, the Russo-Japanese War—well, none of these things moved us. Yet all of them, plus events of which we were totally ignorant during our growing years, foreshadowed a new era in the life of nations and of science and of philosophy.

The year that Ernest was born, Grover Cleveland was serving his first term as President. A brief twenty-five years had passed since Lincoln had issued his Emancipation Proclamation. The guns of the Civil War and Lincoln himself had been silenced only twenty-two years; and it had been a year less than that since the first civil rights act, granting citizenship to all persons born in the United States except Indians, had passed over the veto of President Andrew Johnson.

Also in the year Ernest was born, Pearl Harbor was leased from Hawaii as a naval base, and free delivery of mail was provided in all communities with a population of at least 100,000.

Eighteen years later (1905), when Ernest arrived in Boston, Theodore Roosevelt had been inaugurated for his second term, and the whole world, consciously or subconsciously, was pregnant with the changes that would drastically and permanently affect the destiny of mankind in general and, although he couldn't know it then, of this very young man from the Maine woods in particular.

It was during this period of eighteen years that the great political and social upheavals took place in Russia. The German socialist Karl Marx, author of *Das Kapital*, had died in 1883, and events were ripening that would result in the rise to power of that ruthless fanatic, Lenin, who would in 1917 put teeth into Marxism until it would become Russian Communism.

It was in this period, too, that Belgium forcibly took over the Congo; the dissolution of that union is plaguing the United Nations unto this day. Ernest was only seven when the Sino-Japanese War broke out, ending in a victory for Japan, complete independence for Korea and the ceding of the Island of Formosa to the victor. Korea, Formosa, Man-churia, were only names then for faraway places, if we had heard of them at all. Eleven years later when the Russo-Japanese War ended in a treaty arranged by President Theodore Roosevelt in which Russia was excluded from Manchuria and Korea was ceded to Japan, they were still just names.

Yet all this while it was as if the collective hand of man was setting up a giant chessboard, moving a piece here, a piece there, placing in the hands of each player a loaded and cocked gun that would be fired when the real contest began.

The United States, too, had been collecting and placing strategic chess pieces around the world; the Hawaiian Islands were annexed, the Philippines, Guam, Puerto Rico. Cuba had been granted her independence by us, but we retained the right to interfere in case of government instability. Con-struction of the Panama Canal had begun, and the Republic of Panama had sprung full-fledged from the busy brain of President Theodore Roosevelt, the Rough Rider who wanted to "tread softly and carry a big stick."

At home new forces were emerging. In the summer when Ernest was five years old a strike at the Pittsburgh Iron Works in Pennsylvania was suppressed by state militia amidst great suffering and privation for the families of labor. In the White House at that time sat Benjamin Harrison, who had replaced Grover Cleveland after the latter served a single term. In the presidential election following that troubled summer, labor showed a political power that resulted in the reelection of Cleveland, the second Democratic administra-tion since the Civil War. From this beginning, labor de-veloped a consciousness of the value of organized power, bringing forth great unions, a matter of continuing social and political importance to this day.

A second force of which Ernest also approved in later life was already apparent when he reached Boston. The popular song in 1905 was "Everybody Works But Father," and it was not so much a moral finger pointed at laziness in dear old

Dad as a social commentary on the number of women who were replacing men in office and factory jobs. They were beginning to win, little by little, the equal rights they had sought so long. The best seller of that day was the autobiography of Helen Keller, *The Story of My Life,* a story of grandeur and courage and spiritual light that put this amazing woman into sharp focus. Evangeline Booth had just been appointed commander of the Salvation Army in the United States. Mary Baker Eddy was living in semiretirement near Boston in the waning years of her remarkable accomplishments. When former President Cleveland, writing against woman suffrage in the *Ladies' Home Journal,* said: "Sensible and responsible women do not want the vote. The relative positions to be assumed by man and woman in the working out of our civilization were assigned long ago by a higher intelligence than ours," many, including my brother, looked to Helen Keller, Evangeline Booth and Mrs. Eddy, and wondered. Perhaps that higher intelligence was releasing into the consciousness of this epoch a new creative force, free women.

Two mechanical emergences that were to change the size and face of our globe and the air above it were in the toddler stage. True, there were over 77,000 automobiles in the United States, but they were still called "devil-wagons" and considered a "luxury for the man who does not need one," while the 1903 flight of the first heavier-than-air craft by Orville Wright was a subject for ridicule. But they had been born, and their growth would affect the shape of the world.

Boston, in 1905, was, as she always had been, a hub of culture and a center of dynamic thought. During the second half of the nineteenth century it was said that she suffered the twilight of her gods with the passing of such giants as Longfellow, Whittier, Holmes and Lowell. Yet she remained a hub and drew to herself all that was new or controversial in a time of mental upheaval.

The year 1905 provided the hinge of science, for it was in that year that Albert Einstein, a youth of twenty-six, published a paper on the *Special Theory of Relativity* and began the career that was to revolutionize science and eventuate in control of the atom, which in turn produced the atomic and hydrogen bombs and changed the course of history. Sigmund Freud was publishing his reports on psychoanalysis, which were to effect another kind of revolution; and from his headquarters at Columbia University the influence of philosopher John Dewey was being felt in the schools throughout America as progressive education, a controversial trend that was to continue during Ernest's entire life.

And so, in that year, straight from the back country, the stony farms and rich forests of Maine, bringing with him a suitcase full of clothes and a head full of questions, young Ernest Holmes came to Boston. Perhaps the shape of things to come was not clear, but the very air here was charged with the stuff of which they would be made. And from the moment he arrived Ernest breathed it deeply.

If the ferment in Boston, which had only trickled up to us in the back country, was immediately felt by Ernest, he found Aunt Carrie Steeves, with her big family, as placidly impervious to it as if she were home on the farm. She was the same easygoing, untroubled soul he had visited before; her altar was the kitchen stove except on Sunday, and the satisfying answer to her own limited questions in the peace that reigned under her roof.

Ernest received a warm welcome from the whole Steeves family, unpacked his single suitcase, and settled down to get better acquainted. Aunt Carrie's husband, a big, good-natured man, was in the meat business and led a sedate and uneventful life except for an occasional round at a saloon. On such occasions he would be brought home petrified and lie like a stone for a day or two, and Aunt Carrie would say quietly at breakfast, "Your father is sick." No one would ask further about it, because they knew already. Theirs was a large family of big, handsome young men and one sister. They, too, had their own grocery and meat stores where they worked through the winter, with wide-open doors to keep the meat automatically refrigerated. Ernest immediately went to work for one of them, and put in mornings, evenings and all day on Saturdays. But this left him free on most afternoons. This was his time for the library.

When I visited Boston on a couple of occasions, I used to admire his strong shoulders and his endurance of the cold. He had the most expert hands. They were not only skillful but were a graceful accompaniment when he talked. He and my cousins used to provide their own entertainment by bowling, wrestling at a gymnasium and playing pool—his life here was full and his appetite prodigious.

He showed me all around Boston, first to the library, of course, then by subway and the elevated to visit Bunker Hill and out to Concord to the bridge that Emerson immortalized in the lines I read chiseled in stone:

> By the rude bridge that arched the flood,
> Their flag to April's breeze unfurled,
> Here once the embattled farmers stood
> And fired the shot heard round the world.

Religion and the philosophy of religion, together with a natural inclination to worship, attracted Ernest to the church, and as Aunt Carrie was a Baptist, he went there with her. They had a famous preacher, an eloquent man by the name of Bustard, whom John D. Rockefeller later persuaded to take over the pulpit in his own city; and they had an assistant by the name of Page. Ernest soon was popular with them and the Page Bible class of young men. He had a good fund of Yankee stories and a whimsical humor on his own account; he was a natural entertainer, so he soon captivated the Baptists. They wanted him to be baptized and join the church. He was inclined to membership but sheered off from baptism like a skittish horse.

"Is baptism by immersion really necessary for salvation?" he asked Dr. Page.

This was the reply: "I don't know whether a man could be saved without it, Ernest, but I wouldn't take a chance."

Ernest wasn't really afraid to take a chance, because he didn't believe in hell anyway. Shortly before his death he and I were discussing this subject when he remarked that strangely enough Jung and Kunkle had flirted with the concept of a devil; but we agreed that this was psychological rather than theological, being the tendency of the libido in certain cases to reinforce and even to personalize dominant ideas, as with the child who excused its conduct by saying, "I didn't do it, Mama; the devil dot behind and puthed me."

To this Ernest added, "Dualism never bothered me as a philosophy, but belief in dualism was a part of the religion of the time. I never did believe it, although I was just a kid when I went to Boston. I used to say to Dr. Page, 'How do you know there is a hell? I don't believe it.' "

"He would answer, 'Ernest, you mustn't talk that way. It's in the Bible.' "

Then Ernest would ask, "Who wrote the Bible? If it's in the Bible, then somebody made a mistake. Something inside me knows it isn't true."

However, he had no prejudices at that time against traditional religious rites. "I felt that nobody could be hurt by water unless it was too cold. And I was influenced by the young men in the Sunday school class. I had already joined the famous Page Bible class and had been made one of 'the greeters.' I had been brought up as a Congregationalist and I saw little difference in the Baptist teaching except for the devil and whether you should be immersed or only sprinkled, so I decided to take the leap."

On the appointed Sunday the candidates assembled and the minister, wearing a waterproof suit over his Prince Albert, went down into the pool below the pulpit floor and received them one by one. Placing one hand beneath the neck of the candidate and the other on the boy's clasped hands, he plunged him beneath the surface of the baptismal waters.

Meanwhile the choir was singing:

Down in the waters with Jesus,
Buried in depths below,
I shall arise with Jesus
Whiter than driven snow.

The young men then changed their clothes and resumed their seats to listen to the sermon on "Salvation." Ernest told me that he was disappointed that the baptism didn't do something to him.

"I didn't feel more 'saved' than I had before. I didn't feel different at all, although I tried hard and I was sorry that nothing happened to me."

"Had you ever taken part in other church rites?" I asked him.

"Yes, the communion service in the Congregational church. That was Mother's church, as you know, but none of us believed in transubstantiation."

"Did the Baptists?"

"Some did, but I couldn't say about Dr. Page. I met some who believed the bread and wine were actually the body and blood of Christ. I didn't understand what it was all about at that time. It was only long afterward that I interpreted the meaning of the Lord's Supper for myself as the Spirit and the substance—the universal Spirit and the visible form."

There was a great deal still that he did not understand, study and read as he would, question Dr. Page as he did. And then, the second summer after he had gone to Boston, the glimmer of an answer dawned for him. And he found that glimmer, not in Boston, the hub of culture, but in Lincoln, Maine, where he was born.

We were together, Ernest and I, in the summers of 1906 and 1907. Father was doing quite well with his potato farm and the boardinghouse, and we were able to live comfortably and pleasantly in the cabin on Mattanawcook Lake, where we continued with our picnic parties, charades, boating and fishing. Jerome, too, was at home. He was a brilliant personality, and he was a fine-looking young man. He not only had taught Latin while still an undergraduate, but had taken over the duties of a full professorship in chemistry immediately upon his graduation from Bates College. Jerome and Ernest were a striking pair as they would come striding in from a swim in the lake. Neither of them, however, was conscious of it.

Ernest throughout life was not interested in his physical appearance and his body. He looked upon the body merely as the instrument of mind; put it to bed when it got tired, fed it when it got hungry and washed it when necessary. His intellectual curiosity, I found, was as keen as it had always been; he read to all hours of the night and still was fresh and vigorous in the morning.

But the great event of that summer for Ernest came through our brother William and his wife Rose, who were spending the vacation nearby in the village. Ernest was twenty. William was twenty-eight. Ernest had been a husky, carefree youngster. William had been a slight, timid, appealing child with an intense interior nature and a devotion to Mother that lasted a lifetime. He had grown into a quiet, serious young man, and though he was primarily a teacher and educator, he never lost that deep interior life. Different as were these brothers, no one, I believe, had so great an influence on Ernest's first adventure into metaphysics as he. William was a student of psychology for four years at Yale, an advanced thinker, wrote on metaphysical subjects and was for a time in remarkable years yet to come, a confidant of Ernest's.

His wife Rose was part Indian and had grown up untouched by Christian orthodoxy. She was well educated and unconventional in clothes, habits and reading. Her living room table was covered with such books and periodicals as might not be found anywhere else in the county, among them *The Philistine,* a magazine written and published by the iconoclast Elbert Hubbard.

When Ernest went into the village to buy provisions for

the lake cottage, he would drop in on William and Rose. He liked to talk with them because they had points of view that were new to him. William was the only one of her sons with whom Mother had shared her "secret book," and he well remembered reading Drummond's *Natural Law in the Spiritual World*. This led to an exploration of Darwin's theory of evolution, *The Origin of Species* and *The Descent of Man*.

And it was following one of those discussions in the cottage of William and Rose that Ernest discovered on their living room table a copy of Emerson's *Essays*. He read all day and late into the night while his brother and sister-in-law went quietly about their affairs. He returned the next day to read more. It was at that moment that life really began for Ernest Holmes. He had entered the foreground of The Idea.

BOOK TWO

THE GROWTH OF AN IDEA

I

∾

Ernest Discovers Emerson—And Himself

THE HISTORY of an idea is rooted in infinity. You cannot say, "It was created here or there on a certain day in the mind of an individual." You can only say that this man or that man perceived a truth at a certain time with such clarity that we call it a discovery or a revelation or the birth of an idea. It is at that particular moment that the subjective becomes the objective, just as a green shoot in the garden pushes up into visibility, although it has been incipient there for quite some time. The warmth and light that nurture it often come from the thoughts expressed by the developed consciousness of those who have already turned toward their own roots in the Infinite and brought forth the fruits of truth. There were three major contributors in this regard to Ernest's early unfoldment, and the first of them was certainly Ralph Waldo Emerson.

It was at the moment when he discovered Emerson's *Essays* that life really began for him. He not only read and absorbed them avidly, he also talked about his discoveries with suppressed excitement and exuded some of it at our cottage.

Mother was quick to realize what was going on and went to William and Rose asking them not to disturb Ernest's religious faith. She acknowledged that she had a rather broad view but "not that broad." She had not given up her basic faith but had seen it in its broader implications. While Emerson was widely accepted as "one of America's great poets," he was almost anathema to the evangelical churches, and Mother was afraid Ernest might lose some fundamental beliefs.

Mother's appeal to William to leave Ernest's mind untroubled by Hubbard's *Philistine* magazine and Emerson's *Essays* was not owing to any extensive reading of either author. She knew that the first was an iconoclast and the second had taught principles alien to a faith founded on Jesus Christ as the sole instrument of salvation. Her views were far from liberal enough to contemplate a Christianity without a redeemer. "Everyone would become his own savior," she protested.

She might well have been echoing Emerson's Aunt Mary, who at the age of sixty-six was angered by his essay, "Self-Reliance" asking, if "this strange medley of atheism and false independence was the real sane work of that man whom I idolized as a boy, so mild, candid, modest, obliging."

What would Mother have thought in those tense moments of concern for Ernest's soul if she had been able to foresee her own destiny? By coincidence she would be exactly the age of Aunt Mary—sixty-six—when she would become converted to the very philosophy that filled her now with alarm.

Whatever fears Mother may have felt, there was no stopping her youngest son, no way to pull him back. Ernest had discovered a new world! He had, in fact, discovered himself! Not that he had reached a basic philosophical understanding or knowledge of the "self," which was to gradually develop, but he had the skeleton key that would eventually unlock the mysteries.

Nothing is more important in understanding Ernest Holmes and the growth of the ideas that blossomed into Science of Mind after many years than to look at Emerson's "Self-Reliance" as Ernest saw it then. On the face of it and from the standpoint of a beginner, it was a disquisition on one phase of the psychology of personality, the central theme being the necessity of independence of mind, a determined effort to resist the temptation to "conformity" and even of personal "consistency" in coming to the decisions of life and acting upon them. "Be yourself," he said. "It is easy in the world to live after the world's opinion; it is easy in solitude to live after our own; but the great man is he who in the midst of the crowd keeps with perfect sweetness the independence of solitude."

This was what Ernest got on first reading, just as millions can quote this sentence from Emerson though they may never have read his essay. It supported the thesis that a man's own reason and intuition are of equal value with any other's; including, Ernest felt, those of Dr. Page, the young Baptist minister in Boston, and the authorities quoted. The time would come when Ernest would be as deeply influenced by the metaphysics of the essay as he was by its psychology, for he never ceased to study and teach from his writings, but it would be years before he could define the subtleties of the philosophy of Emerson.

Ernest was immediately entranced with the psychology of Emerson but puzzled at first by such terms as "the soul becomes" and "inasmuch as the soul is present, there will be power not confident but agent," implying adequate causes already existent in oneself. He was totally unprepared at that time to think in the terms of immanence here implied, to say nothing of the transcendental philosophy that characterizes Emerson. Only in after years, when he had become acquainted with some of Emerson's original sources in the mystical literature of India, did he come to a full recognition of the significance, and as late as 1958 I found him emphasizing the importance of immanence in transcendence. Yet, in 1907, at the age of twenty, he fully rejoiced in the feeling of freedom from the chains of ecclesiastical opinion and authority that the psychology of Emerson provided.

Ernest's new life stemmed from that hour. There was a

subtle change in his manner. He began to voice opinions as well as conundrums, not loudly, not aggressively, but with conviction. I think this was typical of him throughout his career. Even though he knew what he himself believed and did not veer from his course, he was tolerant of the opinions and beliefs of others. He was not scornful nor sarcastic. Throughout life he would discuss such matters in the evenings with his friends either at home or as a guest, preferring this to any entertainment whatsoever. He never showed rancor but took his position firmly and held up the shield of his faith in his own opinions.

A strange experience followed Ernest's conversion to the psychology of independence, something he had not anticipated. He had had no acquaintance with mental therapeutics, knew nothing of the psychology of suggestion or of the New Thought movement and its method in healing disease, but shortly after his return to Boston he discovered that a throat irritation that had afflicted him for years had disappeared.

He was always convinced that throat trouble was due to sensitiveness. He had been sensitive to the opinion of others, and when he learned not to be affected by it, he was automatically freed from its effects.

In connection with the psychology of an independent mind, Ernest later described its results not only in conduct but in faith in his own convictions of truth.

I will say that another thing Emerson did for me that had a profound affect upon my life—reading Emerson for the first time, the first half dozen lectures or essays—gave me a realization that in a certain sense every man has to interpret the universe in terms of his own thinking and personal relationships, and that in order to do it, he has to have *faith and confidence in his own interpretation,* because it is the only one that can ever be true for him. He will read much that will support his intuitions and convictions, but unless what he reads has a relationship with his immediate self, it will have no essential meaning to him. He who pursues the opinions of others will find himself in a revolv-

ing door and come out where he went in. Nothing has fundamental "meaning" to the individual until it becomes a part of
his own living.

Although his interpretation of Emerson was at first a
matter of psychology, it brought about new inquiries and
directed his search into new channels. For the first time he
glimpsed a goal.

It was the early study of Emerson that convinced Ernest
that life itself has a purpose and a meaning, and he determined to find it. This became a glorious pursuit and demonstrated to him that the joy of the pursuit is not only glorious
but satisfying; and since life expands to infinity, there is an
endless happiness in store for him who understands its progressive unfoldment. It was to this understanding that he
dedicated his life henceforth.

It was fortunate for him that many of the answers to his
questions could be found in a deeper understanding of
Emerson's "Self-Reliance." To a young man just emerging
from his "teens," life *is* a conundrum; he wonders what it is
all about, and his body and mind alike are filled with an
inexplicable ferment that frequently results in melancholy.

Ernest seems to have escaped this melancholy entirely by
dipping deeper than the surface psychology or the social
psychology that first appealed to him in Emerson. He felt no
frustration after having glimpsed possible answers to his
inquiries.

Ernest attempted at one time to explain it.

I began to realize that Emerson was talking not only to men
but also *about* "man." I did not know anything about the subtleties of the "self," but I had a definite interest in the "soul."
My religion had had definite dealings with the soul; it could be
saved or damned, I was told, but I had no concept of it. The
soul had been pictured to me in art as a half-naked and trans-
lucent man trailing white draperies en route to a cloud, in and
on which other similarly clad figures were blowing trumpets and
singing choruses. It used to chill me. I had seen no correlation

between soul and self and "man." But when I read "Self-Reliance," I found that I had taken short excursions into the fields of abstract thought—not in those terms, to be sure—and it rang a bell in me. It corresponded to something I had felt but had not thought. It is otherwise impossible, I think, to explain the impression made upon me—we can read a thing but if there is nothing in our consciousness that recognizes it, it has no meaning. Perhaps it was the appeal to me of something that I wanted to be, that I ought to be, that I was determined to be that drew me with almost dramatic intensity. I became suddenly aware that Emerson was talking about *me*. I instinctively linked the words, self and soul and man and me. It didn't spring up in my mind like a flower full-blown but it filled it like a rosy mist.

I supposed the Essay was about *everybody*, but that thought did not concern me at all until long afterward when I began to feel the urge to tell others what I had discovered for myself. At the moment all I could think of was this—there is more to a person than he realizes, that is beyond ordinary experience. Here is a mature man, a great man, a terrific man and he affirms that there is something in you that is great, too. For the first time in my life I thought that whatever was going to happen to me would be due to *something that was already in* me. It was vague, and I admitted to myself that whatever it was, needed a lot of investigation but, nevertheless, I believed that I was on the track of an entirely new thing. "Here is a new field of consciousness," I felt. And even at that moment I knew I would get the answer to some questions that the church had not given me.

But I did not attempt to compare Emerson's teachings with those of theology, at first. I was too interested in discovering *his* meaning.

This was, for Ernest, the breakthrough from the midnight of theological questioning into the twilight of metaphysical thinking and philosophy. Up to that time the answers given him were traditional theology. "Soul" had been accepted as a given fact, and no one had discussed its *nature*. The chief function of religion had been to save the soul from sin and eternal punishment through acceptance and obedience to dogma. Ernest had read the Psalmist's cry, "What is man, that thou art mindful of him? and the son of man, that thou visitest him?" *as poetry*. But now his mind pounced on the word *man*. *What is man?*

No one realized better than Ernest himself that this was the beginning of a new mental life and the turning point in the stream of consciousness that flooded out into his river of writing and teaching in the coming years. He all but memorized the essay and went on to read "Spiritual Laws," and one essay after another, always concerned with the what and whence and why and whither of human life. It was not a question now of "Is life worthwhile?" but rather, "How can I make it worthwhile to me and the world?"

At the time, he was still one massive question mark. One question answered gave birth to two more in geometrical progression. He began to get new names for God, thus directing his inquiry from religion to the philosophy of religion. He saw God in ontological terms as First Cause, as Being, Impersonal Principle and Spirit. Of course, the words *ontology* and *transcendentalism* as applied to Emerson, Kant, Hegel and Berkeley meant nothing to him at that time. In place of such terms, to indicate that knowledge can go beyond phenomena and appearances to reach the ultimate principles of his own being, he employed the simpler terms of *Law, Principle, First Clause*. It was inevitable that the word *purpose* was dominant in his mind. If the soul is in the process of becoming, as Emerson said, there must, Ernest thought, be purpose and worthwhile goals. Even so, he was wary of "plans" and "purposes" as applied to God.

So Ernest spent his happy midnight hours that summer in the light of the oil lamp beside his bed, reading and wondering and thinking, a habit that he followed throughout life.

Above all he was learning *to believe in himself*. As he once told me, "Every man becomes his own philosophy, his own institution and what he has is conditioned by what he is. I learned at the age of twenty that you are married to your soul for better or for worse, for richer or poorer, for life and death now and forever; and sometimes the thought frightened me; I didn't always like myself but I couldn't get a divorce."

Occasionally that summer he voiced such thoughts to Mother, to Jerome or me, to William and Rose at their cottage. He explained that he felt there is something in man that belongs to the universe, that is related to him and that this unification made him something special. "You yourself are an individualization of this thing; there is a depth and meaning to your own being; if you can discover it, it will answer your own questions. You may as well accept it and get to work for they will never get answered outside yourself—never."

He was not a fatalist but a practicalist. "Man cannot escape the fact that he is *here*. Something has to be done. He is the only one who can do anything about it." For himself, he found life good because he was pursuing an idea and was beginning to do something creative with it.

It was at this time that he ran across a phrase in the Bible that appealed to him: Jesus, speaking of Spirit, affirmed that men must "worship the Father in spirit and in truth: for the Father seeketh such to worship him." Ernest pondered over it in the light of his new understanding. Did not that suggest the possibility that there is something in the universe that presses in on man, seeking to express itself *through* him? It was a vague but exciting idea that was later to expand. He was sure, however, that Emerson had made it plain that *"there was* something in me already that could enlarge and expand. This was, I sensed, my soul, and I felt it swelling until I almost burst. Having had some light from the Bible, I began a more thorough study and got a lot of help from it and often found confirmation of my new ideas. This was in itself a worthwhile pursuit and I followed the practice throughout life."

When he went on from "Self-Reliance" to Emerson's "Spiritual Laws," he understood "soul" to be its main theme. The first paragraph stated that "the soul will not know either deformity or pain . . . For it is only the finite that has wrought and suffered; the infinite lies stretched in smiling repose."

How often I have heard him quote it! And he was inspired with the concept that "a higher law than that of our will regulates events" and that by obedience to it, life is made easy and happy. Emerson said: "God exists. There is a soul at the centre of nature. . . ." A man's contact with that is his genius and determines for him "the character of the universe."

It was confusing, it was delightful, it was extravagant, it was true! These were Ernest's thoughts as he loosed anchor and ran full sail across the unexplored ocean of Emerson's thought. "We know that the ancestor of every action is a thought . . . to think is to act."

God and man and soul and thought! These, he felt, were what Emerson was writing about. It was his introduction to a world new to him, the creative power of pure thought! The importance of this revelation cannot be overestimated. Suddenly, it was clear to him that *thought* was the power that ran the universe, thought was the weapon of individual mind. In some way they were related to each other.

It would be an arrant error to conclude that Ernest derived from Emerson more than the barest suggestions that led to the system of applied metaphysics that he developed in succeeding years. There was no more than the vague feeling that a man's mind could initiate a stream of causation that would result in control of health and environment.

Hidden beneath his epigrammatical and picturesque language, Emerson had indicated the concept of a law of cause and effect. It was vague, indefinite to the average reader, but it pointed to something significant, which is that creative thought produces an effect in exact measure with the cause. Such action is not confined to physical or material forces, but obtains as well in the field of mind.

But where Emerson was vague, Ernest was explicit. He knew instinctively that this was the master key—creative thinking, progressive action toward a goal! It was not by coincidence that his first book, *Creative Mind,* written ten years later, was the direct result of this inspiration.

If this was true, and if he could understand and utilize this corelationship, life would be a creative adventure. There would lie the goal, the answer to the great question, "How can I make it worthwhile to me and the world?"

II

Dramatic School and Growth

IN SUCCEEDING months after his return to Boston, Ernest found young friends with whom he discussed metaphysics. Some of them were indifferent, some turned away from the subject because it interfered with their snug little pattern of theology, and others "heard him gladly." The latter were found especially among the group of young men and women he met in the Powers School of Expression.

Deeply interested in dramatic entertainment, Ernest attended a recital by Leland Powers one night in 1908 and was astonished and entranced with it. Here was a man who could people a platform with a cast of eleven characters, all of them invisible but himself, and make them stalk the stage and speak their lines with such realism that in imagination the spectator could see them there. He was the most famous single entertainer on the Chautauqua Circuit of New York and New England and also conducted his own School of Expression.

Ernest then and there decided that he would take up the profession and within the week had applied for admission. Powers asked him to read a few things he had already memorized, and Ernest recited selections from "Hiawatha" and some other pieces he had used at church entertainments.

Powers was impressed and called his wife, an accomplished dramatics teacher whose rich beautiful voice and diction had given her the position of second reader in the Mother Church of Christian Science in Boston. She immediately expressed interest in the tone quality of Ernest's voice, and both of them admired his use of his hands and said "the hands would talk for him any time whether he remembered the words or not."

So the Powerses accepted him as a student in spite of the fact that he had no money for the tuition of $150. I remember the time some years later when he acquired money enough to repay them. It was a happy day for him.

Almost immediately he attended service at the Christian Science Church to hear Mrs. Powers. His intellectual curiosity was aroused by the message. He bought *Science and Health with Key to the Scriptures* by Mary Baker Eddy and became deeply interested in it. Soon he could quote from it as he quoted from Emerson. It was not long before he noted points of similarity between her writings and Emerson's *Essays.* Emerson both accepted and defended an "Over-Soul" while Mrs. Eddy began with God but interpreted Him in terms of a Universal "Principle." Both of them inspired right conduct from the standpoint of an Absolute and Perfect Good.

It was characteristic of Ernest that throughout his life he would permit no unfair criticism of Christian Science to go unchallenged; yet, even at the beginning of his investigation, he found many things that he could not understand or with which he could not agree. One of the first stumbling blocks was the apparent contradictions in the teaching of "One Mind." On a plaque attached to the Mother Church in Boston, Ernest had read: *The human mind alone suffers and is sick and the divine Mind alone heals.*

It seemed to him that that was an acceptance of dualism. Ernest found it all very puzzling.

What, then, was it that appealed to him so strongly in

The Holmes family taken when Ernest was about eight years old. First row: Jerome, Mrs. Holmes, Ernest, William Holmes, Sr., and Guy. Second row: Luther, Charles, Fenwicke, William, and Walter.

Ernest at thirteen

Ernest as a professional entertainer
1912 at age 25

Ernest Holmes, about 1930

rs. Anna Holmes, known
"Mother Holmes"

Dr. Ernest Holmes

Josephine Holmes

Augusta E. Rundel

Ernest Holmes in the 1940s

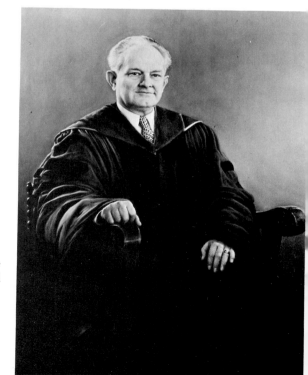

Ernest Holmes, 1948. Portrait in oil by Ferdinand Earle

Dr. and Mrs. Ernest Holmes about 1955

Mrs. Ernest Holmes and
Mother Holmes

Ernest and Fenwicke Holmes in November, 1959

Side view of Founder's Church

Christian Science while he was a student in the Powers School?

It was a new concept of *prayer*.

There is no clearer evidence of religious genius, I believe, than was shown by Mary Baker Eddy in beginning her *Science and Health with Key to the Scriptures* with a chapter on "Prayer." People of all faiths and of no faith believe in prayer or at least know something about it. The approach is disarming. No one is against it. Ernest was fervidly for it. If it offered solution to any problem, a person ought to use it. But clearly, the prayer advocated here was different from the kind he had repudiated back in the church in Bethel, Maine. In fact, the whole nature of the book was new and surprising to him. He had never before read a book that was so strictly devoted to the theory of religion. The word *theology* meant nothing to him, but he could easily believe that prayer does something if you know how to pray for what you want. It was evident that the kind of prayer he was accustomed to had had poor results for he had observed meanness, sickness and poverty among church people who had prayed for spiritual and material blessings with the greatest fervor. Evidently they had prayed the wrong way. What, then, was the right way? The first chapter was fascinating, because it attempted to explain just that. It stated that the answer to prayer lies in the mental attitude of the man who prays. It is not God's Mind that needs to be changed but our own. God is to be looked upon as Love, impartial and universal; He answers all who pray with real faith, not in God alone but *faith in the answer as well*.

The stumbling block to Ernest was in calling God or Love by the title of Divine Principle. This he could not understand. It seemed to remove God's *personalness*, and he thought a better term would be *Person*. He did not know that he had put his finger on the exact center of all "mental science systems," that is, the Law of Mind in Action: what is Principle, how does it work? Is it "personal" and in what sense?

Without understanding the principles involved in his search, but by a sure intuition, he set himself to the task of finding out the real meaning and significance of a Principle freighted with such immeasurable possibilities. He did not know, he had no reason to know, he did not even possess the classical instruments of research, nor could he foresee that his inquiry would eventually lead him to an appreciation of Christian Science and beyond this to a deep knowledge of all religions—their history and application to the direct personal needs and problems of human life—and finally to his own formulation of the Principles and Practices of Science of Mind and the ultimate institution of a new church.

When Ernest came home to the cottage on the lake that summer, he brought Mrs. Eddy's textbook as well as Emerson's *Essays* with him. I do not recall any great curiosity among us about the matter. Mother, I think, was a little disturbed. She had heard of "the new religion" through Aunt Mary, whose sister, Mrs. Carr, lived in Boston and who had spent a summer on the Buck farm a few years before. I think Aunt Mary had confided some small alarms to Mother, but Mother would have forgotten about it if Ernest had not brought the book home. However, she believed it was a matter of intellectual curiosity and said nothing about it.

The boys passed a few general remarks, as we did about all the books we read, and that was all except our annoyance that he read so late into the night: it bothered our sleep.

We had a wonderful time together again that summer. Everybody got home, although some stayed in the village scattered among our numerous relatives. But the summer was gone all too soon, and we had to separate again. It was painful to all of us, for we had an exceptional family affection and loyalty. Jerome went back to teaching chemistry at Bates College. I became the head of the Latin department and teacher of English in a Massachusetts high school. Charles returned to his schoolteaching in Massachusetts and William to superintend his string of schools in Connecticut and attend his psychology classes at Yale. Walter still ran his hardware store and bought and stored the potato crops of Lincoln Township. Guy and Luther remained in Lincoln, and Mother and Father lived on at their boardinghouse.

Ernest was off again for Boston to continue his education in dramatics at the Powers School of Expression, working in the Steeves' store part of the day and reading deep into the night. This lifelong habit actually gave him the wide and deep education that drew degrees and honors from many institutions throughout the world in later years.

Through his study and through his reflections he had come to the conclusion that there is *a spiritual law or principle* that could be called upon for healing, independent of any particular religious faith, and that anyone could use it—including himself. He was convinced that such a law or principle must be "simple—as simple as I was."

In later years, he told his students:

I had a strong feeling that there was some simple method which I could use without resort to the formulas I had found in books. Neither then nor afterward did I put much stress on formulas, because I believed that a statement of divine truth did not belong to any group or organization. Whatever power we use, I thought, must be impersonal and simple. . . . That fitted my need exactly and I determined to use it. This was really a breakthrough in my life. I escaped from the bonds of traditional church religion and entered into a new field of consciousness. It was, to be sure, a half-metaphysical use of faith and prayer, but how glorious was that first moment when I consciously used it!

It came about in this way. Although he now avoided religious discussions with the Steeves family, who thought that his reading was strange if harmless, he still had plenty of opportunity to talk with the students who went to the Powers School. They, too, had attended services at the Mother Church to hear Mrs. Powers read, and some had become Christian Scientists. When Ernest spoke of "giving a treatment," instead of "healing prayer," they looked at him with surprise.

"You have to take classwork," they said, "and learn a lot more about it than you know."

"How do you know how much I know about it?" he asked. He had the "feeling that if there is something anyone knows, then anyone else can know it, too. I felt it then as I have always felt it: there is no mystery to anything except Life Itself. Anyone can decide the way Life will work for him."

"Well, if you know enough, give me a treatment to overcome timidity and self-consciousness on the platform," one of them said, half-jokingly.

Ernest looked at him appraisingly. He was an earnest-faced young fellow, too slim for his height, his skin too white from indoor life, but good-looking enough and with a pleasing timbre in his voice.

"All right, if you want it," Ernest said. "Stand up like a man when you get on the platform, and I'll work for you."

It was a strange use of the word *work*, but somehow it carried the idea; and Ernest clung to it throughout his career —"I'll *work* for you. I'll do something in my mind that will take away your self-consciousness."

It "worked like a miracle." The young man forgot himself, concentrated on his delivery and was "cured" permanently.

"How did you do it?" he asked Ernest.

"It wasn't anything," Ernest said. He didn't feel sure *he* had done anything. He pondered on it. He was aware that he himself was never self-conscious on the platform, he was not concerned with how he looked or how he dressed but was wholly absorbed in the presentation of an idea.

In later reflection about the success of his treatment, Ernest concluded that all he had really done was to get the young man to "think the same thing I was thinking. He was reflecting my mind, I guess; what would have happened to him if my mind had been a blank, well, that would have been the ruin of a promising career—my own. If I had failed in the treatment, I might have given up. As it was I was eager to give it another try!"

His next opportunty came from an unlikely quarter—the Steeves family. Although they still could not fathom his unusual literature, nor the strange words he used, they all respected Ernest and were soon asking his spiritual help.

"I don't know what you do, but please do it," they said, and eventually all the family got in the habit of confiding in him, outlining a problem and relying on this semimysterious power he had "dug out of his books." And the growing number of successes proved to him that he was really "giving treatments in some sort of way and getting results as well. So I kept on."

Our Mother, still suffering from the heart trouble that had brought us so much fear as youngsters, was one of the first persons to get a thorough-going "treatment" from him, one in which he worked up a complete "argument" beginning with some reading from the Bible and other books, repeating "promises" from the Bible, denying the reality of any negative power and affirming what he conceived to be "the truth." He told me about it in later years:

As I look back on it, it appears like a "formula" but it was spontaneous and more in the nature of a prayer except that I had already learned not to beg God. I merely stated to myself that "no evil shall befall thee, neither shall any plague come nigh thy dwelling"; I thought about Mother and how good and kind she was, and that God had nothing against her. There was no need for her to be sick, and I half *asked* God to heal her and half *affirmed* that He would.

The treatment worked. Ernest was elated, of course, and with his insatiable curiosity began to probe his own mind, asking himself what he had really done. Mother got over her heart ailment permanently and lived for some forty-odd years afterward, passing on at the age of ninety-eight.

For one thing [he decided], I was praying, God came into the picture, but I prayed *positively.* I believed it was the Father's good pleasure to give Mother the kingdom, and I said so. This would be called affirmative prayer today and even some of the orthodox churches are using it. But church people of my day and a large part of them today prayed negatively, bringing Deity up-to-date on the wickedness of the world and the symptoms of their own suffering, and trying to get God to change His mind instead of changing their own. What happend in Mother's case was that I changed my own consciousness about her and in some way it reached her. I didn't know then how it happened but it did.

I pressed him years later to recall what actually went on in his mind at that time. "You didn't have a full-blown philosophy," I said. "How much philosophy did you really have?"

"It was in the egg, an embryo half-hatched but pipping through the shell. I still didn't know at that time what the writers on applied metaphysics meant by Divine Principle. But there was one thing they had made plain to me from the start and that is that 'God is good.' I don't mean 'holy,' for I had always believed *that,* but I mean 'good' toward you, toward everybody and anybody. It was really a new concept for me, and it thrilled me, too. It helped to answer a lot of my problems: 'God is good from the start, you don't have to win Him over.' It gave me greater confidence in the universe and answered more of my questions than anything I ever heard, because I could take the goodness of God as a starting point and work up from there. I felt at once that this was true and practical as well. Yes, the first and greatest result of all my study was 'God is good.' "

"But you never had fear of God, none of us feared God."

"That's true, but I had thought of God as *passive* good, not *active.* Now, I believed He was *working* at it and you could go along with Him. Besides, my association with others had colored my earlier thinking, of course. They were really afraid of God. They didn't feel safe in the universe, and most of them felt that both God and the universe were against them, and the first thing I had to do was to throw off the negative suggestion."

"Did you really understand all of that?" I asked.

"Not at the time, of course, not fully, but I intuitively worked along the line of affirming God's goodness and that sickness and suffering are not His will. I think it safe to say that I accepted the idea of the Divine Presence as much as I did the Divine Principle, but it was, as I said, mostly intuitive.

"There was a woman who talked with me then. She had an unhappy, agonized face. I learned that she had had a dissolute son who had been killed in an accident. It was not the death of the son that agonized her so much as it was the belief that he had gone to hell and was in torment there.

"I had already read somewhere that explanation can be the 'cure' and I felt that that would be the real treatment. I learned one of my first lessons right there. It isn't easy to change the religious habits of a lifetime, even if the other party is willing. It took time, and I remember reading where Jesus said to a boy, 'Son . . . thy sins be forgiven thee'; and then he read the minds of the scribes who were thinking, 'This man blasphemeth'; and he said, 'For whether is easier, to say, Thy sins be forgiven thee; or to say, Arise, and walk?' Then he healed the boy.

"It took *work* to remove the woman's fear and belief in hell and damnation. *I learned more while doing it than I got out of my studies at that time. It developed more faith in the goodness of God.* In fact, by the time I fully realized it as a living truth, the woman, too, was cured of her agony. You see, I was growing in my understanding. I had to work it out alone because I didn't know anyone with whom to talk it out. I had to ask and answer my own questions. My answers were probably only about half right, but I gradually began to figure out that there is a way of establishing a relationship between yourself and a 'good God.' It was more than 'having faith.' Lots of people in the church 'had faith,' but they were sick. This poor woman was sick but she had faith—faith in God and hell, too.

"I was forced to go back over everything I had read and try to work out some kind of Principle. No doubt I had read it before—often—but I hadn't developed a deep enough conviction. But from my rereading and thinking and from the experience of actually *working* for the afflicted woman, I began to get the concept deep inside of me that there was a Divine Presence with whom I could *commune*, but there was also a Divine Law which I could *use*. I even connected it up with Browning's 'All's love, yet all's law.' "

Ernest, at twenty-one, was already a dedicated seeker for truth, a pilgrim with his face set toward the Infinite; and it seemed with him, as with every honest seeker, as though the Infinite responded with intelligent and careful arrangements for his progressive education. The steps for inquiry, experiment and spiritual growth, each related to the previous one, opened sequentially, and he took each one in a spirit of high adventure.

Following his effort to help the grieving mother who believed her son to be in hell, it was natural for Ernest to search for the answer by an attempt to pierce the veil between time and eternity.

"*Where* was the boy who had died?" Ernest asked himself. He could not believe in hell; but did anybody really know where the soul went at the time of death? "Were the answers to be found only in the Bible and religion? Were there any reputable scholars who claimed to have had contact with the departed soul? If so, had they really learned anything from the entity?"

He was not content to leave the answer to religion or philosophy. The question ought to be studied by psychologists and physical scientists, he thought, but he determined to make personal inquiries whenever possible. If there was anything known about the future life and if it were possible to find assurance of survival of the soul beyond the grave, then all humanity ought to know about it. This was the beginning of an inquiry that lasted through many years and culminated in his eventual positive stand for immortality.

At the period when his interest was first aroused, inquiries into "psychic phenomena" were not foreign to the times. The expansion of spiritual mediumship had been rapid in the years between Ernest's birth and his twenty-first year, and Bostonians were openly and honestly fascinated by the spiritualists.

There was a man by the name of Wiggin who held spiritualistic meetings in Jordan Hall in the Conservatory of Music Building on Sunday nights. Ernest attended regularly and was, as he says, "terrifically impressed by him." To the wondering audiences, the man seemed to be in communication with the so-called dead. He gave "messages" or words of comfort and advice to people who were in attendance and was able to call "the spirit" by name and to give the name of the person in the audience to whom the message was directed. He often went into detail about the families concerned and revealed a knowledge of matters known only to them. It was weird, breathtaking and often frightening, but it was also fascinating. As usual, Ernest began to philosophize about it.

"I was impressed," he says in one of his notations, "but I did not believe there were 'spirits' talking to him. I argued to myself that this man is a spirit now as much as he will ever become. Then, if there is only one universe, he has access to the same knowledge that these so-called spirits have. But I don't know how he gets it."

Ernest concluded, however, that the arguments were as strong for the evidence of survival of the soul as they were against it and continued, "He certainly has something that is worth following out." In later years he did follow through and attended seances on unnumbered occasions only to find in regards to Spiritualists that

. . . They got just so far and never any farther. Once in a while someone [the medium] seems to break through and get a little more but it is a limited field. I still think that Spiritualism as a religion gives more comfort than most churches, because they believe in the extrasensory experiences described in the New Testament such as the appearances of angels, and the scene of the Transfiguration in which the patriarchs appeared to Jesus and the disciples. The Spiritualists, in other words, believe firmly in immortality and get more comfort from their religion than the communicants of the average church.

Ernest was, as usual, correlating his thoughts, trying to decide what he himself believed about survival and immortality and coming to the sensible conclusion that he didn't know enough to put up an argument with himself at that time. He used to say whimsically in the after years, "I knew more then than I do now; why didn't I settle the whole business while I knew so much!"

At that time, he was convinced, however, that he had hit upon the right answer to the suffering mother, that there was only One Spirit, that no soul could be lost out of It, and her son would find himself in Eternity. He knew that his philosophy was unclear and probably would not stand the test of theology, but he had no fear of "authority" and believed he could solve the problem completely, given time to do it. Besides, the woman had recovered her peace of mind, and he figured that "by their fruits ye shall know them."

It can be seen from the foregoing that Ernest imitated no ready-made system and followed no formula except what he created for himself. In fact, it was to be nearly ten years before he had perfected an organized expression of his own ideas and begun to teach his system to others. It was to be a half-century before his work was completed and he could commit his full-fledged philosophy to his followers and to posterity. Yet one of his last statements was this:

Do not adopt the letter of my teaching but the spirit and you will find as I did that you will begin to formulate a system that is true for you. My earliest recollection of my application of the principles of metaphysics to practical problems was the insecurity that follows the effort at imitation even of the best. I learned that you must develop faith and confidence in your own interpretation of God, man, and the universe.

III

Religious Background of the Idea
and Fields of Knowledge in 1909-1919

ERNEST, during his years at the Powers School, had no future plans beyond the field of public entertainment and the satisfaction of the inquisitive mind. Although he had not penetrated the big Chautauqua circuits, he was having success in neighboring cities by giving recitals of Browning's *Saul,* humorous verse and short popular plays like *The Perpendicular Farm.*

His mental life, however, was like a river into which big and little streams alike pour their waters. Some of these streams originate in obscure mountain springs of history and have run a long, long race with Time. Others are short-lived, like flash floods. Nor are they to be graded by volume, with the inpouring streams growing larger as the river progresses. By virtue of Ernest's destiny, the waters of wisdom, either ancient or modern, large or small, poured into his mind at just the moment they were needed.

He went on with his explorations in the field of mind, because his imagination and enthusiasm had been captured; there was no turning back. Here was a natural philosopher who was unconscious of philosophy as such, whose philosophy was from the first of a spiritual character. It was already becoming practical, for he was putting his ideas to the test in

actual efforts at healing among his friends and acquaintances.
It was not long after this that his reading began to expand
with such writers as Christian D. Larson, Ralph Waldo Trine
and Horatio W. Dresser. The influence they had upon him
can best be evaluated against the background of the movement that was known as Higher Thought, New Thought
and The New Philosophy, including some research into
psychic phenomena and psychology and the prevailing concepts in the field of religious philosophy of that time.

It is neither necessary nor possible to give a history here
of this evolution in great detail nor in chronological order,
but rather to make note of them only in connection with the
state of the world-soul during Ernest's formative years, and
the conditions under which it flowed into his unfolding consciousness.

The period around the turn of the century might be described as an age of struggle, with scientific materialism on
one side and religion on the other.

Unable to find answers in the orthodox churches, large
numbers abandoned their membership during this period
and drifted away or turned to new sources of faith.

A considerable number termed themselves "humanists"
and attempted to escape from supernaturalism and to discover in the natural world and in man the answer to the
riddle of the ages. They looked upon man as the end-product
of evolution and found no need to posit the concept of a God-
idea.

Others were drawn to the spiritual teachings of the orient
and the Theosophy movement flourished under the leadership of Mme. H. P. Blavatsky. Poets of the caliber of Sidney
Lanier and Walt Whitman had a major impact; and serious
students of the philosophy of Robert Browning formed themselves into "Browning Societies." Spiritualism as a religion
was at its zenith and the infant science of psychology was
beginning to have impact.

Even a partial study of the history and evolution of psychology and applied metaphysics leads to one of the most

fascinating streams of consciousness that ever took rise in a single desert spring where waters flowed out into the fields of history. The common source of all the movements that we have been discussing was the mind and theory of Dr. Friedrich Anton Mesmer (1734–1815). The period in Ernest's life when he first studied in Boston was a century after Mesmer's death.

It is not pertinent here to give a detailed history of Mesmer, the Austrian physician who created such a furor among the medical practitioners of his day; although he is worthy of all attention, for he began those investigations into drugless healing that started an ever-expanding research, which circles the world today. But, it is pertinent to outline the four stages of the historic development of his ideas.

Mesmer's own experiments form the first stage. He had noted certain phenomena that led him to believe that an unknown magnetic force was emitted at times from his own body and passed into his patient, bringing relief and often complete physical healing. His first method was to attempt to control this force consciously and at will, using his own body as the healing medium, but he was soon led to attempt to create a mechanical source of magnetism, using specially arranged substances of silk, wool, glass and iron filings, which reached the patient by means of a rod. The reaction of his patients to the stimuli that he created and that he believed imparted healing properties was often emotional and convulsive, but doubtless many of them were healed.

In making his theories known, he was met with bitter hostility and attacked and repudiated by his fellow physicians, who tabbed him a charlatan. A sincere and honest investigator, he stood by his convictions and from time to time interested others in his research. Although his work was physiological rather than psychological, it was the initial step in the evolution of psychology.

The second period began in 1814–15, when a man by the name of Abbé Faria, a Portuguese priest, appeared in Paris and exhibited certain mental phenomena. He believed that the source of his power lay not in him but in the individual himself and that it was possible to activate it by a command. He presented public exhibitions of what we now call somnambulism by giving a loud command that affected not only one but several individuals at the same time, using the one word *sleep*.

In 1841 the English physician James Braid accepted as genuine the phenomena but concluded that they were owing not to magnetism or occult physical forces but to some action of the mind. He noted that a fixed gaze and a suggestion brought about a sleep state, and he therefore applied the word *hypnotism* (Greek *hypnos*, sleep) to describe it.

A third period began about the middle of the nineteenth century. Of chief interest to us is the work of a New England clockmaker by the name of Phineas P. Quimby (1802–1866). He read in Maine papers reports of mesmerism and hypnotic healing and began to make experiments on his own account. He discovered that a hypnotized subject was able to diagnose certain forms of disease and that in this same state it was possible to induce healing in the patient. Quimby himself, having been healed, began to practice psychotherapeutics. He soon found that it was unnecessary to induce hypnosis and that by diagnosis and oral suggestions he was able to bring about the desired results.

The fourth period in the development of a psychological science embraces the investigations of F. W. H. Myers in the field of psychic phenomena. In his effort to explain telepathy, clairvoyance and supernormal powers, he rejected the traditional theories of occultism and possessing entities and tried to find some latent power in the normal mind that would account for the phenomena. Up to that time academic psychology had not achieved a knowledge of the dual powers of mind —conscious and subconscious. But Myers noted that those who exhibited psychic powers always did so in a subjective state as though it were another mind or secondary personality that was in control. He therefore concluded that a hidden or "subliminal self" took control of consciousness. That he gave it the title of "subliminal self" does not invalidate his discovery of the *subconscious* mind.

It was exactly in 1887, the year of Ernest's birth, that Myers formulated this theory and gave it to the world. The principles and practice of psychotherapeutics profited not only in dealing with abnormal states but in the whole field of hypnotism from that day to the present.

Sigmund Freud (1856–1939) employed the term *unconscious* in his writings around the turn of the century in dealing with subconscious mental states. He affirmed three states of consciousness—conscious, preconscious and unconscious—and declared that primitive impulses and strivings are embedded in the unconscious. The term *unconscious* had been employed by Harald Hoffding (1843–1931) but not in the specific sense of Myers' *subconscious*.

Every scientific discovery is followed by a change in philosophy of some sort, and this philosophy is determined by the attitude of the philosopher toward the physical sciences in general. If he is inclined to the mechanistic theory of evolution that stresses the function and behavior of the organism he will be a materialist. If, on the contrary, he is inclined to view man as a spiritual being, he will develop his philosophy in the direction of idealism. Freud became atheistic, while William James was an idealist.

The undoubted genius of Phineas P. Quimby is brought into clearest focus by the apprehension of the foregoing facts, for he antedated Myers, James and Freud in the practical employment of the psychology of analysis and suggestion in the healing of a patient. And in addition he formulated a religious philosophy based upon his observations and practice, which he named "Science of Health" and "Christian Science" as early as 1862. Quimby possessed an original capacity of observation and deduction, which enabled him not only to perform genuine and remarkable cures but also to develop the cornerstone of a body of belief that would eventually be followed by many schools of metaphysical healing.

In concluding his textbook, *Psychology,* William James not only noted that in 1910 there was no "science of psychology," only "the hope of a science," but predicted, "When the psychologists of the future come, as surely they will come, the necessities of the case will make them metaphysical." It was a prophecy of some forms of psychosomatics of our day, and later Ernest Holmes was to work valiantly with psychiatrists to fulfill this prophecy by correlating psychology and metaphysics.

At this point, if we call our chariot "Truth," we need to bring our horses into breast-to-breast position before following P. P. Quimby as he traveled the road from hypnotism to mental and metaphysical healing. Let us then look at kindred healing movements of this era.

The practice of mental healing and the philosophy of religion associated with it are not to be confused with the faith healing that was widely practiced in religious circles, often in connection with revivalistic campaigns then prevalent. Faith healing in the Western world has almost always been identified with the Christian religion, although it was practiced in Greek temples like that of Aesculapius' several thousand years ago.

The "mountain evangelist," George O. Barnes (born 1827), practiced faith healing in the 1880's and taught that the devil sends sickness and that God is the healer. In Shiloh in our own state of Maine when we were boys, F. W. Sanford (born 1863), a clergyman of high scholastic attainment, created a famous Home of Healing (1893) as a part of "The Holy Ghost and Us" movement of the Christian and Missionary Alliance.

Joseph Smith, Jr. (1805–1844), founder of the Mormon Church, began by exorcising evil spirits and practiced faith healing by the laying on of hands, prayer and baptism.

Francis Schlatter (1856–1909) was healing by faith in this decade. A strange spiritual man with the outward appearance of the traditional Jesus, he healed untold thousands. I have stood in Denver, Colorado, at the spot where in 1895 as many as five thousand people frequently assembled in a single day and passed six abreast along a fence where Schlatter stood. He clasped the hand of each as he passed, prayed for him separately.

John Alexander Dowie (1847–1907) formed the Christian Catholic Apostolic Church of Zion and was busy in San Francisco in Ernest's infancy (1888) organizing branches of the Healing Association. His message was threefold: Salvation, Healing and Holy Living. He was a man of vast talents and used them to promulgate what he believed; and he is said to have healed thousands of the sick by laying on of hands and the prayer of faith.

There were other influences stirring in the years pivoting around the turn of the century. In 1884 a book was published in America by Daniel Hack Tuke, M.D., F.R.C.P., on *Influence of the Mind upon the Body in Health and Disease,* a reprint from a London publication. This book by a medical practitioner and psychologist was probably the first of its kind in the field of psychosomatic medicine but is still fascinating reading with its case histories.

Twenty-odd years later an experimental activity called the Emmanuel Movement was being carried on in a Boston Backbay church by an Episcopalian minister, Reverend Elwood Worcester. This work was based on psychological "science" in collaboration with Dr. Isador H. Coriat, with whom Worcester wrote the book *Religion and Medicine,* which had been published the year before (1908) and was directed toward "The Moral Control of Nervous Disorders." They especially stressed the therapeutic power of prayer and treated such diseases as tuberculosis with great success. But Worcester stood aloof from metaphysics and was unsympathetic toward both New Thought and Christian Science because of a misconception of their philosophy. This pioneer experiment in pastoral psychology dried up, leaving, for the moment, no living water flowing into the great stream.

To find the living water, to penetrate the mystery of consciousness from the standpoint of the psychology that was begun by Mesmer like an artesian well flowing to this day, we must recognize the several streams that originated in it. One stream was the psychoanalytic movement developed by Bauer, Freud, Jung, Adler and their successors. Another stream, that which most closely affected Ernest Holmes, passed through the consciousness of Phineas P. Quimby and emptied directly into the mind of Mary Baker Eddy, who transformed it into a new religion, Christian Science; and into the minds of a Swedenborgian minister, Warren Felt Evans, and a newspaperman, Julius Dresser, who transformed it into a New Philosophy, which came to be known as New Thought or the New Thought Movement.

The faith healing, the search for a soul, the timid stirrings of psychology in the fields of medicine and religion certainly indicate that something was "in the air" at Ernest's birth and that the crystallization or synthesis still lay waiting in what Jung later called "the collective unconscious" at the time of Ernest's first inquiry into mental-spiritual science. It is important to reflect upon the practical aspects of this striving toward a new spiritual philosophy as distinct, let us say, from the metaphysics of Meister Eckhart (1250–1328). Eckhart perceived, even at that date, a Unitary Cause and that It indwells all men equally and that the *Only One* is forever begetting the only begotten son and "is begetting him in me today," but there was no healing significance attached to such awareness, nor was it expressed by any other person until Quimby!

In many, if not in all, religious movements, healings have occurred by means of faith and prayer, in the fields, in churches, at shrines and in hospitals for the sick, but a *definite system of spiritual mind healing* was never announced until it was voiced by the one-time clockmaker of New England.

IV

Foreground of the Idea

The New Philosophy

It was in 1840 that Phineas P. Quimby began his experiments with hypnosis. Eighteen years later he had progressed so far with his theory and practice that he took up the regular healing work that he carried on for the rest of his life. During this period he not only gave mental-spiritual treatments but wrote down his experiences and his interpretations of them in the now well-known book *The Quimby Manuscripts*. He declared that he gave no medicine but explained to the patient that his disease was the result of "error," and this knowledge could cure. It was his belief that body fluids were affected by opinions induced by fear or by medicine and that the condition was corrected by discharging these opinions from the mind. It was his belief that man is made up of truth and belief; and, if he is deceived into a belief that he has, or is liable to have a disease, the belief is catching and the effect follows; that the source of the belief may be from parents, the public or the patient and therefore there is no fixed rule of procedure. "Therefore it requires great shrewdness to get the better of the error: for disease is the work of the devil or errors. . . ."

Mr. Quimby possessed extraordinary powers of intuitive perception such as today are of interest to the investigator of extrasensory perception. He required no description nor recital of symptoms and no diagnosis and was able to tell the patient what the latter had already been told by the medical diagnostician. Then he proceeded with his "mental treatment"; many wonderful reports were made of his cures.

He was a natural philosopher, for he pondered much on the science and religion that underlay his technique. Being a religious man, he began to compare his practice with cases of healing in the Bible and concluded that the results were due not to miracle but to "a science of mind." Part of his technique, therefore, was shaped toward removing fear from the patient, releasing his emotional stresses and distressing memories and replacing them by positive or affirmative mental states. He believed that each negative state could be replaced by its opposite. By successful experience with hundreds of patients and constant effort to understand the *modus operandi*, he worked out the principles that became the foundation for future "healers" or "practitioners" of his science, including denial and affirmation, "spiritual realization" on his own part and acceptance on the part of the patient. There was here no charlatanism, psychism, "faith-cure" or hypnotism. Because of his honesty and the fact that his theory developed from and was not the source of his practice, he created a practical science.

It should be recalled here that Quimby was working with principles that had not yet been defined by psychology, that the term *subconscious mind* had no scientific significance until 1887, and Freud had not brought forth his theories of the "unconscious."

What was it that enabled this man, narrowly educated in the schools, to found a system destined to outlive Freud's psychoanalysis and expand into unlimited future service to the world? This factor was his spiritual and religious faith and his interpretation of Christianity from *above* rather than *below*. In other words, he sought to demonstrate that man is of divine origin, not merely an aggregate of emotions, instincts, and reflexes, without a soul, but a living spirit, related to God and to eternity.

It seems strange that this obscure genius should have known and practiced so many principles of psychology before the scientific verification of the subconscious mind by Myers (1887). He anticipated many of the findings of Freud but arrived at different conclusions, perceiving man as a spiritual entity and not a compound of atavistic impulses.

He created a "science of healing" based on psychology and religion. He was able by intuition to put himself *en rapport* with the patient and to diagnose him, not from the standpoint of physical disease but rather from the patient's *belief* in the disease. Holding that belief in a disease, acquired through suggestion, was the cause of the malady, he made it his practice to "analyze the belief," to consider the patient's mental attitudes, his temperament and the various sources of what he called "error." He then sought to restore wholeness by explaining the cause ("The only medicine I ever give is my explanation and that is the cure."), to build confidence in his recovery and help him to meet the character defects that fostered his malady. To this end he made use of his knowledge of the Bible, having discovered that the Scriptures reported healings of similar maladies, and he added to it by sitting with the patient and silently meditating in what he termed "spiritual realization," from which a practice of "meditation" developed.

Quimby's philosophy was slanted toward idealism, because it repudiated materialism; and he stressed mental causation and the spiritual nature of man. But his rejection of the power of matter over mind could not be denominated a philosophy, although in his reaction against materialism he no doubt anticipated the idealism of the eighties, which was of similar origin.

Reverend W. F. Evans, the Swedenborgian preacher, having met and conversed with Quimby, came to the conclusion that his position was in harmony with the philosophy of Bishop Berkeley, with which he had been conversant before his conversion in the Swedenborgian Church, and he affirmed that Swedenborg himself held the same opinion.

Through Reverend Evans' influence, Emanuel Swedenborg, the Swedish seer, scientist and mystic who founded the Church of the New Jerusalem, exercised a strong influence on the early literature of the New Philosophy. Swedenborg possessed remarkable powers now known as ESP, while at the same time demonstrating scientific skill that has won for him recognition as father of several modern sciences. His so-called "law of correspondences" is most familiar and acceptable to metaphysical practitioners. "As below, so above," he says. This is in harmony with the theory of "thought patterns" that was later accepted and elaborated by Ernest, the object of treatment being to create or release the inherent pattern of perfection so that it shall find its correspondence in the body.

Reverend Evans became not only a disciple of Quimby's, but one of the early and influential writers, along with Julius and Horatio Dresser, who attempted to expound and develop Quimby's findings, but the Quimby manuscripts themselves were not published until 1921.

Evans interpreted the teachings of Quimby into philosophical terms, denying the reality of disease on the grounds that there was no material body to experience it. He declared that "Men err when they suppose objects exist independent of a perceiving mind." His inference was that if you do not see a thing, it will disappear. This was a misinterpretation of Bishop Berkeley, who held that an object can be verified only by perceiving it and who maintained that cosmic objects have permanent *being* in the Divine Mind. Evans' greatest error lay in denying the body instead of the disease. Later practitioners of the metaphysical schools cautioned against denying the body.

"Disease being in its root a false belief," said Evans, "change that belief and we cure the disease." And Mary Baker Eddy, who had experienced healing through treatment by Quimby and been his follower and disciple for some time, later elaborated this by affirming in effect that disease is an image held in the mind until it appears in the body. In these instances the denial is not of the body but of the disease.

Mary Baker Eddy became the most celebrated among those who further developed the theory and practice of spiritual mind healing. In 1875 she published her *Science and Health with Key to the Scriptures* and in the same year founded an institution in Lynn, Massachusetts, but transferred its seat to Boston in 1882—this magical epoch of the eighties—where she developed a religious organization that has spread throughout the world.

Mrs. Eddy appears to have been in general harmony with the psychology, religion and technique of Quimby, but she found it necessary to reject much of his picturesque language and some of his practices. She repudiated the principle of dualism, that man is a composite of spirit *and* matter. She declared that matter is not a thing-in-itself and is incapable of sensation apart from the cognizing mind. In her *Scientific Statement of Being,* which is both a doctrine and a treatment, she declared that "There is no life, truth, intelligence, nor substance in matter." She completely rejected hypnotism as a method of treatment, since it was based upon the concept of "minds many" instead of relying solely on the One Mind. She was not content merely to reject matter as cause, but followed up with a positive statement of being, which affirms that "All is infinite Mind and its infinite manifestation. . . ."

Mr. Quimby had no organized system of philosophy, yet the elements of a system were implicit in what he said, furthered no doubt by his contact with Evans. "Matter," Quimby said, "is an unsubstantial appearance and is created and governed by thought. Men err when they suppose objects to exist independent of a perceiving mind." He thus quoted from Reverend Evans, but there is no evidence that he denied reality to an experience.

For further clarification we should remark that Evans seems to have communicated Berkeley's philosophy both to

Quimby and Mrs. Eddy without knowing that Berkeley had himself misconceived Kant—what Kant affirmed was that the mind is led into illusion in its effort to demonstrate the existence of a real world—and Evans promoted the thesis that "if you don't see it, it isn't so." It is important to observe this misconception, as it is the basis of the "system of denials" that forms the major rubrics of many schools of metaphysics.

Quimby did not deny the experience, as we have said, but he nonetheless looked upon disease as the evidence of "a false belief" and concluded that the *cure of the belief* would result in or actually *was* the *cure of the disease.* To which Mrs. Eddy contributed that "sickness is a delusion."

The various metaphysical movements that rooted in this philosophy accordingly instituted their system of "denials" or refusal to acknowledge the negative. Ernest Holmes did not accept this concept and, as we shall later see, built a different type of metaphysical practice.

Evans, who was deeply impressed by the word *idea,* which Quimby used in the sense of a mental picture, interpreted it in the terms of philosophy as used by Plato and Hegel, that is, as an absolute principle or divine pattern. He fostered the philosophic rather than the psychological concept and taught that nothing existed outside the perfect and the ideal. Everything else was unreal; this included disease and limitation, evil and even death. Everything that denied perfection was an illusion and disappeared in the light of truth by means of the spoken word, which denied the false and affirmed the real.

For convenience a sort of pseudo-mind was permitted, but this referred only to habit-thinking or misconceptions of reality. There was here the tentative recognition of accumulated impressions that were part of the race memory; and those which had a destructive tendency could be eliminated by rejection and denial of their reality and therefore of their power to control the health or well-being of the individual. All that was needed was to recognize the existence of the beautiful, the good and the true—these only—and the slaves of misconception, poverty, disease and death would be set free.

Psychologists of the school of suggestion accounted for the cures that so often resulted from these religio-psycho-philo-sophical principles, while the skeptical denied them alto-gether. The proponents of New Thought, however, did not practice suggestion in which one mind submits to the direc-tion of another either consciously or unconsciously, but rather taught meditation, self-realization or "the silence" as a means of realizing perfect states of consciousness that would auto-matically release the person from destructive states of disease and limitation.

The principle of any philosophy is that it maintains a position or *point of view* that is the key to its system. It must have the assurance that it takes into account and explains more of the facts associated with it than any other theory or principle, and it must make sure that no elements are included that contradict it. Nor can facts be excluded for convenience of the arguments.

The New Thought or Metaphysics accepted the demonstra-tion of the presence and reality of a soul independent of the vehicle in which it functions and emphasized that soul is not to be looked upon as a by-product of evolution, a composite of chemical reactions and instincts, a pawn of nature. All branches of the movement accepted *soul* as *an entity* emerging from and yet immersed in Infinite Being and not subject to death or annihilation. It is related to God, for it *is* God in individual manifestation that confirms the words of Jesus, "I say ye are gods," and the quotation from Paul the Apostle, "For in Him we live, and move, and have our being. . . ." As such, man possesses the *powers of God* in all affairs that con-cern the well-being and satisfaction of the individual both as to health, wealth, freedom, love and survival.

The new emergent in the metaphysical field differed from both the Oriental and the Grecian concept of Plato in one respect; that is, it claimed the scientific demonstration of the existence and nature of the soul and developed a system for the purpose of applying the powers of the soul to the attainment of health and abundance. This system was an entirely new concept in the field of religion.

It was inevitable that such concepts and practices led to a further study of the nature of mind and of matter, illuminated by the newborn principles of psychology and fostered by the almost universal effort of religion to free itself from the death clutch of materialism and find new stars and safe guidance upon the seas of faith.

The movement had spread rapidly, and was adopted in part at least by many clergymen. It was called in Boston the "Mind Cure" or the "Boston Craze," but magazines and books published to teach its tenets had wide circulation.

Scholarly preachers whose denomination permitted excursions into the philosophy of New Thought frequently applied it to their discourses, and as understanding widened, it was not unusual during more than a half-century to hear sermons strongly influenced by it.

It was bitterly repudiated by orthodoxy in general, however, because it endowed man with power to personally solve some of his problems without recourse to miracles, theology or Christology. It did not leave enough room for the devil, salvation by the blood, predestination, nor damnation for nonconformity. They also criticized the New Philosophy because it taught that "sin" was not inherent in the human soul and failed to support the ancient doctrine that "in Adam's fall, we sinned all."

The dominance of inherited theologies was overcome at that time by such men as Reverend Dr. John Randall, a Baptist preacher in a Fifth Avenue Church in New York, who wrote *The Spirit of the New Philosophy* and other such books and lectured on the subject in his own church. On the other hand, even those who accepted New Thought found it difficult to cast off old theological traditions. Horatio W. Dresser, in his *Handbook of the New Thought*, unconsciously damns it with faint praise in the first half of the volume and saps it at every other joint in the second half. "Choice," he says, "is only half relative, . . ." "man proposes and God disposes" (of his plans).

These were not the only problems faced by the pioneers of the New Philosophy. There was one in particular with which they wrestled and of which Ernest Holmes was aware from the very beginning. It was the problem of *semantics*.

Those who taught and practiced body healing by mental means found it necessary to develop a language to describe it, and the word *metaphysics* was given a new and special meaning. Aristotle had created it to define what came *after* (*meta*) physics. His *physics* had dealt with objects of sense. His *metaphysics* was a term to describe abstract thinking or philosophy, but it had no reference to the science of mental healing. Except for isolated cases as at the Temple of Aesculapius no one had practiced healing without the use of medicine. When the practice of pure mental healing originated in America in the last half of the nineteenth century, words that described the theory and practice were added in glossaries to the textbooks for that purpose.

Leander Edmund Whipple began to teach in Hartford, Connecticut, in 1885 and early wrote books under the title of mental healing and mental science and later published the outstanding *Metaphysical Magazine*. In 1896 Horatio W. Dresser published the *Journal of Metaphysics*. The organization that later became The International New Thought Alliance, a loose grouping of independent metaphysical teachers and churches, was first known as the *Metaphysical Alliance*. In 1895 mental science leaders founded the Metaphysical Club in Boston, which took an important part in later forming the INTA.

Later Ernest and I named our work *The Metaphysical Institute of California*. The word *metaphysics* was (in our usage) to be correlated with *idealism*, which is the philosophy basic to the Science of Mind and accepted by those who heal by the word only. Idealism as used in metaphysical practice maintains that the objects we see are actually ideas held in the Mind of God. Metaphysics explains the nature of these ideas. It also provides a theory of knowledge and attempts to explain the nature of being itself. It disputes the nineteenth-century claim of materialism that "all is infinite matter" and asserts on the contrary that "all is Infinite Spirit." This is also in line with transcendentalism and the essays of Emerson.

Bertrand Russell, noted English philosopher, once said that we live in a monistic universe and that everything must be either spirit or matter; it cannot be both; that is, all is spirit or all is matter. He preferred to call it matter. On the contrary, the monistic idealist or the metaphysician prefers to call it spirit. Lord Haldane, the great English scientist, said, "nothing exists apart from mind and without mind it has no meaning."

It was not long after the time of Quimby that the great writers in the metaphysical movement saw that it was in harmony with the teachings of the Germanic philosophers of idealism like Fichte, Schelling and Kant or like Spinoza and Bishop Berkeley; yet it was not that school of idealism that brought the multitudes into the metaphysical movement. It was a human and desperate need to escape from materialism: it was existential, rising out of the fact.

And they came to metaphysical churches in those early days by the hundreds. By the time Ernest Holmes had reached mature years they came by the thousands. By then the Idea, too, had reached maturity, and he was prepared to receive them. They were still looking for faith, for healing of mind and body, for the full and abundant life promised by Jesus. And Ernest, by that time, had proved he had found a sure way. Meanwhile, his preparation and his search went on in quietness and confidence and the spirit of adventure.

V

꒱꒱

The Holmes Family Moves West

Growth of the Idea

DURING THE early years, Ernest and I were like two streams flowing through alien lands of intellectual inquiry. I knew nothing of the New Philosophy but was inducted into a new theology just the same.

We met seldom, except in the summers at the lake, or when I stopped off in Boston en route to a quick trip home to Maine. While Ernest was following one stream of inquiry, I was following another, and it seems strange in retrospect to observe how soon those two streams were to unite on the opposite side of the continent and for many years flow together as one.

I was at that time studying philosophical and theological problems in the more conventional manner by attending Hartford Theological Seminary, a Congregational school for the ministry. It is necessary to speak of this at this point because of the unquestioned bearing my conventional training had upon both Ernest and myself in our very near as well as our distant future.

In 1908 and 1909 the theological world was in a period of change and adaptation to the requirements of the new age of science, and my own professors were taking a strong lead in it.

The ancient concepts of dualism were under scrutiny. Physical science had forced a reexamination of old concepts. The problems of mind and matter were being discussed as much in the pulpit and seminary as in the Metaphysical Club or the laboratory and university. Theories of good and evil flew about like swarming bees or hornets. The inference is obvious, each stinging the other for holding an opposite view. In contrast with present-day tolerance in the contest between traditionalism and existentialism, there was a kind of spiritual bitterness between various factions.

Men like Josiah Royce, the noted Harvard professor of philosophy, were accepting the principle of monistic idealism but coming to strange conclusions about it. It was like freeing an imprisoned man by striking off his shackles and then putting him into a different cell. Royce yielded to the proposition that all we can know with certainty is drawn out of mental experience. He properly deduced this from science itself, which had provided the grounds, by observing that we have all manner of mental experiences that have no counterpart in nature, such as softness and hardness, fragrance, light, sound, color, perspectives of distance or nearness or direction. An object in water can be wet but there is no "wetness" as a thing-in-itself. The physical world, idealists like Royce claimed, was not what it appeared to be, and reality could be determined only by mental means. Therefore, Royce concluded, a Cosmic Mind is necessary to make the world intelligible and real.

A new position in philosophy plunges its proponent into the theological problem of evil, and Royce became curiously involved. Having taken the position of absolute idealism, he concluded that all things existed in the mind of God, and, therefore, evil has eternal existence and God is in an eternal struggle with it. God is, of course, eternally in the process of overcoming, and He "pays the cost in unutterable suffering."

It is to be presumed that he had no acquaintance with New Thought, which also propounded an absolute idealism, but which argued that evil is not inherent in the universe but in man's inharmonious relationship to it and that, therefore, evil *per se* has no existence. This was one of the assertions of Mrs. Eddy and New Thought that the theologians of the evangelical church struck out against. Their arguments were not only absurd but futile. The successors of these theologians have since changed their attitude, but we must take it into account at that period, nonetheless, in order to follow the contrasting philosophy of religion developing in Ernest's mind.

While I was struggling with the New Theology in Hartford, Ernest was progressing with dedication but without strain into the New Philosophy.

It was in 1909, when he was twenty-two years of age, that we see Ernest in the act of picking up a book by Christian D. Larson called *The Ideal Made Real* or *Metaphysics for Beginners,* which was published in that same year, and launching out into the stream of New Thought. I cannot overstress the importance of observing this step-by-step unfoldment of his understanding, for in so doing any reader can automatically and progressively develop his own.

No one could read Larson's *The Ideal Made Real* without experiencing a high spiritual feeling and a confidence in the value of faith in attaining a better life; Ernest was no exception. The determined student can find the "method" embedded in it. It avoided ecclesiastical terminology and the word *God* was seldom used. On the other hand, the student was urged to see "the spiritual kingdom" and to develop "the Christ Consciousness, finding the true source of the life more abundant in health, happiness and perpetual increase in power." He wrote, "Perpetual harmony is necessary to attainment in every field, and success is founded in large measure upon the continuous expression of gratitude."

Ernest's comprehension of Larson was made easier by his knowledge of Emerson. Emerson had led him into a concept of a spiritual universe and a spiritual "self" and a need for a faith in a universal Consciousness responsive to demands made upon It. Ernest was ready therefore to derive an enormous inspiration from *The Ideal Made Real,* and it encouraged him to go forward in learning and practicing the art of mental treatment. At that time, as he says in his manuscripts, "My treatments were half metaphysical and half the use of faith and prayer. I now felt more strongly that my treatments would work—and they *did* work—which encouraged me to more work!"

His mental measuring stick was still Emerson, and he declared that the discovery he had made through Emerson of the uniqueness of the self and the freedom of the individual to adopt a new doctrine enabled him to accept what Larson had to say. Ernest knew little or nothing at this time about the principles of conscious and subconscious mind, but he had accepted from Emerson "the principle of a new field of consciousness, something in my own mind and my own being that was one with a universal consciousness"; and he was ready to accept the inspired teaching of Larson that the power to control health, happiness and environment was resident in his own mind.

There were three particular points emphasized by Larson that broadened Ernest's understanding and made a great impression. The first was instruction on the subject, "Pray Without Ceasing," advocating the practice of the highest states of what he called "the silence" and indicating a *method* of treatment:

"Relax mind and body, close your eyes and be perfectly quiet; turn your attention on the inner life of the soul and gently hold your mind upon the thoughts of stillness and peace." He then proceeds with statements of truth about oneself—statements that can, of course, be made about another person.

Larson concludes, "When you know that you are in the *image of God* your thoughts will be right. See yourself as you are in your true being and that you are, even now, in full possession of all good and all health; and it will soon express the way you think."

The second point dealt with "contradictions," or the

appearances that would deny an all-good God and man in His image. Larson said: "To think the absolute truth at first seems a contradiction, because we are so used to judging from appearances, but when we find that appearances are simply the result of thought . . . we shall no longer see contradiction."

The third point, however, was the most stimulating to Ernest's expanding consciousness. Historically considered, *The Ideal Made Real* was one of the first full book expositions on the subject of "the control of conditions." While such a possibility was implicit in Emerson's essays and in the principles of New Thought, it was not *explicit*. Early writings stressed the healing of mind and body; but Christian D. Larson indicated strongly the use of the same principles as applied to life situations.

In a chapter titled "Create Ideal Surroundings," Larson taught that one must first of all think in terms of the ideal, and this eventually by a natural law will affect and control his environment.

Ernest found inspiration in applying the principles of metaphysics to other matters than healing the body, for Larson handled the subject so delicately and spiritually as to remove any feeling of commercialization of the truth.

Ernest himself had not formulated in 1909–10 a systematic method or technique of treatment and did not do so until four or five years later. He was always wary of formulae, anyway, lest they lead to formalism and to meaningless repetition like a Buddhist prayer wheel.

He went on with his study of Emerson, and abandoned the Christian Science textbook for the New Thought writings of Larson, and another fine book, *In Tune With the Infinite* by Ralph Waldo Trine. Julius Dresser and his wife Annette had already published *The Philosophy of P. P. Quimby,* but Ernest did not read it at this time. He had skimmed Dresser's *The True History of Mental Science,* but found it more controversial than inspirational. He was in no way interested then or later in the human antagonisms or organizational

difficulties that developed between those who had been ex-
posed to the early teachings of Quimby and the disciples'
disciples. He believed and stated that there was "no copyright
on Truth." He himself sought truth wherever he could find
it and gave what he had wherever and whenever it was asked.
This consistent attitude enabled him all his life to place
principle before human personalities and to separate the
wheat from the chaff.

It was in 1909 that a remarkable personality, Sigmund
Freud, visited this country and set Ernest to work winnow-
ing the grain. Ernest did not know of the theories and techniques of Freud until the autumn of that year; none of his
influence as yet had invaded the literature of metaphysics.
Freud lectured on psychoanalysis in Worcester, Massachusetts, on the "Interpretation of Dreams." Ernest did not hear
the lecture but read it from published writings and was
impressed with the fact that Freud had freed consciousness
from physiology, thus changing it from the science of brain
to the science of mind. But it seemed to him that Freud
propounded two minds in place of two aspects of the one
mind. It appeared to him as a form of dualism of conscious
mind and unconscious mind.

He felt that both Freud and New Thought were mistaken
but finally determined that it was more a question of semantics. He concluded, however, that Freud was in error when
he failed to support a "super-mind" or an "Over-soul" with
Emerson. A second inconsistency, he thought, was Freud's
accepting a "sick self," for he had denied a *self* that could get
sick, and concluded that Freud's materialism was in direct
conflict with the concept of a spiritual universe.

If this seems to show a deeper and more penetrating
analysis than we would expect from a young mind untrained
in the academic approach to logic and philosophy, it is all
the more important to note this early evidence of his rational-
izing ability as he approached those years in which he would
formulate an original philosophy of science and religion.

Although it was not evident at the time, for Ernest was

still enthusiastically attending dramatic school and reciting *Saul* and *The Perpendicular Farm,* he was in truth moving steadily toward that destiny and further and further away from the Chautauqua Circuit. The next actual move, however, in the unfolding pattern of our lives, was mine.

In 1910 I was compelled by ill health to leave Hartford Theological Seminary. The doctor held out the hope of recovery in a warm climate, and I secured a job on a ranch through a schoolmate whose father lived in Ventura, California. I made the journey by "tourist train," in which the passenger cooked his own meals and slept on the cane-bottomed seats.

My employer met me with a horse and buggy and drove me to his dairy ranch seven miles distant. Here I stayed for some months, but I was not happy there and went to Pasadena to live with a clergyman and his family, through whose influence I was invited by the superintendent of the Southern California Congregational Conference to become a home missionary in a country-farm neighborhood called Prado, near Pomona.

Mother came out from Maine to join me there, rejoiced to find me improved in health, and here we built a cottage-type church with chapel and living rooms. We lived in Prado that winter, and the whole countryside pitched in to help us and make us happy. A fresh ham or other food was often left at our door at night; one evening there was a big party, and twelve women each brought a laying hen. Thereafter we were constantly supplied with Egyptian corn to feed them. We ate forty dozen eggs that winter.

The inland heat of summer was too great for me, so we moved to Venice, where I was soon asked again to act as home missionary and build up a congregation. In a very short time we had a sizable attendance, holding services in a barnlike structure that had once been used as a bathhouse or "plunge." I got along well with the people in the city and soon filled the hall to capacity on Sunday night.

I had not been in Venice long before Ernest came from Boston to visit Mother and me. The year was 1912, and my brother was now twenty-five, an exuberant, robust young man, not tall, but extremely dynamic, with thick curly brown hair, a strong, sizable nose and chin, merry blue eyes and strangely eloquent hands, which all combined to give the illusion that he was handsome. Handsome, Ernest never was. Not even our mother nor later his devoted wife claimed this distinction for him. But he always had an enormous charm that made mere regularity of features look pale by comparison. Such is my memory of him that I can see him today as I saw him then—young, vital, intelligent, alive with affection and good will.

Little did I think when I met him at the station in Venice that our lives would be so closely bound through so many years. He himself was as little aware. He was prepared for the profession of platform entertainer, and I as a preacher. We went to the parsonage where Mother was waiting, and it was a happy occasion for us all.

The parsonage was a two-story beachhouse with two bedrooms and a pull-out bed in the living room; it was so inviting that Ernest wanted to stay on. He had no money, but as he said, "I am full of work and funny." I thought his staying on was a splendid idea and within a few days had window cards printed to advertise him as an entertainer. Soon he secured an engagement to entertain at a Pomona church, where one of my friends was the preacher.

This part of the story comes to an abrupt end. He didn't like it! He came back late that night and said, "It's too much work for too little money. It's my last time." I was disappointed, because I had eighty dollars invested in it!

I tell it as it happened, because it was always characteristic of him to make abrupt changes when he felt they were called for and not to argue about it. He did not then know what he *would* do, but he had discovered in one trip to Pomona what he would *not* do. Meanwhile, there was plenty he could do to help me with my church. So he stayed on with us, and we all lived together for many years.

In Venice, Ernest helped me in the organization of the Junior Church, which was a unique adventure in those days and widely reported in current religious journals like the *Congregationalist.* It was perhaps the first of its kind. All the officers were children under sixteen years of age. The morning service was given over to the youth exclusively, with a youth choir and special music. My sermons for them were sometimes written in story or dialogue form with such titles as "The Quest of the Noble Heart," in an extended series, and the youngsters were intrigued by this type of presentation.

Ernest was popular with both the youngsters and the adults. As early as January, 1913, he gave a dramatic recital for the church. He helped decorate the platform, and I recall one occasion where he hung canary cages among the flowers all around the auditorium. They sang with the choir, and created so much of an impression that the Los Angeles papers reported it the next day.

It was necessary for him to find paying work, and he secured a position on July 12, 1913, as Playground Director for the Grammar School. He admitted that he didn't know what to do or how to do it, but he'd soon find out. And he did. All he had to do was play with the kids and they loved it and him. He had some acquaintance with a ball and bat and could call balls and strikes with anybody. The boys, especially the batter, didn't always agree with him; but they liked him immensely, and that was enough.

Meanwhile Ernest went right on with his reading in metaphysics when he could. I was so absorbed in organizing and building up a church congregation in the beach city that I paid little attention to what he was reading, and we did not talk about it at all during his first year in Venice.

He was always ready to do anything for the church, especially in the field of entertainment, and our mutual activity centered there. We had organized a men's club, called The Goodfellows, which included members drawn both from the

church and businessmen of the city. I find in my old scrap-
books that on March 17 of that year he had given humorous
readings from Maine poets to the club, and on April 13 he
had put on a banquet and made a short speech with a large
number of notables present, including officials of the city
and Los Angeles.

Mother added to the church by assisting in the organization of the Ladies' Social Service Circle, which did an immense amount of work for the local needy and raised a
considerable amount of money for the church. Mother's
participation must be noted, because she was later to become
widely known in the social and charity work of the Institute
of Religious Science. She was given the name of "Mother
Holmes" among unnumbered thousands in Southern California.

Ernest helped in the founding of the young men's club
called The Lagoon Lobsters, composed of church members,
who challenged the High School debaters and won a decision
over them.

In June, 1913, the Fellowship Club staged a play called
The Waiter Who Didn't Wait. The newspapers gave it a lot
of attention and spoke of Ernest as "an experienced teacher
in dramatic expression."

It was in that month, too, that Jerome stopped off briefly
with his bride on their way to Japan, where he was to act
as a foreign missionary and conduct a language school in
which English-speaking men and women could learn Jap-
anese, a language in which he soon became proficient.

Jerome and his wife Jennie stayed with us for the summer,
and in August Father and my brother Guy with his wife
Emma and their two children, Josephine and Lawrence, appeared on the scene. We had a compact household by this
time. We stretched out our sleeping facilities by using my
study and a storage room, and we were all happy, intensely
happy.

Guy immediately joined Ernest in working with the young
people, whom they took to Topanga Canyon for an outing,

which was the beginning of the establishment of a permanent camp there, and where Ernest took the Boy Scout troop that he organized for the church a year later. Ernest's interest in the Boy Scouts was manifest with his usual enthusiasm. He was cheerful, untiring, half-worshiped by the troop; and weekends saw them taking off into the canyons or along the beaches. When they disbanded for the night, there was often one left over to be fed and watered at the parsonage.

This troop included one very special youngster, Reginald Armor, who later became Ernest's protégé and has been associated with his work for many years.

It was in October, 1913, after the departure of Jerome and Jennie, that we began to get into local politics. It was a campaign to prohibit prizefighting in Venice, which, as a Congregational minister with a young flock in the area, I supported; for several weeks there was a debate between us and the promoters, which was carried on in the daily press. I wrote our arguments and rebuttals for the Venice *Daily Vanguard,* and we took the lead in the campaign and eventually won, the vote being heavily in our favor. This was a very important matter so far as Ernest was concerned, for although he never stated how he felt about the issue, he was, as usual, willing to lend me a hand; and this brought him into new friendships that were of critical importance in his life.

Among the local supporters of the campaign was the city engineer, a man of good education and character by the name of H. B. Eakin. He was not a churchgoer but a believer in religion, and we received a letter of congratulation from him. Ernest had worked with him on some political details, and a friendship ripened between them.

Eakin was also a city playground commissioner. He suggested that Ernest take over the city purchasing department and storeroom, which he did, eventually giving up his playground duties. It was this contact with Eakin which resulted in Ernest's most intensive period of study and experimentation to date, his contact with the second major influence in his unfoldment and eventually in his first public lecture on metaphysics and his active entry into the particular ministry to which he would dedicate his life.

VI

Our Life in Venice

Ernest Discovers Troward and New Theory of Prayer

THE FIRST BENEFITS of the new job Mr. Eakin offered Ernest were reading hours, even at work. After he quit the playground Ernest had plenty of time, because the tasks involved as purchasing agent for the city of Venice were negligible. He was not even required to make a choice between rival supply houses, because the political machine took care of that. All he had to do was to transmit and record the orders. So he read and thought during his hours on duty.

He had discovered the Metaphysical Library, run by a Mrs. Reeseburg in the Brack Shops in downtown Los Angeles. Mrs. Reeseburg, her library and the Brack Shops were to figure largely in his first giant steps into a new world, but for now the ability to borrow books was in itself a large step forward. He was an omnivorous reader, and sitting quietly at his office desk, he ingested an enormous body of literature on the mental sciences.

Ernest and I began, at this point, to have long, fruitful dialogues, in my library. Ernest was himself tolerant of diversity of opinion and found it difficult to understand why the different sects were intolerant of each other and of the new emergents in science and philosophy. As for himself he was determined to keep an open mind on all phases of religious philosophy and to share his discoveries with me, checking the concepts against my formal theological training. Many of the books that interested him he brought home, although we were careful at that time not to disturb Mother's peace of mind by discussing the theological implications. She was not at all narrow-minded but was very proud of my position as a clergyman in the Congregational Church and did not wish to see it jeopardized by implications of the New Philosophy—which eventually happened anyway. As our interests and experience flowed so closely now, it is possible to relate in accurate detail what Ernest read and learned at this time.

One of the books Ernest brought home was Hudson's *The Law of Psychic Phenomena*. This book greatly impressed me because of the intellectual treatment and scholastic approach. I was so convinced that the philosophy was basic that I adopted three of the major principles in the first book I myself was to publish some five years later.

Ernest was equally impressed, and he also became interested in an approach to mental science that was new to him in the writings of a man who called himself Swami Ramakaracka, whose real name turned out to be William Walker Atkinson. His books explained the Yoga philosophy of India in occidental psychological terms.

In recalling these books Ernest once said, "There were so many wonderful teachers at that time in the New Thought movement! I had already read so much that was remarkable and new to me that I was overcome with a great desire to find out: What is the great *fundamental* thing in them all that is *so*, something you couldn't leave out."

It is interesting at this point to note that Ernest's inquiry had changed from the earlier quest of "Why?" like Kant (of whom he knew nothing at that time), to "What can I know?" and "What ought I do?" The question of "How?" intrigued him. And he was doing all he could to search out answers. But if his head was in the clouds at the office, his feet were on the ground in my Venice parsonage, and he continued his very practical help.

It was only a month after our successful political campaign against legalized prizefights that we employed the wide publicity we had received to enlist the whole city to help build a modern church building to house the services, the clubs, the Boy Scouts and other activities. It became a city project, and the list of donors included almost everybody of prominence and all the business houses in Venice. As head of the purchasing department of the city, Ernest was in a position to urge the local street contractor to "do the big thing" for us. Though Ernest had no actual control over contracts, still he was a friend of Eakin's and the City Council; and among us we negotiated the gift of all the reinforced concrete, worth ten thousand dollars and more. Russell, architect for the new high school buildings, donated the drawings, and we were able to build a modern tapestry-brick building with stained-glass windows, opera-type seats, velvet carpet and hangings—the most beautiful church on Santa Monica Bay.

Before its completion there was a fire that demolished the building next door, in which we had been holding our services. We escaped personal injury and cast about for temporary quarters. Some of our social activities, including the Boy Scout work, were transferred to buildings on the same street. In negotiating for the use of these buildings, I was brought in touch with the owner, Mrs. Augusta Rundel, a woman of considerable means, who had made her fortune in real estate in Venice and Los Angeles. Her home was in Los Angeles, but she lived part of the time in Venice in a fine cottage. "Gussie" Rundel was a society and club woman of the old school, forceful, dynamic, a woman who "got things done," handsome and sophisticated, with a voice like a foghorn and a heart like butter. She had a sister, Annie Gillan, who later became important in Ernest's life and was the mother of Hazel Foster, a widow whom Ernest later married.

From the day I negotiated the use of her buildings until

the day she died, Gussie Rundel became a devoted friend of mine—and of my brother's. She helped us then in our emergency, and assisted in building my church. Later she helped greatly in the early activities of the Institute of Religious Science headquarters in Los Angeles where she personally served for over thirty years.

It was June 8 of 1914 when the cornerstone of the Venice church was laid. The dedication took place in November of that year with a great conclave of noted leaders of the Congregational Church, whose building society had contributed five thousand dollars toward the building fund. On all occasions Ernest acted unobtrusively, helping to carry out the infinite details, assisting with the decorations, directing the ushers and looking after the celebrities.

On a visit to the Metaphysical Library, Ernest had laid his hands on a copy of *The Edinburgh Lectures on Mental Science* by an Englishman, Thomas Troward, formerly a judge in the Punjab, India. This and a companion book, *The Doré Lectures,* filled him with overwhelming delight.

He had felt a philosophical weakness in all the books he had read on the subject. Some of the authors were confused, he thought, failing to build up a confidence in the Principle they advocated and "often coming to inconclusive conclusions." He liked close and axiomatic reasoning and took the position that the slightest break in the argument invalidated all that followed thereafter. He was no religious existentialist who begins with Nothing, demonstrates that "God is dead," comes to an impasse and then *leaps* across it! Ernest was willing to support and demonstrate his major principle, the *a priori* existence of God as Wholeness, Goodness and Truth; but once accepted, he demanded clarity and sequential logic to a rational conclusion. Later in his career he spoke much on "the axioms of reason," a phrase he borrowed from the metaphysical writer and teacher, George L. Burnell.

We shall better understand what the Troward lectures

meant to him when we study what he believed or knew before his discovery of Troward.

Almost from the first he had accepted or constructed his own *theory of prayer*. It was true of him from first to last that he believed that the analysis of the fruit would give a knowledge of the tree; "by their fruits, ye shall know them." He considered it possible to discover the Principle if you studied the Practice. During his entire career he always asked the student to explain to him what was going on in his mind and heart when he was in the process of a treatment. He tentatively concluded that Principle denoted a Law of Mind in action, *the way* by which faith becomes effect. Expressed in simple terms, he was persuaded that the harvest is potential in the seed; it *is* the seed come to fruition. The *form* is conditioned by the thought. "Thoughts," as he had learned from reading the great metaphysical poet Ella Wheeler Wilcox "are things."

He had reasoned that the way to plant a seed was to *plant* it. It is unnecessary to inform God of what has been going on. Most introductions to prayer in the churches had been a process of bringing God up-to-date on the latest sins and transgressions of the congregation as a whole, not so revealing that the rest of the people were let in on the secret of the offender but enough to expose evil in all its luridness or lure. In his opinion negative prayer must be replaced by affirmative prayer. Basically such prayer was not merely affirmations of faith in the Beautiful, the Good and the True nor a rosary of I-believes, I-ams or I-affirms, but rather the affirmative *state of consciousness* in which the individual makes his declaration. The purpose of prayer, he felt, was not to change God's mind but to change your own consciousness. It was something that established a different relationship between the self and the Universe. After this state was realized the "word" or prayer became the word of God in meeting the condition and bringing about a state of wholeness.

He began with the transcendental position of Plato, Jesus, and Emerson, the acceptance that the real nature of being is Goodness, Wholeness and Truth, an impersonal Source or Reservoir from which all persons might draw directly and not by some fickle choice of Deity itself. "God is more ready to give than we are to receive," he believed, and one of the aspects of prayer is to put oneself into harmony with the divine Law of Life and Abundance, to permit the outflowing waters to fill our cisterns and our systems.

These reflections are not my own but the recollections of my brother in an interview on October 11, 1956. He was asked at that time if the orthodox church had not now accepted this point of view. It was his opinion that there was indeed a wide wing of the church that did accept it, but old habits of thought and traditions of worship often resulted in positive affirmative prayer in the morning and old-fashioned prayer at night.

"If you go to bed with lumbago in your mind, you are likely to wake up with lumbago in the morning," he said. It was his view that affirmative prayer works even for the ignorant, and expressed his gratitude that this is true, saying, "The law of growth holds no hostility to the seed; it accepts your word and brings it to harvest." He concluded, "I believed this from the very first."

If Ernest, then, liked close axiomatic reasoning, if he felt that the slightest break in the argument invalidated all that followed thereafter, if he demanded clarity and logical demonstration of a consistent principle by a lucid and consistent mind and a rational conclusion, then those who have encountered already the works of Judge Troward will know why he became the second major influence in Ernest Holmes' unfoldment.

Thomas Troward was a singularly interesting man as a man.

The personality of any individual is the lifeblood of his message, and if we possess no portrait of the prophet, we are constrained to create one by the brush of the artist. We look to Raphael or Michelangelo to portray Elijah or Moses or Jesus or Paul to identify the man and his words. Or in more modern times we record the tones of his voice on tape and his personality on celluloid.

With Thomas Troward we have a different story in between these extremes—there is something, but it is meager indeed. We have his physical portrait, but except for the few personal recollections set down in print in 1948 by Harry Gaze, an English writer and lecturer, we have little else. It seems strange that this is so, seeing that Troward did not die until several years after Ernest began to read and study his works. Troward was the most human of humans, possessed of wit and laughter, love and sympathy. His photograph tells us that he was an Englishman with that fineness distinctive of the upper classes, his face well proportioned with full but not round cheeks, his forehead high, his eyes wide and clear, his lips partly covered by a mustache. He is seated with his family, his wife and six children, three of them by his first marriage.

He was the son of Richard and Sarah Troward, was born in Ceylon, India, in 1847 and lived to be sixty-nine years of age. He was brought back to England to attend Grammar School, and in 1865 at the age of eighteen he graduated from college with gold-medal honors. Four years later, at the age of twenty-two, he took examinations for the Indian Civil Service and answered questions on metaphysics that attracted the attention and approval of the famous Professor Jowett.

Admitted into the service as assistant commissioner, he advanced to divisional judge, which title became so identified with his name that in America he is always referred to as Judge Troward. His justice was administered with kindness and understanding, and he won the good will of the people of the Punjab of Northern India, where he was stationed. Here he learned the language of the country, studied the sacred and historic writings, including Raja Yoga, the path to union with the Absolute. His further pastime was the study of Hebrew, which provided the foundation for his later works such as *Bible Mystery and Bible Meaning* and the book posthumously published, an interpretation of *The Psalms.*

This religious bent was a part of his life. From boyhood he had practiced reading from the Bible daily and, like Abraham Lincoln, was often on his knees. His daughter Ruth recalled that when she was approximately three years of age, in the year 1879, the whole family knelt for family prayers around the breakfast table. Ruth remembered his love for children and how he told them fascinating stories. He had a fine sense of humor and would often surprise his wife by what we would call a practical joke. He would come to the kitchen door, pretend to scratch like a cat and utter a pitiful *meow.* At prayers one morning, the cat jumped on his back, and he lost his glasses, on which he sorely depended. He picked up the cat, spanked it with a felt slipper and dropped it out the window. Feeling quite embarrassed before the children, he decided against family prayers at the breakfast table.

His whimsicality spilled over in the most serious situations, and one of his friends used to remonstrate with him for his jokes in lecturing—much as would happen to Ernest and myself on numerous occasions. I have often chuckled over Troward's humor in dealing with the problem of recognizing yourself as Being.

. . . to realize your being you must have consciousness, and consciousness can only come by the recognition of your relation to something else. The something else may be an external fact or a mental image; but even in the latter case to conceive the image at all you must mentally stand back from it and look at it—something like the man who was run in by the police at Gravesend for walking behind himself to see how his new coat fitted. It stands thus: if you are not conscious of something . . . then you are unconscious, so that to be conscious at all you must have something to be conscious of. This may seem like an extract from *Paddy's Philosophy,* but it makes it clear that consciousness can only be attained by the recognition of something which is not the recognizing *ego* itself—in other words consciousness is the realization of some particular sort of *relation* between the cognizing subject and the cognized object. . . .

Here we see humor softening the problem of consciousness in contemplating the nature of Being itself. And here enter the ghosts of Fichte, Spinoza and Bishop Berkeley.

An old lady was incensed by hearing Judge Troward declare in a lecture that "there was no such being as the Devil." When the lecture ended she came out with it indignantly. She got this reply: "What do you want the Devil for, for yourself?" . . . "Of course not," she replied. . . . "For your friends, then?" . . . "No!"

"Then what the Devil do you want him for, Madam?"

Now perhaps I have made Judge Troward too facetious. But we must not forget that we are talking about one of the great geniuses in the field of philosophy, of whose writings Professor William James said, "Far and away the ablest statement of the philosophy I have met, beautiful in its sustained clearness of thought and style. A really classic statement."

The necessity of being a person is expressed by Troward—of being a living example of what you teach—and he insisted, "It is just the same with anything else. No book can do more than tell you about a thing; it cannot produce it. You may study the cookery book from morning till night, but that will not give you your dinner."

Troward himself was willing to exchange ideas with those who had already entered the lists in defense of a great new philosophy of life, and in 1914, the year Ernest first read *The Edinburgh Lectures,* we find the Judge attending the International New Thought Convention in London to speak on the subjects of "The Higher Law" and "Threefold Man."

Troward was definitely a man of the hour, the hour for Ernest, and in a short time, for me as well. After his discovery of Troward, Ernest studied with even more concentration. He continued to appear at his office. He continued to help me in my Orthodox pastoral work, but once again a new dimension had been added to our lives; and looking back I realize that "The Pageant of Venice" was in many ways a victorious farewell.

The dedication of the church was hardly out of the way when we began, in January, 1915, a very ambitious project, the enlistment of the whole city in "The Pageant of Venice." We opened headquarters in one of Mrs. Rundel's store buildings, and she supervised the extensive costuming of hundreds of actors, including the children of the local schools, and the employment of a theatrical teacher for the many songs and dances. The wintering circus provided several acts, including Indian dancers, and the motion picture industry of Hollywood contributed actors. I myself wrote the lyrics, which were set to music by the composer Chiaparelli and played by the city band, and Ernest read preludes to the acts, including:

> Behold a city of laughter,
> Rippling rivers of laughter,
> Pacific Ocean of laughter,
>   City of fun.
> Streets overflowing,
> Coming and going,
> Everyone knowing
>   A pageant's begun.

Those were the days when oratory was in style, and his rich baritone speaking voice rolled like thunder across the vast audience; and I was so proud of him! Besides, he made my lyrics sound like poetry!

The affair was a great success, which not only profited the church financially but gave it wide and favorable publicity. Among other benefits it brought Ernest into contact with a number of prominent people, some of whom remained his friends throughout his life, including Thornton Kinney, a well-known figure today in the Religious Science Headquarters activity.

Late in 1915 Ernest and I subscribed together to a course of studies by mail with Christian D. Larson, whose *The Pathway of Roses*, given me by a deacon of my church, O. C. Melton, had had as much of an influence on me as *The Ideal Made Real* had had on Ernest.

I was in something of a quandary, now, with my ear becoming more and more attuned to this new truth, my eye on its great possibilities and my feet planted in the Congregational Church. The stirring new concepts began to creep into my sermons, some members of my flock hearing it gladly, others, including our mother, watching me with wary eyes. My heart was fully dedicated to God and service, but the way, for now, was not clear.

The library dialogues between Ernest and myself became lengthier and dived into the deeps, for Ernest, with the advent of Troward on the horizon of his mind, had begun to see ever more clearly.

VII

❧

Ernest Simplifies Troward

THE IMPACT of Troward was one of the greatest and most exalted experiences in Ernest's whole life.

It was Troward's proclamation of a *neutral principle* that excited and inspired Ernest's mind. The terminology was strange to him, but both his reason and his intuition told him that Troward was right. "So right," he said, "that it eclipsed anything I ever read; in fact, I couldn't help saying to myself, 'This is exactly what I feel. This solves the problem of dualism. This is the real meaning of 'Principle.' This is the Law."

Ernest, giving in his own words the gist of Troward's *Edinburgh Lectures on Mental Science,* said, "Troward has not destroyed the Science of Mind, but he has made the teaching clearer. A beginner might find it harder at first because he deals with it from the standpoint of psychology and philosophy rather than from the religious approach. Broadly speaking he follows the psychological law of suggestion as laid down by Thomas J. Hudson in *The Law of Psychic Phenomena.*

" 'Psychic' can mean 'mental.' Hudson taught that there are two modes of mental activity, one conscious and the other unconscious or subconscious. The subconscious mind is the builder of the body, the seat of emotions and storehouse of memory. He laid down three rules, 'This mind is impersonal, it is creative and it is controlled by suggestion,' that is, by the strongest impression made upon it. In other words, it does not have an individualized *will* or the power of choice but acts creatively upon any thought that is impressed upon it. That is the way by which healing can be brought about!

"Troward used psychological science as a means of approach to metaphysics. He does not think that 'will' is the creative faculty. He merely used 'will' to emphasize the necessity of sticking to the choice we have made. It is the business of the will to maintain the position we have taken long enough to allow the law of growth to carry our decision into effect. It does not mean that we are to make 'resolutions of the will' nor use what is called 'will power' but rather to permit the law of correspondences or the law of attraction to draw to us the external results whether we are asking for health or anything else.

"Contrary to the opinion of many practitioners, Troward's primary purpose was *to teach a theory of mental healing* rather than to promote a philosophy; but to do so, it was necessary for him to produce the philosophy of Mental Science. And he does just that! No wonder Professor James of Harvard praised his clarity. Troward began by showing that there is no such thing as dead matter. The finest particles are in motion and there is a 'livingness' in everything. This livingness is Life, Intelligence, or Spirit in action.

"Troward thus resolved all things into one universal category, that is pure Thought or Spirit. Spirit is independent of time and space and therefore is present in its entirety here and now. There is no such thing as 'distance' within the One Mind and as we also are in it, we can say that everywhere is right here."

Ernest paraphrased a saying of Troward that he used to repeat many times through the years. "The effort of Nature was to produce an individual who could repeat the creative process. Evolution was at first on the basis of the law of aver-

ages—that is, without conscious volition. But the time came
when an individual, that is man, had reached the point of
intelligent individual volition. From that point man took
over and has been able to control the conditions of his individual world ever since. He is one with Spirit, Cosmic Intelligence; he creates as God creates—by the word or thought.
As the Gospel of John says, 'In the beginning was the Word,
and the Word was with God and the Word was God . . . All
things were made by Him . . .' "

Ernest stated, "The thing I like about Troward is that he
gives a scientific or logical explanation of whatever he claims.
Take the idea of 'Unity,' for example. He quotes from the
ancient teachers of India, the Vedantists, saying that it is impossible to have two infinities, for if there were two, neither
of them could be infinite. Therefore there is only *one*. Then
it follows that *individual existence* is but a mode of self-
recognition within the universal. God and man must be one.
Troward admits this is a philosophical abstraction and affirms
it is not only true but necessary for the student to understand
if he would produce practical results in healing work.

"Troward shows that if the originating Life Principle is
infinite, or limitless, then the whole of spirit must be present
at every point in space at the same moment, it must be omnipresent in its entirety. . . . All spirit is concentrated at any
point in space that we may fix our thought upon."

Here Ernest showed that power of memory that was typical
of him throughout his long life. He could quote at will from
any printed source when he felt it was more convincing than
his own words.

But his next statement was his own. "What an inspiration
to believe in the power of absent treatments—everywhere is
right here! The individual who can realize the truth in his
own mind does not need to concern himself about impressing
it upon the mind of the patient whether the patient is present
or absent. This truth, once realized, removes all doubt and
all speculation."

It is well to pause here and answer a question often asked

in regard to whether or not Ernest was ever a Christian Scientist. I am able to answer this question. He believed in its major principles, he was aware that the genius who had formulated it had been compelled to employ a language not adequate to express her beliefs and that her use of terms had been a major source of the criticism leveled against her and her teachings. Thus, he was not a Christian Scientist, although he deeply respected Mrs. Eddy and her movement.

Ernest had early come to the conviction that the *application* of the principles of any science of mind was by far the most important aspect of that science. He believed that mind could heal, and he constantly inquired of himself, in regard to all his reading and study, "How do you work?" He believed that something went on in the mind of the practitioner besides "waiting on the Lord." He felt that no problem was to be solved by standing before a blackboard and asking the principle of numbers to solve it. You had to go through a mental process to arrive at the solution. He wanted to know what *process* was used in treatment.

"The basic principle of spiritual-mental healing is the recognition and awareness of Divine Mind," he said. "The whole effort of the practitioner is concerned with bringing his own thought into harmony with the Eternal Presence. He assists the patient in understanding that it is not his own mind nor that of the practitioner but the Truth that will set him free. There is nothing from outside to do the work but only something inside. He does not rob the patient of his individuality by use of suggestion designed to drive out some evil supposed to be there, nor to implant new life and truth in the effort to heal the patient. Life and Truth are already there. Once the thought is turned away from false concepts of sickness and limitations, from belief in disease to belief in perfect life here and now, it is possible for Divine Mind to assert itself and restore the patient to the consciousness of health and wholeness. '. . . the basis of all healing is a change of belief.' " Here Ernest quoted directly from Troward.

"To this end it must be explained to the patient that the power being used is not the power of the practitioner nor even his own human mental power but the power of Divine Mind. He must see that he has limited himself by his false thought about himself, and he must be guided to a new point of view. But this work is not the treatment. The treatment itself is in inner self-recognition by the practitioner." This also was Quimby's thesis.

"Therefore the practitioner has his work cut out for him. He must escape from the influence of suggestion and world-thought about disease. He needs to revert to the primal nature of cosmic man and realize himself as a son of God. He himself is pure living spirit and therefore his power is unconditioned since 'I can of mine own self do nothing . . . but the Father that dwelleth in me, he doeth the works.' [Jesus] '. . . Spirit [is] not hampered by conditions of any sort, and therefore not subject to illness.' [Troward] It may take time to escape from the narrow circle of race thought or what is called 'mortal mind' because 'all our life we have been holding the false belief in sickness as a substantial *entity* in itself and thus as being a primary cause, instead of being merely a negative *condition* resulting from the *absence* of a primary cause; and a belief which has become ingrained from childhood cannot be eradicated at a moment's notice.' [Troward] It may happen that there is a temporary improvement, but the old symptoms often return. When at length the Truth is fully realized, the symptoms will disappear. A single treatment would be sufficient if the patient were able permanently to retain the belief in the perfection of being, but too often the belief in sickness is reestablished in the patient's mind and further treatment is required.

"The practitioner must not be discouraged nor lose faith in his own principle, and to this end he may deny the evidence of his senses and affirm the truth of perfect being. To actually 'see disease' is to believe in it. 'If we concentrate our mind upon the diseased condition of the patient we are thinking of him as a separate personality, and are not fixing our mind upon that conception of him as pure spirit . . . We must therefore withdraw our thought . . . from his corporeal personality altogether, and must think of him as a purely spiritual individuality, and as such entirely free from subjection to any condition, and consequently as voluntarily externalizing the condition most expressive of the vitality and intelligence which pure spirit is.' [Troward] The practitioner must always realize that he performs his 'work' by knowing there is no 'work' for him to do. In other words, 'the Father that dwelleth in me, he doeth the works.' The intellect as such has nothing to do with it.''

He illustrated this by telling of his experience in the playground with the boys under his care. He had not been with them long before they began to look upon him as half-father, half-pal and talked over their problems with him. Some were worried about acne, some were resentful about a teacher, while others were inclined to escape it all by running away not only from school but from home. He talked seriously with them but with no condescension. He was near enough to their age to understand and also to build up their faith in him. It got around the playground that he was "a wizard on warts." All the boy had to do was to show his warts and say he wanted to get rid of them. Ernest would look at the growth with serious attention and say, "Now I can tell this to go away and it will go away. Do you believe it will go away?" and they would answer, "Sure do; do it." He would look at the boy to see if he meant it—in other words that he had faith. Then he would say, "Go wash your hands and keep them clean. The wart is going away. Get rid of the dirt."

"Does it grow in dirt?" asked one little fellow.

"What do you think?" Ernest asked.

"I guess I'll go wash up now."

The supreme quest of Ernest's life in his early twenties had been to find out what went on in the consciousness of a great healer. But from the first he knew that all people used the *same* power. As he said to me, "I was convinced that

Troward spoke for all schools of metaphysics and Emerson
when he said that there is only One Mind in the universe
and we use it. There is no such thing as an individual mind
or an individual anything in its ultimate essence. If there
were, then all individuations would be so separate and apart
that they would have no way of communicating with each
other, they would jostle each other in space and still not know
of each other's existence."

I now became interested in metaphysics, was doing considerable reading and had found inspiraton in *The Pathway
of Roses* by Larson as well as in his correspondence course.
I began to feel safer about the changes that were taking place
in my own theology. My theological point of view took a
radical change. I had a new incentive to *know* more, although
it would be a little time before I would put my new knowledge into practice.

VIII

∼≈∽

Ernest Conceives the Great Idea

So it came about in this year of 1915 that Ernest, through trying to find out "the fundamental thing in them all that is *so*"
came into possession of and was possessed by his great idea—
the fusion of metaphysics, psychology and philosophy. It
would be a synthesis into one harmonious whole of the teachings of Emerson and Troward, the religions of East and West,
the spiritual tenets of Christian Science and New Thought
together with whatever he knew or could learn of the
"Mother Doctrine" that had survived in the various deposi-
tories of ancient wisdom like the Hermetic teachings, the
Bhagavad-Gita and the *Zendavesta*. He would relate them
with the teachings of the great poets like Whitman, Wordsworth and Browning.

He was like a mountain climber alone among unfamiliar
peaks. Everything was new to him; he knew smatteringly of
psychology and philosophy, only a little of psychic phenomena, nothing of mysticism and had little real knowledge of
religions beyond Christianity when he began his adventure
into the unknown. So far as he knew he was the first person
to conceive of this idea. It was his very ignorance of traditional philosophies of religion that was to be his greatest
asset, for he approached the whole subject from the original
point of view that was to distinguish his career.

While Ernest maintained always his concept of a religion extracted from the highest and best thoughts of man throughout history, he came eventually to look upon the synthesis as a "new emergent in the evolution of spiritual consciousness." He observed, too, that the contemporaneous theology of the Christian churches was undergoing vast changes leading to a common melting of the minds of all denominations. Man, he believed, was himself emerging into a new creature, and he affirmed that the new findings and teachings of science were contributing to it.

Ernest's fresh ambition led him to even more reading and to search out the history of the modern metaphysical movements in deeper and wider detail than he had found up to that time. He turned back to study the philosophy of Phineas P. Quimby, whom he held in veneration and reread his principles of theory and practice, acquiring a lasting respect for his genius.

How thrilling his ambition and his search! His excitement could hardly be contained. It was too great a secret to be kept to himself. He had to tell it to someone, and so he told it to me.

His enthusiasm moved me deeply, even though my study of Larson's works and my sermons based upon them had already brought me under the suspicion of a wealthy deaconess of my church as leaning toward "the horrors of New Thought." I was interested in the fruits of this new faith, and I asked Ernest repeatedly if he had been *practicing* his new theory.

"Yes," he said, "and you know very well you yourself sent one man to me. He had asthma and asked you to pray for him. He came up from Arizona. Been there for a cure, but no good. Couldn't lie down; gasped for breath all night. I gave him one treatment in my office at the storeroom. He went home and slept eight hours without a break and his trouble never came back. Made me a present."

Just the telling of the story to someone else seemed to en-

thuse him; it made him more confident he was on the right
track.

Before long, a strange woman arrived at the parsonage door
demanding to see Ernest and "get treatment." I told her
where she could find Ernest but she said she was too ill to go
there. Mother came to the door and, seeing the woman's sick,
tired face, let her in. It didn't have anything to do with
Mother's interest in metaphysics—at this time she didn't have
any—but she did have a heart.

"I'm too sick to go on," said the woman, who identified
herself simply as Mrs. Brown. She tottered to the door and
spoke to her chauffeur. "Bring in my bags. I'm going to stay.
You and Mr. Brown go back to Ojai."

Mother and I were speechless, shocked into inaction, but
when the short, fat lady began to mount the stairs from the
living room, Mother gave a queer little laugh and followed
her. I went to get Ernest. The rest of the story is in his own
words as he told it in a taped-recording years later:

When I got home I said to Mother, "Well, where is she?" Mother
pointed to the stairs. I found the woman in the guest room.
When I came into the room I saw a short, very fat person lying
on the bed with a hot-water bottle perched on her stomach and
great tears running down her face. She looked so funny that I
sat down and laughed. And she asked, "What are you laughing
at?"

"You look so funny."

She had a great sense of humor and she laughed, too, with
the tears running into her mouth.

She told me that several years before she had had an abdominal operation at the Mayo Clinic and came out from the
ether long enough to hear the doctor say to one of the nurses,
"She'll die about five o'clock." Then she "went under" again.
Her husband, an engineer of a huge project in the Northwest,
was deeply in love with her and had been sitting at the door
just outside her room. When he heard the doctor say this he refused to believe it and kept repeating to himself, "She is going to
live, she is going to live!"

But every afternoon she would have the abdominal pain and be at the point of death. She had it on the hour—five o'clock exactly! I can't brag of the cure. She had been under the influence of pure suggestion—or impure, whichever way you take it—and I told her so. She stayed two weeks and went home perfectly well. I followed it up for years because we became firm friends. There was no recurrence of the sickness.

Mother, of course, was interested in Mrs. Brown's recovery, but she was even more interested in how a strange woman had found her way to *our* parsonage. I don't know whether she suspected a heavenly design or foresaw a most unheavenly horde invading her parlor, but she gave us no rest until Ernest discovered that Mrs. Brown had heard of him through Gussie Rundel, and her sister Annie Gillan.

My chief interest was in Ernest's practical application of his theory to Mrs. Brown's case. I remember asking him at that time if suggestion and treatment are not after all the same thing. He was very explicit in his denial. I have notes on what he said, and it seems to me wonderful that he had progressed so far in his understanding.

It is done *unto* you as you believe, Jesus implied. A treatment is not a transference from your mind to another, whether you call it suggestion or anything else. It goes on within yourself. It has nothing to do with your will power, it is concerned solely with what goes on *in your own mind*.

Because it goes on in your own consciousness, it is also going on in Universal Consciousness, and since it transpires in the One Medium there is no absence between the thinker and the thing thought about. Everywhere is right here simultaneously with your thought. The action is instantaneous. So the person for whom you are knowing the truth within your own consciousness—and therefore within Universal Consciousness—must know what you know. That is all there is to it and if you knew and understood and practiced this principle, you would reach the ultimate understanding. This is what Troward made so plain and which I adopted from the start, that since there is only One Mind in the Universe, there is only one mind you need to concern yourself with and there is no such thing as an individual mind apart from the All-mind. If there were such, then all individuations would be separated and apart and have no way of unifying with each other. It is problematic if they would actually know of each other's existence.

ERNEST BEGINS TO LECTURE

It was only a short time thereafter, late in 1915, that his friend H. B. Eakin, who had been noticing Ernest's reading for some time past, engaged him in conversation about it and asked him if he would give a talk to some friends he would invite to his own home. Eakin, a highly respected and well-educated man, was not formally religious. He had given money toward our church building but had never attended. Nor did he attend any other church. He was free of all theological prejudices, and Ernest was surprised at the invitation.

However, he accepted and gave an explanation of *The Edinburgh Lectures,* adding a few of his personal views, to about twenty people, including the fully recovered Mrs. Brown. The magnificence of conception and the clarity of expression of Judge Troward in dealing with abstract principles of Spirit and Soul, of Love and Beauty were enough in themselves to inspire interest and conviction. But Ernest himself appeared to be an incarnation of the principles involved.

He was in his twenty-eighth year, magnetic, positive and yet with a disarming modesty that had an impact on men and women alike, and he was all the more effective in that he made no studied effort to be pleasing. This impersonal pronouncement of his knowledge and convictions was destined to be typical of him. He told Mr. Eakin's guests convincingly of his early efforts to understand the principles taught by Troward and how he had found in *The Edinburgh Lectures* the first clear explanation of ideas he had developed in his own way up to that time. There was no showing of erudition except the simplicity and thoroughness of his own understanding.

He told them that Troward taught that we are surrounded by what Troward called Impersonal Mind, or what we mean by Universal Subjectivity, which receives the impress of our thought and then acts upon it. "The way we do it," he said, "is to impress our thought upon It, and It in turn reacts to us. There is a process by which thought can be turned to form. Our action upon the universal medium is really a process of self-knowingness." He hesitated on this because it was difficult to explain self-knowingness. Everyone studied his face at this moment. They sensed that he was feeling after something he wanted to say. He smiled. "It's a tall order," he said, "to explain Troward, but what he said was that the self-knowingness is really Spirit knowing Itself in us. Because, after all, the Spirit in us is the thing that knows at whatever level we know it. We have to be careful to note that we do not deal with any mind but our own. We do not believe in Divine Mind and human mind as two minds but only one; and there is danger when reading Troward or any other Higher Thought teacher that you get misled by language. There is no truth in thinking of conscious and subconscious and superconscious mind as such, but in remembering that these are merely expressions or levels of Absolute Consciousness. If you dealt with all the aspects of mind separately and spread them all out on the floor, you would have so many pieces you couldn't find any room to walk unless you walked over them, and that is a pretty good thing to do."

He told me that naturally he left them in about the same ignorance as when he began, but they applauded him and some asked him privately for treatment. He himself was far from being pleased with himself. He wondered if he would ever know enough to give a real lecture and whether he would really ever want to, anyway. Eakin, however, was delighted and thereafter they were the firmest of friends for many years.

WE CREATE *The Uplift* MAGAZINE

In 1916 Ernest urged me to help write and edit a magazine. It didn't seem too much of an undertaking, and I agreed but refused to use my name as editor, being still a Congregational minister responsible to a specific flock. So we put out *The Uplift*, a magazine of metaphysical healing, to which he contributed a special article each month and formulated some treatments. Both of us used material from it three years later in writing our first books. Readers of *The Law of Mind in Action*, which I wrote, and of *Creative Mind*, which Ernest wrote, will note the close affinity. We continued to issue it for two years.

The magazine began immediately to draw people to Ernest as a practitioner. At first he did most of his "work" in the quiet of the city purchasing department, but because he was disturbed by occasional interruptions, we gave thought to finding a more suitable environment. We discovered a place through Gussie Rundel. Our relationship with her had continued with such warmth after the pageant that most people thought she and I would be married, although neither she nor I subscribed to the idea. Through her, our friendship with her sister, "Aunt Annie" Gillan, had deepened. She not only sent us Mrs. Brown, but now persuaded Aunt Annie to rent us her summer cottage on the canals nears our house for a rest home.

When Ernest was not working for the city, he used the roomy cottage both for treatments and private teaching. Some people came from other cities and boarded there while taking metaphysical treatment. Through them and others the magazine enlarged its circulation and drew still more people so that it was necessary to secure the help of another practitioner.

The practitioner, Mrs. Graham, was a remarkable woman and did fine healing work; she had been trained in the Denver Colorado College of Divine Science. Both Mrs. Graham and her teacher, Mrs. Agnes J. Galer, at that time an ordained minister in the Divine Science Church in Seattle, Washington, were to have a direct bearing on Ernest's immediate future—and the Divine Science movement was to play a most important part later in my own. But we little suspected it at the time. We only knew that we were grateful for Mrs. Graham's assistance at the convalescent home, and Ernest approved of both her method of treatment and her results.

Neither Ernest nor I lived at the house ourselves but had a housekeeper and a cook to assist Mrs. Graham. Everything was successful from the start. People came from everywhere to the home; but Ernest still went on with his city job, and people sought him out there.

I recall one man who visited him at the storeroom office. He had suffered over a long period of time with a pain in the neck. It sounded laughable, and Ernest smiled. "We all do at times," he said. But the man was in great distress. He begged for help.

"I've been to one doctor after another," he related, "and I'm like the man in the Bible Jesus talked with—the fellow who had suffered many things from many physicians—"

"That wasn't a man, it was a woman," Ernest corrected.

"Well, sex doesn't come into it, anyway." And the man actually growled. "But the Bible says that she suffered many things from many doctors and didn't get well but on the contrary got worse. I'm in the same boat. If you can't help me, God help me!"

Ernest gave him a treatment, but nothing seemed to result at that time. A few nights later Ernest thought of him in the middle of the night and gave him a treatment. He felt that something had happened, but he did not see the man for a week. They met on the street.

"Funny thing happened last week," the man said. "About two o'clock in the morning I was sound asleep and something snapped like a pistol in my neck. I woke up, of course, and do you know that pain was gone and it hasn't come back. What do you suppose happened? Did you have anything to do with it?"

"God did," Ernest said, but he didn't elaborate. That had been the very hour he had given the treatment.

Meanwhile an event with humorous overtones was taking place in Los Angeles, which was eventually to change the whole course of Ernest's life and ultimately my own. It happened in the Metaphysical Library in Los Angeles, which was owned and operated by Mrs. Reeseberg. She had known Ernest casually only as a borrower of books; but on this day Mrs. Graham described him as a good lecturer, and Mrs. Brown told of her own healing with so much feeling that Mrs. Reeseberg issued an invitation for Ernest to give a lecture. Mrs. Brown accepted for him offhand!

Ernest was astonished when Mrs. Brown visited the purchasing department and told him what she had done. "I am acting as distributing agent," she said. "You are to speak at the Metaphysical Library in Los Angeles at high noon next Thursday."

"I was speechless," Ernest informed me that night. In spite of his experience in talking about Troward's lectures on mental science at the Eakin home, he had not thought of giving public lectures, and he was really disturbed. But he decided to go.

Those were the days of noon-talks by visiting lecturers, and sometimes as many as 150 persons would crowd into the Library. After the lecture, the speaker would announce an afternoon class in an adjoining room, which could be rented for three dollars. Ernest told Mrs. Reeseberg that he had never taught. "I wouldn't know what to teach," he said.

Mrs. Reeseberg advised him to give a class that afternoon explaining the philosophy and theory of treatment by Troward.

To his surprise and considerable embarrassment thirteen people showed up and paid their twenty-five cents for admission. I can see him now. Whatever was going on inside him, he was as always composed on the outside. One thing that never bothered him, then or thereafter, was what people thought about his looks. It is true that he had a distaste for "dressing up" and had always disliked the formal evening wear that custom demanded in his early days as an entertainer; he had spoken of it not as "full dress" but "fool dress," and in later years refused to put on a tuxedo until his wife Hazel took him in hand. He was otherwise indifferent as to how he looked. His intellect, however, was in full control of the thoughts and words that expressed his ideas. He was always more than a man with knowledge; he was a man with convictions and faith in the power of thought to change the conditions of life. This was evident even in that first lecture-lesson.

It is not necessary to repeat his words. The substance of his talk was the same as what he had given at the Eakin home. His thoughts were clearer and his terminology forecast already the originality of expression that was to distinguish his career. One listener that noon so long ago told me that in the intervening half-century, she had never forgotten, when he wished to impress on them that there was "no great, no small" in the One Mind he had said, "from a planet to a peanut." And original examples like that, she said, *stuck*.

After the lesson an announcement was made that he would give personal treatment to anyone who wished his help, and he wound up the afternoon with a clear profit of five dollars. It was always his habit in dealing with "metaphysical money" —in the days before gold was taken out of circulation—to ask to be paid in gold pieces, and this was the day he started the habit! This was the kind of money he used for years thereafter in securing private coaching by college professors in various subjects in which he was interested.

Everybody was pleased with the lecture, Mrs. Reeseberg most of all. This was the real beginning of his career as the public exponent of Practical or Applied Metaphysics. He continued to lecture at the circulating library and was so successful that he decided to give up the city job he had held for the past three years. He was at that time making exactly the same income in each place and believed he could earn a satisfactory living now from teaching and healing.

So here he was, quite unexpectedly launched upon a professional career, which broadened rapidly. He lectured one day a week at the Vista Del Arroyo Hotel in Pasadena and another day in the Schuyler Hotel in Long Beach.

While he took an immense enjoyment in lecturing and was pleased with his growing knowledge of the science of mind, he had a special interest in the theory and practice of healing. As he observed to me much later, in speaking of the early days, "The thing about Jesus that has always impressed me is that he *did* what he talked *about*. He might have come down in history as a good talker and even the best storyteller or parable-maker who ever lived, but the poor sick people who appealed to him needed what the rabbis couldn't give them, and that was *healing*. So he healed them. Like him, from the very beginning, I tried to practice what I preached.

"I remember," Ernest continued, "there was a man came to me and said he had cancer. Now I didn't know anything about cancer; all I knew was that it was something that *grew* in you or on you. So I took a thought—"

He stopped here to explain, "Hazel doesn't like the expression, 'took a thought,' and I wouldn't use it now, but I did then; and this was in the words of Jesus. 'Every plant, which my heavenly Father hath not planted, shall be rooted up.' The man got well. One thing I've learned from years of practice is that it isn't *what* you say that counts, it is saying something you believe in. It's the conclusion you arrive at by thinking and saying it."

And so "his preaching was sanctioned by his practice."

ERNEST ORDAINED IN DIVINE SCIENCE

As his following increased, however, this sanction was insufficient to fill the needs of his growing number of followers. He was requested to perform marriage ceremonies and he required legal authority. This could be obtained only by ordination from a legal and incorporated church. Mrs. Graham recommended that Ernest make a trip to Seattle, Washington, where her teacher, Mrs. Agnes J. Galer, was conducting a successful work authorized by the Divine Science Church and chartered by the state. So Ernest went to Seattle, met the minister, Mrs. Galer, who was so impressed by him and his state of spiritual consciousness that he was duly ordained as a Divine Science Minister.

A series of coincidences often creates the illusion of fate and sets a pattern for destiny. Our introduction to Divine Science through Mrs. Graham and Ernest's meeting with Mrs. Galer in Seattle are worthy of note, since events within short months were to interweave our personal destinies for a while.

The Divine Science Church had been founded by Mrs. Malinda Cramer, who had formerly lived in San Francisco, California, and had by meditation and prayer healed herself of an apparently incurable condition. This was in 1885, and the following year she had founded a Metaphysical Institute in San Jose, California. Mrs. Cramer began formulating her own metaphysical theories, based on her own experience, with frequent quotes from the Bhagavad-Gita, the Cabala, Hermetic philosophy and Jacob Boehme. She considered her philosophy entirely original but must have listened to Mrs. Emma Curtis Hopkins, one of the great early teachers, and a name to be remembered, who conducted a class in San Francisco the very year of Ernest's birth, 1887. The next year Mrs. Cramer founded the "Home College of Divine Science," and soon began to travel and lecture. In Denver she came into contact with "the Brooks sisters," Nona L. Brooks and Mrs. Fannie James, who were teaching some of the principles of New Thought origin. She soon persuaded them to take the name of Divine Science. Ten years later the sisters decided to hold Sunday services, and Nona L. Brooks went to San Francisco to be ordained by Mrs. Cramer and went on to become an internationally known figure in the New Thought movement as well as head of the Denver College where Mrs. Galer taught and our Mrs. Graham was trained.

And so, through ordination by Reverend Galer, Ernest's healing treatments were sanctioned by law.

IX

❦

We Buy a Sanitarium in Long Beach and Open Offices in Los Angeles

MEANWHILE I was continuing my own preaching at Venice. But I was deeply interested in what Ernest was doing and so sympathetic with Mental Science philosophy that I not only wrote for *The Uplift* but also spoke so broadly from the pulpit in the terms of New Thought as to disturb some of my congregation; but I had given no metaphysical treatments either in the church or outside of it.

I had now been minister of the church for over five years and wished to undertake some greater enterprise. I decided to resign and either broaden my education at Harvard Theological Seminary or join Ernest's activities publicly. For some time he had been eager to have us work together as a team. He thought I had already passed the deadline of orthodoxy and said, "You know you don't believe in it any more. Why try to preach it?" So on June 10, 1917, I resigned. I was grateful for the regrets expressed by the community and the church and learned how beautiful are tears when they are shed over you in parting.

I suppose that in my heart I knew I would go on with Ernest, for it took little persuasion from him for me to join in expanding the work he was doing. As a matter of fact, I was half in it already because of *The Uplift*. Yet I felt very

uneasy about it on two accounts, first because of our limited
finances and second because of the world situation.

Ernest and I had the normal American's interest in national politics, and I recall the intensity of my interest in the
campaign of Woodrow Wilson, both because I admired him
personally and because I felt he would be an instrument of
peace in a world threatened with war. Like many other
Republicans, Ernest and I became "Wilson Democrats,"
voted for him and rejoiced in his election. It was a tragic
period in the history of civilization, for in 1914 all Europe
became a maelstrom of war, and the nations allied against
Germany made every effort to get the military support of
America.

The star of anti-Christ was rising in Russia. The sequence
of events was rapid—the death of the monarchy, the failure
of Kerensky's democracy, the return of Lenin to Russia and
the conversion of the peasants into Soviets, followed by Trot-
sky, who turned them into Bolsheviki; then carnage and
bloodshed that destroyed the church and set up Communism
and worship of the state. The Russians and the Germans, and
most of Europe, were at each other's throats, and in the midst
of world holocaust America could not remain neutral. Many
factors conspired to inflame public opinion against Germany,
the most dramatic of which came when Germany declared
unstricted submarine warfare and the unarmed passenger
ship *Lusitania* was sunk by a German submarine. On April 6,
1917, the United States declared war on Germany, and we
became engaged in the bloody struggle.

As Christian clergymen, we participated in many activities
that supported the government, as the purchase of war bonds,
and sustained the morale of the soldiers. Our chief concern
was to support the Red Cross and other instruments of peace
and to help innocent victims of war through personal and
international organizations operating throughout Europe.

But more important to me, when I resigned my church in
Venice just two months after we entered the war was the fact
that the metaphysical message seemed all the more needed,

and Ernest and I both felt that we had a duty to the times and went about it with singleness of purpose.

The capacity of the Metaphysical Library was already outgrown, and we decided to open our own lecture hall with offices in the Brack Shops on Seventh Street and to speak on Sundays at the Strand Theater.

The Brack Shops were well adapted to our purpose, because the floor space was so extensive you could choose the size of your rooms and the landlord would have walls erected to suit.

I did not immediately begin to speak or practice healing in our new quarters. There was a great deal of work now with the magazine and, even more important, duties at the Metaphysical Sanitarium we had decided to open in Long Beach.

The "home of health" in Venice where Ernest had conducted personal healing and private teaching of Mental Science in Aunt Annie Gillan's rented cottage had been so much of a success that we had decided on a big adventure. I was to trade my Venice house for a big residence in Long Beach and we would open it up into a sanitarium for convalescents who sought metaphysical help. We chose Long Beach, because Ernest had already given lectures and treatments there at the Schuyler Hotel. The house we bought was a huge three-story affair with a round tower on one corner pointing straight to heaven. It was really impressive, and by building rooms in the garage we could accommodate eighteen patients. We repainted and papered all the rooms and bought new furniture. I myself laid all the carpets, because Ernest was too busy in Los Angeles to give much help. I remember, however, his working with all of us—Mother, Father, our brother Guy, his wife Emma, their two children and myself—in "tacking" the quilts for the beds. It was a big job to run that darning needle, threaded with wool, through the fabric and cotton lining, push it back again, cut off the thread and knot it. Ernest was as adept as Mother and spent a good many evenings with us on this job.

No one was as enthusiastic about the success of this effort as Ernest, who prophesied immediate results. And they came! Within ten days every room was full, and we began a waiting list. Except for the financial demonstration we had made in buying the house in the first place, this was one of our first real experiences in exercising "the power of the word" in the control of circumstances.

I myself had uncovered an earlier book, the very first, I think, to deal with prosperity and the control of conditions from a metaphysical viewpoint. It was *The History and Power of Mind* by Richard Ingalese, published in 1902, and he had devoted the last chapter to "The Law of Opulence."

In this chapter he related the story of a still earlier leader of the Mental Scientists, Mrs. Helen Wilmans-Post, who started penniless in the world. The following is a brief quotation from his book:

She went to San Francisco with but a few dollars in her purse. When she arrived there she demanded and secured her first position on a newspaper, then she gradually drew to herself through that center money enough to enable her to live more comfortably than previously. After a while, in answer to her demands she got a better position. In the beginning she used the law of demand unconsciously—by following her own intuitions. Then she began to gain something of a knowledge of the working of the law and soon her brilliant career began as a conscious worker with the law. From a journalist she became an author, wrote several books and finally added healing and teaching to her long list of accomplishments. Through it all she continued to draw more and more opulence to herself until she was very rich.

I was impressed with the theory, but this was our first real effort to develop for ourselves a technique for practice of a "prosperity treatment," and from this hour we both experienced a great joy in the fact that "my God supplies all our wants." As it turned out, we wanted a lot!

We had organized our work under the title of the *Southern California and New Thought Institute* and carried on the Long Beach activities as the Metaphysical Sanitarium. It was at the sanitarium that I began my own systematic teaching. Like Ernest, I started by teaching Troward's *The Edinburgh Lectures*. But each week he visited the Schuyler Hotel and continued his lectures there, and they drew some patients to us. We permitted patients to bring their own nurses, if they wished, although we kept a trained nurse in the house. Naturally we attracted people suffering from psychoneuroses and associated disorders. We did not diagnose but allowed a physician to do so if desired.

Analysis revealed that most of them were afflicted with ennui; the meaning of life was lost, perhaps because their children had grown up and gone out into the world, leaving them with little or nothing to do. So far as possible we turned the place into a beehive of industry, making everyone do some kind of creative work, such as knitting, painting and other forms of artistic self-expression.

The Metaphysical Sanitarium in Long Beach and Metaphysical Institute at the Brack Shops in Los Angeles further provided us in those crucial years of World War I with a channel through which we could use our science in relation to the world situation. We not only followed the course of the war and added our type of "prayer treatment" to the body of prayer being built by the faithful on both sides, but bought bonds and supported local drives for the Red Cross and other service activities and also gave personal help then and after the armistice to soldiers and their families.

Ernest was particularly adept in dealing with psychoneurotic and paralytic cases that were then often attributed to shell shock or war shock. As early as 1917, while the war was still raging, a "disabled" young English officer crossed a sea and a continent to be treated at the Metaphysical Sanitarium. Ernest did not resort to psychonanalysis, not only because he did not know the procedure at that time but also because he could "sense" the cause in a way similar to Quimby's. With a few questions in order to orient his mind and that of the patient and also to heighten temporarily the emotional reaction of the patient, he would suddenly "be aware" of the hidden cause. And it was this faculty that enabled him to diagnose the English soldier.

It turned out to be a case of compounded frustration. It seemed to the soldier that life was pitted against him. Nothing ever turned out right. His marriage had been a disappointment, he smarted with injustice because a higher officer had failed to recommend him for advancement in the service although he had won the right by personal bravery, and when a grenade had exploded near him "life blew up in my head and set fire to my soul."

These facts exploded out of him after Ernest had turned the key, and the Englishman fell into terrible weeping. He had never wept before as an adult, and the very act provided an immense relief. Ernest began the process of reeducation that had as its foundation "an understanding of life as a school of experience; some are quick to learn the lesson, some are slow, some appear more unfortunate than others, but in the end we all pass the examination and eventually stand equal with all the rest. You have walked a hard road and climbed a high hill, but *now you know* what you should have known long ago, that you are not inferior, your soul is free, and you will no longer be held back by self-pity, because you now realize your equality with all men and your capacity to make your life what you want."

The Englishman stayed with us for a few weeks and then returned home not only cured of his malady but full of zeal to heal others.

Later the work of our Metaphysical Institute went on during the great influenza epidemic in the fall of 1918, which took hundreds of lives in California. Schools, theaters and churches were closed, and people went about the streets with white gauze masks, attempting to shut out the germ or virus and escape the contagion. Workers fell ill at their desks in the business places of the city, returned to their homes or to hospitals and were seen no more. We went about our business as usual, and although we treated many people who came or telephoned for help, we did not have a single failure. We loaned Connie, the trained nurse who had been with us in the sanitarium and was a student of our institute, to a military academy where so many boys had died. After her arrival there was only one death. Her animated figure, her face glowing with good nature and her cheery confidence in *life* lifted the spirits of the boys.

It was while I was directing the sanitarium that I met Louis. Louis was a nine-year-old boy, an orphan who had been adopted two or three times, and each time returned to the orphanage. He had been mistreated and had not only resented it but resisted it. He was, to me, an attractive, spirited child, and his spirit made an especial appeal to my heart. My work with orphans and orphan asylums had been one of the most satisfying of my ministerial functions, and I had continued it after I resigned from the Congregational Church. My secret dream, always, was to be able to finance and oversee a home or institution where none of the abuses of improper adoption or discipline could be visited upon these lonely youngsters. Louis was a case in point. Over the months I watched what was happening to him and then decided that, while I couldn't do anything lasting for a large number of them yet, I could start with this one.

And so I, a bachelor preacher embarking on a new ministry, adopted a nine-year-old son and brought him to the big home in Long Beach to be welcomed by the family. Only my father cast a shadow on the happy occasion when he shook his head and told me privately, "No woman will ever marry you now!"

"If she objects to my having rescued this poor motherless boy," I retorted, "then I wouldn't want to marry *her!*"

Ernest was in complete accord with this manner of acquiring a nephew and joined me in treating for both Louis and his easy adjustment and happiness. Just over a year later I was to meet a most lovely lady who was not only willing to marry me but had ample room in her gracious heart for Louis as well. Although she has now been gone from us for many years, he was, and is today, our son.

Meanwhile the demands on Ernest's time were increasing in Los Angeles and in Pasadena. He gave up his lectures in Long Beach. I drove to Los Angeles for a couple of evening lectures each week. But Ernest stayed on in the city and began to live with Aunt Annie Gillan. Aunt Annie was quite prosperous, and, besides the cottage we had rented in Venice for Ernest's home of healing, she owned an apartment house at the corner of Seventh and New Hampshire. She possessed great psychic qualities and often displayed them to Ernest, being able to locate and describe the whereabouts of any one of Ernest's friends by means of her sixth sense, and even possessed the capacity to bring into the room the scent of perfume being worn by the individual. They took pleasure in checking up for accuracy and Ernest accepted it as extrasensory perception, although the term ESP did not come into popular use until years later in association with the work in the psychological laboratory of Dr. J. B. Rhine, who wrote the book, *The Reach of the Mind*. Aunt Annie also spoke often of her widowed daughter, Hazel Foster, who was then living abroad, but short of admiring her picture, Ernest gave little more than a passing thought to the handsome young woman at this time.

Having more work than he could do, Ernest invited Mrs. Agnes J. Galer, who had ordained him and whom he considered a fine practitioner and dynamic speaker, to become a teacher-practitioner at the Brack Shops. She had had her own circulating library and lecture rooms as well as her Divine Science Church in Seattle, Washington, but she was instantly willing to join in the work of The Metaphysical Institute under our direction. She came to live at the sanitarium and assisted in the practitioner work there. She and I became fairly good friends, but she loved Ernest devotedly, not with any sentimental attachment, but as a spiritual genius and inspired speaker.

By this time I was completely out of sympathy with myself

for sitting back as a sanitarium superintendent and publisher of a magazine when my greatest interest was platform work. So I told Ernest what I felt, and he understood and was sympathetic with me. *The Uplift* had served its purpose, spread our message and drawn many people to "the work" and to the sanitarium. But it was time-consuming and seemed now an unnecessary activity, and there were more people to be served at The Metaphysical Institute in Los Angeles than in the confines of the sanitarium. So I gave my time solely to teaching and healing in the Brack Shops. The lecture halls were crowded, and the income from healing treatments was enough to take care of our needs. In fact, we had now acquired a fund large enough to consider buying a home in Los Angeles where we could be near the Brack Shops.

So early in 1918 we sold the sanitarium and purchased a large and beautiful home on Third Avenue, just off Adams Boulevard. Mother and Father, Guy and Emma and their children, Ernest, Mrs. Galer, Louis and I moved into our new home. We had room to spare, and Mrs. Galer's daughter Anne came to live with us late that fall. A new phase of activity began, in which our work unfolded and we found ourselves plunged into a world that brought us into personal contact with some of the great metaphysical healers, spiritual leaders and personalities of that day.

X

Psychiatry, Theology, and New Friends

ERNEST AND I had begun our public appearances together at the Strand Theater in downtown Los Angeles speaking on Sunday mornings to a good-sized congregation. He would speak one Sunday and I the next. I remember my pride in him and a kind of wonderment. He spoke like a man of authority and as one inspired. In spite of my formal education and platform experience, I couldn't hold a candle to him, and I knew it. I dug in with determination, but it took two years before that look of disappointment disappeared from their faces when they came to the door and found I was the speaker of the day. At that time I was too much the minister, too little the metaphysician!

Ernest and Mrs. Galer didn't really need me; still there I was! Ernest was speaking several times a week, and his Tuesday and Thursday afternoon meetings were crowded, but so far there was no real need for me to do weekday lectures. It took time to learn what the people wanted; but I began a systematic study of Ernest and found out that he was very practical, while I was philosophically and psychologically theoretic. It took time to make my own place. I used to listen to Ernest with admiration and wonderment at his flow of language. It was often involved, even to incoherence, but beautiful and original.

"It isn't what you know, but what you make people think," he once said to me. And to prove it he gave a lecture in high-sounding metaphysical phrases and involved argumentation that he couldn't have understood himself. He did it purposely, of course, and people flocked around him afterward and declared it was the best yet. This is no slur on their intelligence. It is more of a confirmation of Emerson's theory that what you *are* speaks so loudly, "I cannot hear what you say. . . ." Ernest was a great teacher—clear, concise, original when he wished to be; but he was a great presence, too, and had no need for "pleasing" an audience. Nor did he use "charm" to win friends and influence people. He was too simple, too natural, for that. He was "just Ernest." This subjective quality of attraction was both personal and spiritual. His love for people was genuine to the point of sentimentality but always natural, and any signs of personal deification upset him to the point of rudeness. I saw him one day when a woman rushed up to him after a lecture exclaiming, "Oh Ernest, you are sublime, I worship the ground—" He leaned forward and pushed the lady's hat forward and down over her eyes. "You're talking through your hat," he said, and turned away smiling.

He was rough sometimes on the platform. Two women came in late; the lecture and treatment were over. They made a great fuss getting settled in the front row. Ernest looked on calmly and said, "Welcome, ladies, you're just in time for the collection and the benediction."

Ernest's figure was robust, and health exuded from him. One day a woman said to me, "Aren't you more spiritual than your brother?" "No," I replied, "I'm thinner." When I told Ernest about it, he laughed.

I have in my hands written notes of some things I heard Ernest say at the Strand Theater. He made use of the Bible in illuminating his teaching, but he did not resort to it for proof texts. He had no knowledge of either Greek or Hebrew, and traditional exegesis of a text was entirely foreign to him. He usually quoted from the King James and from the American revised version. He revered Jesus as an intuitive and transcendent personality and never lost the real significance of a Bible passage, although he was not always accurate in the phraseology. His love for the Bible had developed because of its use in family prayers throughout his boyhood, and in his last years he made a cutting of the Psalms, eliminating the negative and accentuating the positive attitudes.

Although we had great interest in psychic phenomena, we had but little knowledge then of one aspect of it, that is, spiritualism. But many spiritualists attended Ernest's lectures, seeking for any new light on survival and immortality. He did not speak to them as a separate group but freely expressed his views to all. It was Ernest's opinion that a philosophy of religion remains only a philosophy until it includes immortality, because purpose and value are lost and the law of conservation is violated if intelligence ends with the grave.

Members of the Katonia Theosophical Society came, too, and reported back to their leader, Dr. Frank Riley, that our message was in harmony with Theosophy. This resulted in a firm friendship with Dr. Riley. He was a great intellectual and later assembled the teachings of sixty-six religions of the world into one great volume. In spite of all my theological training, this was a complete revelation to me, and I know it was to Ernest, too. Our interests were broadened by reading these pages, and we owed something to their influence forty years later in the biographies of the eight great masters in the second part of *The Voice Celestial.*

Dr. Riley was a nature lover, a mystic of the first water, and I half-believed him when he told in a lecture at the Brack Shops of seeing brownies under the guidance of his own little son. We visited the beautiful grounds where he had his headquarters, and I would have had but small surprise to see one of the "little people" peering out through the leaves of a great sycamore tree, because the Theosophists were a delightful mixture of intellect and other-worldliness. Dr. Riley recognized the need of a more practical application of the principles of Theosophy to everyday problems and encouraged his people to study with us.

Ernest himself wrote the following paragraph in regard to Dr. Riley in one of his notebooks of recollection. (It is interesting not only for his personal impression of the man and his work, but because it states clearly how Ernest felt about those who shared their ideas with him then and in the years to come!)

Early in the beginning of my investigations, it was my privilege to meet Dr. Frank Riley, probably the greatest student of Comparative Oriental Religions I have ever known. Not a student in the accepted term of academic learning, but rather, one whose keen spiritual insight and ability to synthesize were very great.

Born and educated in this country, he went through medical school and became a practicing physician only to discover in those early years much of what today goes under the heading of "psychosomatic medicine," which led him into ever broader fields of investigation and caused him finally to give up medical practice entirely and go into modern metaphysical fields.

He became one of the early great teachers and spent more than twenty years compiling *The Bible of Bibles,* the most remarkable synthesis of similar ideas coming from the great Scriptures of the ages that I have ever read.

Something brushes off from such people when we meet them and come to know them well, and it has been my privilege to have known so many great teachers in our field, every one of whom made an important contribution to our system of thought. Few people, indeed, have been blessed with so many wonderful friends as I have, and I look back with deep gratitude and appreciation to all of them, and look forward as eagerly to meeting more, *for the whole world is filled with wonderful people, every one of whom can make some contribution to the thought of anyone who appreciates the possibility of exploring other people's minds.*

Because of this genuine attitude of open-mindedness, Ernest had friendly relations with many other organizations throughout his life, having been broadened and slanted toward independence of thought by instinct and by Emerson in the very beginning.

By now he read not only the works of Madame H. P. Blavatsky, but of Katherine Tingley and Annie Besant and often quoted Mrs. Besant's affirmation depicting the neutrality of creative mind as "the law that binds the ignorant and frees the wise." Having long ago accepted the subjective-mind theories of Troward, he found in this statement a strong support to these beliefs.

The impersonal nature of the creativity of mind became a dominant feature of his teaching that erupted a year later in the paperback first edition of *Creative Mind*.

It was at this time that Ernest became acquainted with Dr. Hayden Rochester, a young physician who had written a successful book on psychoanalysis, *The Gist of It*. This was the first of those contacts with practicing psychologists, professors of philosophy and learned men from all walks of life which distinguished Ernest's career. They considered him a genius with a new approach to the persistent problems of philosophy, the humanities and the enigma of consciousness, and they were all charmed with the vitality of his speech and his personality. Many of them came later to lecture for him at the Institute of Religious Science and School of Philosophy. As for myself, I was in a constant state of wonderment at his erudition and his capacity to popularize his theories.

One particular conversation at that time stands out in my mind as an interesting example of this ability as well as the pattern for "exploring minds" from different schools of thought in an attempt to synthesize, one of Ernest's favorite methods of learning and teaching.

In those years Ernest was somewhat prejudiced against "Theology," being under the impression that theology was a composite of dogma, creeds, rituals, occultism and superstition. But he made no attacks upon either churches or leaders, being largely content to teach the truth as he saw it and only occasionally giving any thought to deflect the arrows of criticism aimed at him or his system of thought.

Because I had been an orthodox clergyman, some ministers came to study with me at the Brack Shops and were soon intrigued both by Ernest's personality and his wisdom. In a group session one day Ernest insisted that Dr. Rochester join us as a representative of the school of psychological medicine. The ministers were interested first of all in Ernest's definition of God because that is the starting point of theology, and everything else may be said to stem from it.

"Who is God?" they asked.

Ernest looked at me. "You tell them, Fenwicke."

"Why me?" I asked, but was careful not to miss my chance. I had given much attention to theology as I left the old teaching for the new, although I had been so "liberal" at my ordination in the Congregational ministry in 1911 that my best friend whispered to me he didn't think I was going to make it.

"William Clark and Washington Gladden have both been urging the church to broaden the concept of God away from the limitations of human personality," I said.

Ernest interrupted, "We look upon God as Infinite Presence. I understood this intuitively from the beginning. The Congregational Church in which Fenwicke and I were reared never taught of God as a Being with the face and form of a man, but many people think of Him that way and picture Heaven as a place where He sits on a throne and you look at Him and sing hymns.

"I look upon God as Intelligence or Mind everywhere present throughout the universe and beyond the universe. On the other hand, I believe that this Intelligence has the capacity to feel and love and that it does feel and love. It is not personal in the sense of a human personality, but It contains within Itself the qualities which make up personality. It has an infinite personalness."

"What do you mean by that?" they asked.

I felt it was my turn and wished to show my erudition lately acquired from Troward. So I broke in.

"Personality exhibits three qualities—the power to choose, the power to initiate and the power of purpose. God can start a new creation, choose where and what He will do with it and He can have ends in view—teleology, in other words."

They all laughed at my enthusiasm, but Ernest cautioned, "I question the concept of 'plan' in the Divine Mind. God has been at work too long to have any unfinished business. This is one of the most abstract things in our philosophy. *Infinite purpose* is self-contradictory. Divine Mind *is,* has been and always will be both at the point of beginning and at the end of any series. There is no 'purpose' in being *being.* Moses defined God as 'I am that I am.' In other words, the subject and the object are one and the same thing. God is not progressing, He is not evolving into something else.

"Let us find an example in electricity. It *is.* It has no goals. But it can be individualized into light, heat or power. We can say, however, that the Universal Undifferentiated Intelligence contains a quality of being or consciousness which is capable of responding to each of us in the terms of our own approach to It. It, therefore, reflects wisdom to the thinker, peace to the peaceful and love to the lover."

Here, because of his growing understanding of psychoanalysis and the presence of Dr. Hayden Rochester, he used a term that startled the ministers and, I think, startled Ernest himself. It was the word *libido.*

"There can be in Divine Mind an infinite urge, a *libido,* an outgoingness of spirit. There is a principle of emergence, a pressure into expression. Life consists not only in the power to think and to feel but it is essentially creative.

"We do not ascribe to God the same idea of 'will' or 'purpose' we ascribe to man," Ernest continued. "Not a divine purpose to accomplish but a divine nature to express. Ignorance of this fact has misled many practitioners to the belief that in some way they must win the will of God, change the will of God. And in orthodox theology people are taught to bend to the will of God in the case of disease, death or misfortune in spite of the fact that Jesus said, . . . for it is your Father's good pleasure to give you the kingdom, and . . . it is not the will of your Father which is in heaven that one of these little ones should perish.' "

The ministers looked confused, and I did not wonder at it. These things were new to theology over forty years ago. Today it is a different story, owing in part to changing science and philosophy, and in large measure to the influence of the metaphysical movements, New Thought philosophy and Religious Science.

"Let us," Ernest continued, "discharge from our minds the common idea of prayer that it is in some way a process of petition to Deity. It is obvious that 'He is more willing to give than we are to receive,' and that He withholds nothing by choice but only by law."

"What is this law which seems to me to indicate personal will on the part of God?" one minister asked.

"It means only that Divine Mind does not give you what you do not believe in. *What you sow, you reap.*"

"But I thought you people taught that you must concentrate and hold the thought and stiffen the will and all that sort of thing," one minister said.

"You thought wrong. And as for my own teaching, I substitute *attention* for concentration; willingness or *mental acceptance* for will; and in place of purpose, I use the idea of *self-expression.* The 'Universal Principle' is an aspect of God as is the 'Universal Presence.' 'Presence' is the immediate availability of life, love, wisdom, truth and beauty; and 'Principle' is the Law or the way It works. We might expand this new term of *libido* as used by Dr. Rochester and speak of the Universal libido or urge to create or to become."

Dr. Rochester looked at him with pleased surprise, but the ministers looked confused. However, one of them said, "I see you have been reading Bergson."

"Who is he?" Ernest asked and laughed. "We all need to do some more reading; I have just started to study."

"We'll be back," said one of them.

I don't know whether they came or not, but thousands of their cloth did come to him, listen and go away with enthusiasm in the following years.

Ernest took pleasure in his friendship with young Dr. Rochester, and when the doctor proposed that they take a trip to San Francisco and give a lecture series there under the doctor's management, he agreed. I was left to carry on at the Brack Shops, assisted by Mrs. Galer, and for a short period I gave eleven lectures a week, a much needed experience in the field of extemporaneous teaching in Mental Science. For ten years I had written every sermon and lecture in longhand and learned it by heart, assisted by a photostatic memory. But now I had to "make it up as I went along," an experience that was to prove invaluable the next year when we broadened our adventure physically by three thousand miles.

Ernest and Dr. Rochester made the trip to Northern California in the doctor's car, and having arrived in San Francisco, they rented the Scottish Rite Auditorium and began to publicize the campaign by announcing a series of lectures on "God." By billboard, window cards, mail and press, they notified the people of San Francisco of a new kind of science, the art of living and the acquisition of health and abundance through God-knowledge. Some enterprising reporter from the daily newspapers was intrigued by the novelty and made a feature of it. Other papers took it up: "God is being advertised."

There was no irreverence in anybody's mind so far as I can discover. If God was being popularized, I am sure He took no offense either. And He must have blessed the undertaking. The auditorium was filled, the classes were large and the people were pleased. It was also a successful financial adventure.

A sad note must be struck by relating the untimely end of Dr. Rochester. His love and devotion to Ernest was unbounded; he persuaded my brother at a later date to return with him to San Francisco and made an advance trip to take care of the business end. In spite of his learning and profession, he was a great believer in the occult science of astrology and had forecast his own death as to time and circumstances. On the day that he had an appointment with what he considered "his fate," he was driving south to Los Angeles, and his car was overturned. He was thrown out unhurt; but a companion was pinned under the car, and he leaped into the road to get help from a passing motorist. He stood there waiting, and an automobile struck him, killing him instantly.

Like the rest of us, Ernest was greatly shocked and felt the loss of his friend keenly. Rochester's death confirmed our lifelong rejection of astrology as commonly accepted and our conviction that it is the mind of man that lends influence to the stars and that man projects his own destiny regardless of the source of the original suggestion.

In a short time we were conducting by far the most extensive and successful work in metaphysics in the Los Angeles area and perhaps in the country, with the exception of Christian Science, Divine Science and Unity.

The Unity School of Christianity and Silent Unity, a center of metaphysical prayer at Lee's Summit, Missouri, were the outgrowths of the healing of Mrs. Myrtle Fillmore in 1886. Mrs. Fillmore had been medically declared "dying" of tuberculosis when she and her husband Charles attended a metaphysical lecture given in Kansas City by Dr. E. B. Weeks, a student of Emma Curtis Hopkins. Two years later, using what she had understood in the lecture, Mrs. Fillmore had not only had a complete healing but had been helping others. She and her husband had gone to Chicago and studied with Mrs. Hopkins and returned to begin a lifetime work. I later did some writing for one of the Unity publications, my contact being through one of Charles and Myrtle's sons, Royal Fillmore, who died a few years later.

We were friends, too, with Albert C. Grier, editor and

publisher of *Truth Magazine* in Seattle, Washington. When we discontinued the publication of *The Uplift,* we turned over our mailing list of subscribers to him. He was a fine and spiritual man and afterward went to New York, where he opened up a lecture and healing center.

Harriet Hale Rix and her sister Mrs. Annie Rix Militz had established a chain of churches under the title of Home of Truth. They had been assisted in their study by Emma Curtis Hopkins and were not only successful but prominent, especially in connection with the New Thought Alliance, which had grown larger and stronger with the advance of the New Thought Movement.

We also developed a very pleasant relationship with Nona Brooks, president of the Divine Science College and minister to the church in Denver, Colorado. She, of course, knew Agnes Galer well, and at Mrs. Galer's and our invitation, she came to visit us at our home on Third Avenue in Los Angeles and was with us for some days. She was a lovely and beautiful woman, unaffected and full of vitality. I recall that she liked to play card games with us and accompanied us to the Venice beach when we went swimming in the surf. I remember, too, how embarrassed I was when we bathed in the surf because of my bony knees. But she was not the slightest bit interested in my knees. She was intent on studying Ernest's mind, and he was intent on her as a leader and platform power.

"Why do you watch me so closely?" she asked.

"Because I want to find out why you are a leader. I want to discover where you get your power?"

He finally determined its source. "You get it from Omnipresence."

George E. Burnell and his talented wife wrote profusely and with great metaphysical subtlety. They had an exceedingly high consciousness of independence of conditions and held their Sunday services in the San Gabriel Valley so that the congregation had to take special buses to attend. This popular appeal was always a wonder to me, even though I read their manuscripts and they came to speak from our platform at the Strand Theater when we held convocations. I recall how abstruse they were with their *Axioms of Reason* and could not penetrate one of their sayings that "everything is a reflection in a mirror but there is no mirror and no reflection." When Frederick L. Rawson, author of *Life Understood,* came to this country from England, he visited the Burnells, and it is said that they discussed metaphysics, each in more abstract terms than the other.

Two of the most important figures to enter our lives in those days were Dr. Ameen Fareed and Dr. Julia Seton.

Dr. Fareed was a popular and renowned psychiatrist, who came to some of our public lectures at the suggestion of his lovely wife Elaine, who had "discovered" us at the Brack Shops. Dr. Fareed had known both Jung and Freud and had a unique background with his medical studies at Johns Hopkins as well as a wealth of comparative religion in the Middle East and some years of practice in Cairo, Egypt.

The doctor was in every way a remarkable man—and was to be a close friend of my brother's throughout life. I remember him as a young, personable man, dark-skinned, with a beard and deep-brown eyes that looked at you with clear honesty and friendliness. His study of psychology had led him to inquire into the primal meaning of the word *psychology* as *knowledge of the soul* (psyche); that is, of man as a *being* or entity. He had departed from the atheistic concepts of Freud, who denied any spiritual origin to the psychological self, and he believed with Walt Whitman that man is more than that which is contained between the hat and the boots.

He had made inquiries in the field of metapsychology before he came to hear us. A deep friendship developed from this very first contact, and we were frequent dinner guests in his home. I recall my objective interest in his surroundings and was greatly impressed with the luster of his red-tiled porch floor at the entrance and the oriental rugs of his living room. Ernest, on the contrary, lifted his eyes to a higher level and plunged into metaphysical discourse.

I joined casually in the conversation, giving more notice to the dinner and the cook, whom I praised enough for both of us. But Ernest and the doctor exchanged ideas with an eagerness that surprised me. Ernest wanted to know why a man trained in the psychiatric field held any tolerance for metaphysics. "I thought," he said, "that psychiatrists do not even tolerate psychoanalysts because they are often not medically trained and not qualified for diagnosis of the body and its organs."

Dr. Fareed gave a simple and direct answer, "I do not overlook the physical aspects of disease, the cause and cure from the medical point of view, but I am aware that medicine is not a cure-all, nor is a patient cured by analysis of his mental and emotional condition. These are but instruments of healing. I remember reading on the walls of the School of Medicine in Paris the words of the famous Dr. Ambroise Paré; 'I dressed the wound and God healed it.' I was impressed by it, but I felt the necessity of being more specific. The over-all term 'God' seemed too indefinite. I felt the necessity of finding out the nature of God's action, the method by which the healing is accomplished. It was this quest that led me to metaphysics."

"What have you learned so far?" Ernest said.

"I like the word *metapsychology;* it is more individual than metaphysics, which deals with philosophy, because metapsychology deals specifically with the *self in relation* to something above or beyond the human. You may still call it God, or you can call it soul or individualized God."

"In other words, you believe in a divine self, which can be brought into activity in healing."

"Yes, that is so. I think that ordinary prayer is ineffective because it calls for aid from some *outside source,* which may or may not be willing to do the desired work of healing. But if you yourself possess this power, which I call individualized God, and if you stir it up and order it into action, it is compelled to heal you."

"What brought you to this conclusion?"

"I was working on it, and then I listened to you and . . ." His voice trailed off into silence as though he had become absorbed in another adventure into truth.

Ernest was also silent for a long time as we drove back to Los Angeles in our Model A Ford. I knew he was organizing the conversation into a definite conclusion, epitomizing it for future reference. It was a way he had, a part of his unique learning process that gave immense value to those "social dialogues" all his life.

As Ernest piloted the Ford absent-mindedly along toward home, I knew his thoughts were not on the road. Finally we drew into the driveway at Third Avenue, and all he said was this:

> The discovery of God and the discovery of
> the self are the same; when the Prodigal
> Son came to himself he came to the Father's
> house. I and the Father are one.
> No wonder Dr. Fareed is a great healer.

Dr. Julia Seton, the founder of the Church and School of the New Civilization, was important to us from the esoteric-metaphysical point of view. She brought the Ancient Wisdom into practical use in the new age. The philosophy and secret doctrines of Egypt, India and Greece were as well known to her as though she had been an initiate in the ancient temples and schools of philosophy like those of Zoroaster, Osiris, Orpheus, Pythagoras and Plato. She held an open initiation one night not too long after my resignation from the ministry of the Congregational Church, and I helped to light the symbolic candles signifying earth, air, fire and water. I recall that Ernest laughed when I did it, because I seemed to be out of clerical character.

But he did not laugh at Dr. Seton. He recognized her as a great soul, and she in turn exercised a considerable in-fluence on him. He was wary of the esoteric but appreciated her mystico-practical psychology and metaphysics, and he learned from her the original source of many principles that he had thought were born in the minds of Emerson and other nineteenth-century thinkers.

Dr. Seton had twice lectured her way around the world, speaking in America, England, Australia, New Zealand and other English-speaking countries or communities. Everywhere, the masses followed her. She rented the Strand Theater in Los Angeles and filled it to capacity night after night. We went to hear her, and she came to hear us. Ernest was entranced with her, and she with Ernest, not sentimentally but from deeper levels of consciousness. She believed that he was an "old soul," for she supported the theory of reincarnation, a belief that Ernest never shared. He said his soul was new and fresh.

Dr. Seton and I became great personal friends, and I later visited her on her farm on the Hudson River in New York; and more than anyone else she stimulated my faith in myself as a poet. But I can still recall my own feeling when I observed her worshipful attitude toward Ernest's teaching.

We learned an interesting and profitable lesson from our contact with Dr. Seton—that you cannot transfer an audience from one teacher to another. It was her desire that her people should attend our lectures after she left, and she made every effort to that end, with the result that two of her followers stayed with us for about two weeks! It softened Ernest just a little toward organization. Ernest had been and still was opposed to organization as endangering the freedom of the speaker, and he had a justifiable confidence in his own capacity to attract and hold the multitudes. From this and other experiences, however, he later came to realize that the only way an institution can carry on successfully from one teacher to another and from one age to another is to create *a church entity* or membership loyal to the institution itself. The people will then accept a new teacher to guide the institution. This lesson was not forgotten a few years later when he himself faced the problem seriously, but at that time he had no intention of organizing beyond the loose form of our Institute at the Brack Shops.

But of most immediate importance was the fact that Dr. Seton invited, in fact, urged one of us to attend the International New Thought Alliance Congress in Boston. Neither of us considered it seriously at that time. Later we did. And in the end one of us went.

XI

Success in New York

Ernest Joins Me in Boston—Writes Textbook

IN THAT YEAR of 1918 our lives were filled with amazing activity—fifteen lectures a week, short trips to neighboring cities, a constant stream of patients at the Brack Shops, indoor games on an occasional free night and Saturday surf-bathing in Venice. Ernest used to come home as early as possible following the afternoon lectures and help our sister-in-law Emma with the cooking for dinner. He always seemed to enjoy cooking and was noted for his culinary talents throughout his life. He also enjoyed gardening, although at this particular time he made vegetable gardening his main interest, because the government had requested it.

In those early years in which Ernest made short visits or "campaigns" to San Francisco and various nearby cities, he displayed the keenest interest in attracting audiences and leading them into understanding of what we then called "metaphysical principles" but appeared to take little interest in the financial returns. And there was no Internal Revenue Service to force him to mend his ways. When he completed a lecture or lesson he put the collection or tuition money in a paper bag or wrapped it in a newspaper and took it to his hotel room. There he dumped it into a traveling bag and left it in the closet. At one time when he returned home we counted out $3,500, mostly in coins. When I protested he said, "It's mine, isn't it? No one can rob me of my own."

As if this was not enough activity, without telling me what he was doing, Ernest was working into the late hours of every night on a manuscript. All his life he followed the habit of going to bed to read and write. He not only read whole libraries in that way but kept paper and pencil handy to do his writing. It was a joke among his guests in his later years that he saved the cardboards from his laundered shirts to write on at night while sitting up in bed "because they were just stiff enough for it."

And while he was writing this first book, *Creative Mind,* I was locked away in my suite at home, writing *The Law of Mind in Action.* Ernest immediately began another book, to be called *Creative Mind and Success.* Thus it was I, Fenwicke, who took the step that was destined to alter the course of our lives and eventually lead us into the national and international field. When Dr. Seton had urged one of us to attend the International New Thought Alliance in Boston, we had given it much thought. Ernest did not wish to leave his writing and lectures, and it was therefore decided for me to go. We debated on whether I should take my speech from the book I had just written or write a new one. It turned out that I wrote "The Passing Of Spirit Into Form," the basis for my second book, *Being And Becoming,* which we afterward published in pamphlet form and sold at our first New York lectures.

It is interesting to note here that "publish or perish" was more applicable in those days to the metaphysical lecturer and teacher than the academic professor. New Thought was still *new* and, after a brief talk or lecture, the seeker wanted something to take home and study. The audience was hungry and thirsty for truth, and these books were manna in the wilderness to them. Both Ernest and I were eager to have our teachings in print, but it seemed equally important for one of us to attend the congress and take our place among those of like mind around the world. In Boston I was received cordially, and so was my speech; but I was new to the movement, and I did not linger long.

From Boston I went to New York, and through the influence of Dr. Julia Seton, I found myself a special lecturer at the League for the Larger Life, an organization of New York and Brooklyn leaders and writers. I spoke three times a day, and the place was crowded at every meeting, people sitting on the platform and stairways. Here I met many notables in the field who became lifelong friends. It was here, too, that I met Katharine Eggleston (Junkermann), a very successful fiction writer, who a year later became my wife and Louis' mother, in spite of the fact that she had long ago determined not to marry a small man, a blond or a minister. She got all three!

Naturally I was elated at my success in New York, and I returned to Los Angeles and urged Ernest to close the work there and go back with me to New York. It appealed to him as a good plan. He had completed his second book, so early in 1919 we gathered up our three manuscripts and launched upon the unknown seas of itinerant lectureship.

We were merry, bold adventurers. I was thirty-five years of age and he was thirty-one. Mother went with us, and Anne Galer accompanied us as our secretary. We found good rooms at the old Schuyler Hotel and lived there for months.

We rented a hall at the McAlpin Hotel in the heart of the city and put some small advertising announcements into the papers; the League for the Larger Life helped us. From the very first the crowds descended on us in a deluge. We were astonished at the numbers who came to our hotel rooms for metaphysical advice and treatment.

Here was begun the series of successes that attended our lectures in large theaters not only in New York but afterward in Boston and Philadelphia. All we had to do was to place a couple of one-inch ads in the papers, and the theaters would be crowded on Sunday afternoons. I can account for it only on the ground that "the time was ripe," although it sometimes filled me with wonder not only on the East Coast but on the West Coast as well, and in fact, throughout America, Canada and England.

The metaphysical lecturers in those days were a fine, selfless, dedicated lot, barnstorming this country and the world with food for the spiritually hungry, hope for the disillusioned; above all, with *healing*. As in the days of the Apostles, their works did follow them, and they not only spoke great words but bore great fruit. There was a generosity and camaraderie among these independent teachers—a sharing of platforms, students, thoughts, ideas—and they strengthened each other and the people they served.

This certainly widened Ernest's horizons, as well as my own, for I have here a recollection he set down of those days.

I cannot tell you how great was my surprise when I was giving what I believe was my second class in New York City, to discover that Orison Swett Marden and Dr. H. Emilie Cady were members of the group. At that time Dr. Marden's books had sold well into the millions and Emilie Cady's book *Lessons in Truth* probably had the largest printing of any of the modern metaphysical books. This was published by the Unity School of Christianity in Kansas City. Dr. Cady was a practicing homeopathic physician and former schoolteacher who had studied with Emma Curtis Hopkins. Deeply religious, her *Lessons in Truth* had literally helped millions to get started on the pathway of a new spiritual adventure.

I well remember my embarrassment when I realized these two great writers and spiritual teachers were among the members of my class, and I took them to one side and told them of my embarrassment, for I was very young and inexperienced. I shall never forget their reply, for each one of them said, "We are getting so much good from this class and are delighted to be here." It taught me a lesson in the things we all need to learn, that the truly great are generally both simple and sincere. I don't think anything in my entire experience ever produced a greater feeling of humility or a deeper appreciation of those who were the great forerunners of our philosophy.

And when I refer to our philosophy, I do not mean something we originated, but always I consider the contribution we have made or that can be made to our field or to any other similar endeavor, is a great and enthusiastic willingness to accept the Truth wherever we find it, and to apply it in such degree as we understand it.

We have no need of prophets or sages or seers in our movement. There is no place for idle adoration of any single individual. Our belief is too deep and broad for this, too inclusive, and we should never forget that anyone who mistakenly builds a high wall around his very small estate will shut out a broader horizon than he can possibly include.

I always think reverently of these great teachers, for they have a great spiritual reassurance and I am deeply grateful it was my privilege to meet and know so many of them.

We were also impressed with Dr. Marden's quiet humor. One evening he invited us to dinner at the Alpine Club on Fifth Avenue and guided us around the foyer to see a one-man exhibition of art. That the paintings were said to be worth fifty thousand dollars, aroused my curiosity as we stood before one of them. It was the painting of an old shed barn, the night appeared to be coming on and a flock of chickens were making frantic haste to the roost. "This," said Dr. Marden, "is the most valuable picture in the collection."

"What makes it so valuable?" I asked, surprised.

"I don't know," he answered, "but whatever it is, it must be behind the barn."

Dr. Marden eventually became one of our closest friends and appeared on our platform evening after evening to give his commendation to our work.

We also met and came to admire Dr. W. John Murray, who conducted the Church of the Healing Christ to a packed audience each Sunday. His church was affiliated with Nona Brooks and Divine Science, and we had heard much of him when Nona Brooks visited us two years before.

Dr. Murray had an unusual background. A man of short, square build, with black hair, a frank, open face and a very forceful, positive delivery; there was yet an air of gentleness and spirituality about him.

He had been a Catholic priest but left the church of Rome to educate himself in spiritual sciences. He also had studied with Emma Curtis Hopkins and had been ordained by Nona Brooks before undertaking independent metaphysical work in New York. He attracted a large number of people who came to him for healing, and it is said that he was so intent on study that he read books as he walked on the sidewalks of New York. In the early days of his work, the metaphysical movement was subject to hostility from the medical profession, and on one occasion Dr. Murray was arrested and put into jail for practicing without a medical license. Having drawn many prominent persons into the movement, including attorneys, he was soon released, and there was no recurrence of this kind. Ernest, I remember, was impressed with this great soul, an unassuming man who emitted a spiritual power seldom encountered. He had moved some years earlier from small halls and midweek meetings in his own home into the great ballroom of the Waldorf-Astoria, which was filled to capacity every Sunday morning. On Sunday evenings he took the train to Philadelphia and spoke in the ballroom of the best hotel. I have always felt that he, too, was one of those who pioneered the field which we reaped as prodigious success when Ernest and I began to teach in that city.

His Waldorf lectures were taken down in shorthand and became the substance of many books, and it was reported that ministers of evangelical churches frequently attended in the effort to learn his method of reinterpreting the Scriptures.

Not even in my dreams would I have thought that some day not too distant I would be his successor at the Church of the Healing Christ.

At that time I lectured in the Morosco Theater; and Genevieve Behrend, reported to be the only personal pupil of Judge Troward, often lectured at the same hour in the theater next door, to equal crowds, and she afterward toured the country for many years. Harriet Louella McCollum, the psychologist and metaphysician, was also attracting multitudes wherever she went.

I repeat that it is my belief that we were among the fortunate ones who appeared at the flowering of the new age into the inquiry regarding man, mind and metaphysics in the search for ultimate meanings. Like Emerson, who caught the same kind of attention almost a century earlier, we were bringing something new to the world. Whatever may be my estimate of the psychology of the times, we had instantaneous and overwhelming successes and were exultant to be alive in such an age.

And so the lecture season came to a close. My own romance with Katharine Eggleston began to crowd everything out of my mind but love and admiration. I was flattered that she returned it, for she was both beautiful and intellectual. She had written fourteen novels and two hundred short stories and innumerable magazine articles. She was of a noted family, aristocratic, but as devoted to spiritual interests as any one I have ever known, and so we were married and immediately took off for Randolph, Vermont, where we spent the summer.

Ernest and Mother were joined by our young friend Reginald Armor, who came on from California to be with them and accompanied them to the summer cottage in Lincoln, Maine. They took a canoe on Mattanawlook Lake and paddled to the cottage that Father had built for us all twelve years earlier. Although many new camps had been built on the shores and many people from the village had by now learned of the fine fishing, there was no scarcity of white perch, black bass and pickerel. Mother immediately sought out fishing tackle and had Ernest row her to the middle of the lake, where she would fish for hours, stopping only when she had a pail well filled with white perch, which she made Ernest and young Reg clean for dinner. Ernest visited the village and went to the mill, where he had helped Father with the boardinghouse and where our brother Luther was engaged as repairman and carpenter.

As I examine Ernest's life in retrospect, it seems all but incredible that there could have been such a cleavage between his own interests and those of that decade, known as the "roaring twenties."

Yet Ernest, at thirty-two, was preaching and teaching the good news that there was a way, a provable, profitable, joyous way to obtain and maintain health, harmony and all good things.

And when he wasn't doing that, he went fishing.

We rejoined each other in the fall, and we continued our metaphysical campaigns in New York and Philadelphia, where we had continuing success.

Our first books destined to be best sellers in our field for the next forty years had appeared in print.

Stimulated by success and encouraged mightily by the reception of our books, it was in high spirits that we returned to our home in Los Angeles in 1920.

The publication of *Creative Mind* and *Creative Mind and Success*, written in his thirty-first year, showed clearly that the Idea was well past adolescence, that Ernest Holmes had already developed a well-organized philosophy of mind that would later be enriched and supplemented by new knowledge in the fields of science, philosophy, mysticism and psychology, but not greatly modified. These two books verify this, and any student, elementary or advanced, would today find it profitable not only to examine them but to put their principles into practice. He had absolute faith in the power of "mental argument," which would automatically lead the practitioner or student to definite conclusions and convictions. In the opening of *Creative Mind and Success*, for example, he says, "An inquiry into Truth is an inquiry into the cause of things . . . Since we can think, say and feel, we must be . . . If we are life and consciousness (self-knowing)

then it follows that we must have come from life and consciousness . . . Life, then, is all that there is."

Here he anticipates what the great scientist Robert A.
Millikan later affirmed, that "all the universe is alive," and
Lord Haldane, who said that "nothing exists apart from
mind."

Life must flow through all things. There is no such thing as
dead matter. Moreover, life is one, and it cannot be changed except into itself [Ernest wrote] . . . But where does man come in?
He *is*. Therefore it follows that he, too, is made out of God,
since God, or Spirit, is all . . . Man is a center of God in God
. . . We might suppose that God made man to live with Him and
to enjoy with Him . . . It is true, indeed, that those who have
felt this most deeply have had a corresponding spiritual power
that leads us to suppose that God really did make man as a
companion . . . Man's mind is made out of God's mind . . . God
governs not through physical law as a result, but first by inner
knowing—then the physical follows. In the same way, man governs
by the process which we will call, for want of a better name, the
power of his thought . . . he can do with his life what he wants
to do; he can make out of himself that which he wishes. Freedom
is his, but this freedom is within law and never outside of it.
Man must obey law . . . At all times we are either drawing
things to us or we are pushing them away from us . . . "What,"
someone will say, "do you think that I thought failure or wanted
to fail?" Of course not . . . but according to the law which we
cannot deny, you must have thought things that would produce
failure . . . We are making our environments by the creative
power of our thought . . . By conforming our lives and thought
to a greater understanding of law we shall be able to bring into
our experience just what we wish, letting go of all that we do not
want to experience and taking in the things we desire. Every
person is surrounded by a thought atmosphere . . . This atmosphere decides what is to be drawn to it . . . All is mind, and we
must provide a receptive avenue for it as it passes out through
us into the outer expression of our affairs . . . Imagine yourself
to be what you want to be. See only that which you desire, re-
fuse even to think of the other . . . Always combine faith in the

higher power with all that you do . . . When a soul turns to the Universe of unmanifest life, at the same time It turns toward him . . . Believing; thinking what is believed to be true; thinking into Mind each day that which is wished to be returned; eliminating negative thoughts; holding all positive thoughts; giving thanks to the Spirit of Life that it is so . . . these are the steps which, when followed, will bring us to where we shall not have to ask if it be true, for, having demonstrated, *we shall know.*

Here Ernest stressed the importance of getting "still" and listening to the inner voice. Feel and *know* that a greater Intelligence than your own has begun to work on your problem because you have initiated a new pattern or design.

During his lifetime Ernest put these principles into practice in unnumbered cases, many of his clients being men of national importance in the field of business. But he also put these principles into service in his own life and demonstrated a free life and an ample fortune. "It is not difficult to do it," he said. "Commit your way unto the Law and It shall bring it to pass." To illustrate, he told of the case of one of his patients, who was connected with a big business concern that had begun to fail after having enjoyed success for many years. It was slowly sliding into disaster when he sought Ernest's help. He was advised that he himself held the answer, he knew all the details and techniques of the business and what he needed to do now was to "be still and know." The inner intelligence would tell him what a practitioner could not tell him.

The man decided to follow Ernest's advice and told his partners that he was going away for a while to get the right idea from the Infinite. They laughed at him, but he went nevertheless. He retired for three days and "waited on the Lord." He told himself that there was a Supreme Intelligence and an absolute leading of the Spirit. During this time a complete plan formulated in his mind as to the exact method to pursue in the business. He returned to his partners and told his plan. They laughed again and said it could not be done. But they decided it was better to follow his lead than accept failure. Within a year they had developed new enterprises and were far more prosperous than they had ever been. The man of whom Ernest spoke became so successful that he was soon able to retire and give his time to help others.

Creative Mind and Success has passed through many editions of printing since Ernest wrote it, and thousands of people have put it to successful use. Its success is due to the fact that it tells the story in a simple straightforward way that anybody can understand on the first reading. It is safe to say, too, that the whole philosophy and practice of the Science of Mind is incorporated in it. Ernest understood life when he said then, "Life is from within outward, and not from without inward. You are the center of power in your own life."

We returned from New York to our home on Third Avenue in Los Angeles and began a short period of rest and recreation. Every day was like a party. There were eleven of us: Mother; Ernest; myself; Katharine and our adopted son Louis; my brother Guy and his wife Emma, with their two children Josephine and Lawrence; and Anne Galer and her mother. And we always had a guest or two, friends, relatives, metaphysical leaders passing through Southern California on lecture tours, and, strangely enough, our father. Father was a guest for the simple reason that, while Mother was long gone in the East touring with Ernest and fishing in Maine, he, now past seventy, had trekked to Oregon, worked in a hotel, added to his savings and bought a home, this time in a northwestern pioneer state. Now he returned to Los Angeles to attempt to persuade Mother to come away with him. Mother, undaunted still by the thought of the rigorous life, was not, however, prepared to leave for Oregon. During the New York tour she had become positively and permanently "converted" to her son's teachings and had begun to be active in Ernest's work. So instead she persuaded her husband to come stay with her, which removed him from the guest list, and both Father and Mother lived with Ernest for the rest of their long lives.

There was ample room in the big house where fifty couples could have danced on the living and dining room floor. All of us played charades, old-fashioned whist, anagrams and authors, or took trips to Venice to swim in the Pacific.

But Ernest and I were soon restless. We enjoyed lecturing and the stimulation of contact with the public too much to stay away from it long, although each of us was writing another book. Ernest was making attempts to convert his present thoughts and earlier writings into a standard textbook, but I did not know of it until a year later, for he again wrote in bed after retiring for the night.

We cast about for more activity. We did not return to the Brack Shops because we thought the private lecture hall would not be large enough now. On the other hand, it was difficult to find a place in the downtown area that was within a reasonable price. Finally we discovered that there was a hall in the Trinity Auditorium which we could rent and we were permitted to build our private consultation rooms on one side. So we rented it and moved in. People were slow in coming at first, and for a time we ate the bitter fruit of reversal in popularity. Our first success in Los Angeles had been a matter of slow growth, for at that time we did not know how to advertise and gather both old and new students. Personally, I was not even willing to wait for another success and decided to return to the itinerant lecture field.

My decision to make so radical a change was highly influenced by the domestic situation. Katharine was unhappy in her new surroundings. We had no quarrels, but she wanted us to live alone. Under the circumstances it seemed the wiser thing to do, and as the work at the Trinity was faring poorly, I decided to sell all my interests to Ernest, including the home on Third Avenue, and move away. Ernest understood the situation, and the move was made.

So Katharine, Louis and I rented a cottage in Santa Monica Canyon, and I concentrated on my writing and eventually went east again and lectured in New York and Boston, leaving my family in California.

Ernest, meanwhile, temporarily resisted the flattering lure of the eastern seaboard. But he was frank in admitting that he missed the companionship we had had for more than ten years, and when he heard that things were going well with me in Boston he decided to follow.

Strangely enough, although a transient in the city, he had an overwhelming compulsion to get on with the writing of his textbook. So we took an apartment together. It was fun for me, particularly as he was a superior cook and prepared most of the meals.

He changed his writing habits to the extent of having a secretary come in each day to help him rework what he had scribbled out the night before, a practice he was to follow from this point on.

So it was that Ernest worked in Boston on the book that would eventually be rewritten, expanded, and reprinted thirty-two times, translated into foreign languages and used as a textbook in scores of churches and thousands of homes. And while he wrote and rewrote I went on with my Boston classes until the time seemed right for us to go to New York, where Ernest would resume his lectures, meet the third major influence in the early growth of the Idea and put his textbook finally in the hands of his publisher.

In New York and in Philadelphia, great audiences welcomed us. And once again our lives were enriched by the varied and wonderful people we met.

It was natural that the theatrical profession took notice of our work, because our audiences crowded the theaters, like Morosco and Town Hall, and the ballrooms of hotels like the Astor and McAlpin.

Many prominent actors on the legitimate stage became our friends, including Janet Beecher and her sister Olive Wyndham, then playing with George Arliss in *The Green Goddess*.

We were entertained at dinner in their home by their mother, a lovely and loving woman, highly complimentary of our stage presence and delivery. In later years Olive was married to Harry Gaze, the English New Thought lecturer and author who had been a close friend of Thomas Troward's. Together Harry and Olive Gaze toured the world for years, finally settling in Southern California, where our friendship continued.

It was not long before we had many actors in attendance at our classes and lectures, and then they began to come privately in increasing numbers, asking treatments to be cast in a new play, to overcome some handicap like stagefright or to develop personality or overcome a superstition. Only those who have had personal contact with the stage profession can imagine the emotional suffering of some actors, singers and musicians. One case was that of a woman who was to give a recital in Carnegie Hall. This is the dream of any artist, and a single occasion may ignite a lifetime profession. But this woman had no reason to fear; she was already famous, for she had a good stage presence and a magnificent voice. Ernest was really astonished that she came to him for help.

She was scared stiff, she said, "for fear the thoughts of people would affect her."

"Well, I won't treat you against 'malicious animal magnetism,' " he said, "because there isn't such an animal. But I will treat you so that you will not be afraid of anything or anybody. You are a trained and gifted artist. You are an experienced singer. You believe in yourself, for you have already proven yourself. I am going to attend your recital, and I shall sit high in the gallery where all the young students and lovers of music sit or stand just to learn from a trained artist. I want you to sing to them and me."

Then he added with his facetious charm, which often seemed to border on the irreverent, "When you really get ready to let out, don't forget God and the angels just a little higher up. You can reach them with high C."

Her recital proved a great success, and she returned to thank Ernest. "But what will I do next time if you aren't there?"

"God and the angels will be," he said.

XII

⌒ᴢ⌒

Ernest Studies With Emma Curtis Hopkins

EMMA CURTIS HOPKINS introduced Ernest Holmes to the limitless possibilities of practical mysticism. So great was the impression she made upon him that thirty-five years later he gave a résumé of her teachings to an advanced class and ended it with a rhapsody of speech and feelings that deeply moved students and teacher alike.

Later, on a tape, he recorded his recollections of her at the time of their meeting in 1924.

She was nearly eighty, I believe; a very stately woman who wore a long dress and a hat at all times. I am told that she was never seen without the hat. I went to the door of her apartment in the beautiful old Iroquois Hotel, and she received me with a stiff little bow of the head and motioned me to a chair. She sat down opposite me and began to talk. It was ten minutes before I said to myself, "This is the first lesson," and it was. She talked for an hour and, when she was through, got up and made a little bow and walked out of the room. The first four times I went, I didn't know whether or not she even knew my name. In an effort to make our relationship a little more personal, on my next visit I took her a large bouquet of roses. She accepted them calmly, put them on the grand piano and remarked, "They'll be very nice for a funeral I attend tomorrow." Then she sat down, talked for an hour, got up with that little bow and walked out with the roses.

I accepted, then, that this was strictly a teacher-student relationship. At the next lesson she suddenly unbent; and after that I used to stay, and we had long conversations. She turned out to be very witty, cheerful and lovable. At one time she told me of a convention she held in Chicago, and there was a student, an Absolutist who began screaming, "I am God," and she said, "There, there, George, it is all right for you to play you are God, but don't be so noisy about it."

She was a very sweet character, and there was something about her that you felt rather than heard. She was the only one I ever knew or knew about who combined mysticism with the use of the metaphysical principle of healing. There is a common denominator of mysticism wherever you find it, among all peoples and all religions, but the language and applications are individual, and she was the first and greatest to express it in terms that are applicable to healing.

Not too much is known of Mrs. Hopkins' personal life beyond the fact that she was the wife of an Andover professor. She was an influential teacher in the over-all New Thought movement. And her teachings made it apparent that she was not only a woman of broad education, but had the mystic's originality and breathed a grander vision into the consciousness of those who studied with her.

Mrs. Hopkins was widely read in oriental literature, including the Hebrew Scriptures, the New Testament, the Vedas and Bhagavad-Gita and other sacred writings of India; the philosophy and mysteries of the Greeks, such as those of Orpheus, Pythagoras, Plato and Plotinus; and she had intimate and exhaustive historical knowledge of all nations and peoples of all timess—a veritable encyclopedia! Her interpretations of the Bible are masterpieces of esoteric and spiritual wisdom. Her approach is from the point of view of *being,* apart from any vehicle in which it functions, but often *revealed through* its vehicle or through the language of religion, poetry, music and art. I know of no other modern authority who equals her revelation as found in her final *Résumé of Higher Mysticism.*

It was to such an authority that Ernest was drawn by his star of destiny at the precise moment when he was prepared for it as the next step in his metaphysical education. This was in fact the last rubric in his mental composition. It was an advance on his previous training, as is easily demonstrated, and an essential forward step.

At that time he had already known the various stirrings associated with those flashes of intellectual intuition so often confused with mysticism. Nature had spoken to him in the wilds of his native state, on the shores of many waters, and had awakened cosmic feelings, and there had been strange responses in his heart as he had quoted Browning's immortal lines on Saul and Paracelsus. But these were isolated experiences, half-realized and quite uncomprehended. He had indeed been wary of *mysticism,* for he had confused the term with the mysterious, perhaps spiritualistic, perhaps occult; and he was determined to avoid these as such. But now as he studied with Mrs. Hopkins, he was brought face to face with mysticism as a frankly recognized and wholly complete philosophy of life.

With his usual clarity of reasoning from cause to effect, he went back in his mind and reviewed the steps he had already taken in relation to his discovery of this new system of thought. He returned to Emerson, who had first opened his eyes to soul-power and freed him from sensitiveness and an inverted self-consciousness by relating him to the cosmic scheme, and recalled how he had correlated it with his knowledge of God and man as revealed in the Bible. He pondered his conviction of the *active* goodness of God. He meditated on the message of New Thought as he had understood it and how it emphasized the inner life and the unfoldment of individual and personal powers free from theological systems.

But the mystical element was somehow lacking, he thought. It seemed to him that the power used was often psychological rather than spiritual, and that there was too much reliance on denials and affirmations rather than the realization of the Presence or the inner life of the Spirit. He felt that oft-repeated denials tended to sustain negative states of thought.

So it was with this background that Ernest was ready when the teacher appeared. Mrs. Hopkins had been the flame that ignited Murray in New York, the Fillmores in Kansas City, the Brooks sisters in Denver, the Rix sisters in California, and Burnell in Los Angeles, and they in turn had given light to America and the world. Ernest was the last in the line of those noted leaders who came under the tutelage of this great teacher.

Just what Mrs. Hopkins taught him, just how the voice of spirit spoke through her, is hard to delineate. It is difficult to put the intangible into words, to open the door to reality so as to give at least a glimpse of its unspeakable beauty. Mysticism is perhaps the most difficult of all metaphysical themes, for it involves an experience rarely realized and never adequately expressed in words—the *realization of identity with absolute being,* or the here and now *experience* of "union with God." The value of the teaching of Emma Curtis Hopkins, Ernest felt, was the fact that she had not only experienced the consciousness of the mystic herself but imparted spiritual conviction in such a way as to awaken a corresponding consciousness in her students.

In describing the scene to me afterward, Ernest said that none of her students ever "studied" with her, for she offered no debate: "What she said was *it* and that was that; and like some ancient seeress, dispassionate but not cold, she powered it with a conviction so great that it imparted something—a definite impartation, in fact, so great that at times it was almost like a wind, like the 'psychic breeze,' a phenomenon familiar to inquirers. It was something alive, animated and inspiring. It was due neither to her words nor to her manner. She awakened an awe which was at once personal and impersonal, identified with her and yet something more."

Mrs. Hopkins taught Ernest that the first step in developing the consciousness of the mystic was turning the attention away from all things, events and persons toward the Deity ever beholding us . . . "Where is your vision?" she asked. To her "repentance" did not mean suffering. She used the word in its original meaning, "seeking again" (*repento*). The vision turned toward perfection, and purity invited it.

As we attempt to retrace the pathway taken by Ernest under Mrs. Hopkins' guidance, we are impressed by the fact that she lifted the principles of the mental-spiritual healing science to a higher plane. Ernest saw that it was not necessary to reject the principles of mental science; they were true *on their level*, but it was possible to realize their truths on the level of First Cause. "God is a Spirit: and they that worship him must worship him in spirit and in truth." When the ascent is made from thought to Cause, he saw the attention is no longer confined to things, forms or thoughts but is directed to the realization of the "patterns" from which all things are derived. In healing, for example, it is desirable to reflect that every organ has its divine pattern as Plotinus and the Ancients taught, and "when by reason of any fact the organ becomes detached, it gets in pain and its whole longing is to get back to its pattern that it shall be whole."

The foregoing paragraph is an interpretation made by him in later years of the understanding that Mrs. Hopkins conveyed to him through lifting both the thought and the treatment to a higher level of consciousness, that is, to become God-conscious, not as an outside observer but as an inner identity.

Yet Mrs. Hopkins found it necessary to put spiritual truth into familiar terms, and she used the word "remission" to indicate the unburdening of conscience and the direction of consciousness to a higher level. In this respect she taught therefore that "what thou seest that thou must become" and the fact that we must avoid looking upon evil.

It was from the seeds sown at that time that Ernest found his life vastly enriched by a new vision of Reality above the psychological and philosophical plane, seeds that were to grow to full flower through the years.

With the publication of *The Science of Mind,* textbook, in 1926, and his return to Los Angeles, both the Idea and Ernest Holmes had reached maturity. Ernest himself was thirty-nine years old, and nineteen years had elapsed since that summer in Maine when he had opened Emerson's *Essays* for the first time and the Idea was conceived.

Certainly with the publication of the first textbook, neither the man nor the Idea stopped growing, for twelve years later, a carefully revised edition with more than three hundred pages added replaced the earlier work. It is this later edition, done with the editorial collaboration of Maude Allison Lathem, that is in use today. But in a certain sense the first edition of *The Science of Mind* was a complete answer to his early search, for it contained a full explanation of *treatment,* the practical application of all he had experienced and learned thus far.

It also contained a chapter on the law of psychic phenomena. By 1936, when his revision omitted this, he felt no loss of personal conviction as to the authenticity of psychic phenomena but that it was developing into a separate field of research.

It was obvious that his primary concern was to explain the Science of Mind in terms of a spiritual principle that could be applied by *treatment* to the individual demonstration of healing body and conditions and revealing a rich, full life here and now.

He did not then nor later concern himself in his writings with the typical abstractions of philosophy that deaden the interest of the searcher for workable principles in the field of spiritual healing. His work was the outgrowth of personal experience, and its essential purpose was to teach the reader how to treat oneself and others; and every treatment was directed to the recognition that "the Divine Nature is re-enacted in man." Everything is about God. He said, "The

mystics have taught that there is but One Ultimate Reality;
and that this Ultimate Reality is *here* NOW. . . ." He solved
every problem by this *principle,* although he was careful to
point out that Principle is personal to the individual but not
in the anthropomorphic sense.

In rereading the first textbook, it is amazing to discover in
how many ways he was able to repeat the theme of the Allness
of God and Good and the method of realizing it through scientific meditation. He looked upon disease as the experience
of consciousness, having no existence apart from the conceiv-
ing mind.

". . . The sources from which most diseases come," he said, "are
conscious observations, suppressed emotions, subjective inherited tendencies, and, perhaps three-fourths of them, from
race-suggestion." He continued: "Disease is an impersonal
thought force operating through people, which does not belong
to them at all. Recognize that it is neither person, place, nor
thing; that there is no law to support it; that it is a coward
fleeing before the Truth; that there is nothing but the Truth."

He considered it unnecessary to specify the trouble for which
he was giving the treatment, although there might be cases
where a knowledge of the disease in regard to the possible
thought that *lay behind it* could be of value to the practitioner. "Mary Jones comes to John Smith and says, 'I have
tuberculosis.' In answer to this he [the practitioner] declares,
'This word is for Mary Jones. She is a perfect and complete
manifestation of Pure Spirit, and Pure Spirit cannot be diseased; consequently she is not diseased.' "

The statement that "Mary Jones is not diseased," appears
on the surface to be a denial of the existence of a condition
that is to be healed. But closer analysis reveals that it is a
brief form of stating that the body is composed of Pure Spirit,
that the Divine Pattern of the bodily organ remains perfect.
The Divine Mind knows how to reestablish Its control, because Mary Jones as a spiritual being is not subject to disease.

Once this fact is realized, the innate perfection will take over.

That this was in Ernest's mind is shown by the balance of the paragraph that we have been quoting:

This is an argument, trying to bring out the evidence in favor of perfection. It is an argument which produces a certain conclusion in the mentality of John Smith, and, consequently, it sets in motion a certain law for Mary Jones. As John does this, day after day, he gradually becomes convinced of her perfection and she is healed. If he could do it in one minute, she would be healed in one minute. *There is no process in healing. It is a revelation, an awakening, a realization of Life.* Man exists in Divine Mind as a Perfect Image. . . ."

And he offered an inspiring conclusion to the chapter:

There is One Infinite Mind from which all things come; this Mind is through, in and around man; It is the Only Mind that there is, and every time man thinks he uses It. There is One Infinite Spirit, and every time man says, "I am," he proclaims It. There is One Infinite Substance and every time man moves, he moves in It.

There is One Infinite Law, and every time man thinks he sets It in motion. There is One Infinite God, and every time man speaks to This God, he receives a direct answer. One! One! One! "I am God and there is none else." There is One Limitless Life which returns to the thinker what he thinks into It. One! One! One! "In all, over all and through all."

Talk, live, act, believe and know that you are a center in the One. All the Power there is; all the Presence there is; all the Love there is; all the Peace there is; all the Good there is and the Only God that is, is Omnipresent; consequently, the Infinite is in and through man and is in and through everything. "Act as though I am and I will Be."

Ernest stressed what he called "realization," which consists of becoming aware of the Perfect Presence, the *only* Life, and in which the elevated consciousness revealed by Mrs. Hopkins does the work: "God is all there is; there is no other Life."

Above all, in the textbook *The Science of Mind,* he had done what he had set out to do. Not long ago I came across a remark made by Ernest in recollecting his theory and practice in those early days.

Treatment [he said], *is both an art and a science.* Faith is the art of knowing, law is the science through which spontaneous art performs its work. The recognition of Presence is more important than the recognition of Principle. Everything originates and is maintained by Pure Feeling. A perfect healing can be effected at any time by the simple process of realizing the Allness of God as Life and Love; by accepting the truth that nothing can separate you from the Love of God, "Who forgiveth all thine iniquities; who healeth all thy diseases."

He had, in the textbook, written the first and still definitive book on *treatment.* And he and his students used it "with signs following." The Idea now was full-fledged. And the man, Ernest Holmes, was poised for the next step.

BOOK THREE

THE IDEA TAKES FORM

I

⌒✑⌒

The Invisible Made Visible—1927

I HAVE WRITTEN that Ernest Holmes was a practical man, a man of his time, with a direct message for our day.

And so he was.

Truth itself, however, is timeless.

Centuries before Ernest Holmes was born, a disciple of Jesus' wrote: "And the Word was made flesh, and dwelt among us . . . full of grace and truth."

The accuracy of that mystic statement was a cornerstone upon which Ernest built his life and works; but he made it even more relevant for us today. The Word, he said, *becomes* flesh and *dwells* among us. And being a practical man—as was the Master Christian—he went on to prove it, and having done so himself, Ernest also insisted that all men could do likewise.

In his textbook Ernest taught in the words of our time that man, every man, is a center in Divine Mind, a point of God-conscious life, love, truth, and action; that the invisible passes into the visible through our faith in it.

He himself had passed through questioning to belief, through belief by practice and through demonstration to faith; now he had arrived at a conviction—a realization of the Presence.

The word "body," as Ernest used it, meant an objective manifestation of the invisible Principle of Life. With an expanding awareness of the invisible Presence and Principle, he maintained, came a corresponding expansion in the outer forms and varied expressions of the One Life.

And so it was.

It proved true for Ernest. It proved true for his students. The next ten years are a practical example of the growing "body" of the Idea that Ernest had conceived.

There were to be great changes in the outer expression of the life of the boy from Maine who had started on his way with little more than a head full of questions. They included fame, fortune and his one great and lasting love affair.

Ernest was pressed to found an organization in California. It was, indeed, the natural development to embody his Idea, and thus it would grow nationally and internationally with the years, to live on in its physical form long after he had discarded his own. But at that time Ernest, with his democratic insistence on individual spiritual freedom, his personal debunking of any so-called "final revelation" or "personal revelator," his distaste for the bondage of "creeds" and "dogmas," was slow to yield.

It was one man, I believe, more than any other, who by faithfully bringing the matter to his attention finally persuaded Ernest to take a closer look at the value of founding an institution.

That man was Lem Brunson.

In late 1925, on his return from New York and before publication of the textbook, Ernest leased the Ambassador Hotel Theater in Los Angeles and began to speak there regularly each Sunday. He had the courage to go on, although his first audience was only 75 people. But in a few months the theater was crowded to its capacity of 625, and after that his success was assured. Many important persons, among them old friends like Dr. Ameen Fareed, and new ones like Judge Ben

Lindsay, nationally known jurist, began to gather around Ernest, and hundreds of people were turned away from the Ambassador on Sunday mornings.

One of the regular attendants at the Ambassador was Lem Brunson, later known to everybody as "Deacon" Brunson. He was an able businessman, who had made a fortune in oil at Santa Fe Springs and afterward with the same partner by the name of Bell had developed the vast area along the mountain slopes from Beverly Hills to the sea that they called Bel Air. When I met him on one of my visits to California, he had two great interests: landscaping his own estate at enormous cost, and a friendship with Ernest. I recall playing golf with him one day, and when we rested at one of the tees, he turned to me and said, "I think there were three really great men in history, don't you, Fenwicke?"

I smiled, looking at him quizzically. "I'm sure of it. Who were they?"

"Socrates, Jesus and Ernest," he said.

I have often wondered at it. I knew it was sincere, and I concluded that anybody who brings you into a real experience with God must be great to you.

Deacon Brunson was a natural organizer, and he and other businessmen who were taking class work with Ernest felt that my brother could exert a wider influence if he gathered his following into an organization. From their point of view, there would then be nothing left for him to do but lecture and write.

Ernest knew it was not so easy. He felt he had been instrumental in bringing me out of organized religion and he was increasingly wary of getting into it himself. Would he himself not get caught in the machinery? Would his message be tampered with? He felt this was typical of church organization, and he wanted nothing of it. But they insisted out of love and respect for him. And so it stood while he battled it out with himself. I have his own reflections in some manuscripts I have discovered.

The thing that really persuaded me it was best to organize [he said], was my study of the contrast between two great metaphysical movements, Christian Science on the one hand and New Thought on the other. One of them was a close and authoritarian organization, the other was a loose affiliation. No one would question that many leaders in the New Thought Movement have been great speakers and writers. They were even agreed on a body of beliefs, but the movement as a whole went up or down according to whether they had a strong leadership at a given time or did not have.

On the other hand Christian Science had developed a powerful institution and one which has exerted an enormous influence religiously, socially and even politically. I recalled the struggle they had had to establish the legal rights of metaphysical practice, contesting with the established church, state and medicine in all the courts until no one today would think of challenging them. Without question the whole movement owed a great debt of gratitude to an *organization* which had demanded and won the legal right to heal the sick by mental and spiritual means.

On the other hand, I thought that organization tends to crystallize and become authoritarian and I believed that it dwarfed the natural growth and expansion of the message itself. It is probable that the founder of any cult or system of religion if he could live beyond a century would make great changes. For example, many principles of metaphysics or the religious sciences would be modified because of new discoveries in the fields of psychiatry and science. Newer and better understanding might result and overcome the narrowing tendencies of a traditional and orthodox theology which lives beyond its age.

Yet, I myself had never been threatened by secular authority of any kind nor even by the more barbed arrows of religious bigotry. I did not have to suffer with the founders of Christian Science or of Mormonism, for example. I escaped being called crazy or foolish or a schizophrenic or even a Bible-wrecker.

So Ernest mulled over the pros and cons of organization from the impersonal point of view. But there was one personal argument that finally persuaded him, the undoubted fact that organization provides an importance to the work because of the influence of a compact group of leaders and the partisanship of members. He recognized that the public automatically confers more respect upon a group than on an individual, especially if the officers are steadfast and enthusiastic. And he admitted that his work would not outlast his own life unless an organization carried it forward. He decided in favor of organization.

So far as I know he never regretted it. He had no battle royal with officiousness and he himself, through the years, rode organization lightly.

There were other important men besides Deacon Brunson who had urged organization upon Ernest, and in December of 1926, after he announced his decision, they all met at a dinner in the Brunson home to plan and to raise an expansion fund. They contributed five thousand dollars that night and decided on getting a California state charter for a nonprofit organization, which they named the Institute of Religious Science and School of Philosophy. One of the original organizing Board members was Ernest's early friend Reginald Armor, who, through re-election, has remained on the Board to the present time.

Ernest himself proposed the title, because he considered an *institute* to be "a place of learning, *religion* is man's idea of God and *philosophy* is the love of learning." He later defined Religious Science as "a correlation of the laws of science, the opinions of philosophy and the revelations of religion applied to the needs and aspirations of man."

Eleven years after that time in my parsonage in Venice, California, when he came into possession of, and was possessed by, his great Idea for the fusion of metaphysics, psychology, philosophy and the religions of East and West, Ernest was still true to his vision and had forged an instrument for its implementation.

The work of incorporation in February, 1927—almost exactly on Ernest's fortieth birthday—was carried out by Judge Leonard Wilson and Mostyn Clinch, a prominent realtor who was taking Ernest's class. They located a building better fitted for his work. The midweek lecture hall that they rented could seat 250 people, and they took adjoining offices at the corner of Carondelet and Wilshire Boulevard. The faithful Gussie Rundel moved in permanently as a receptionist, a position that she continued to fill until her death thirty-four years later.

The Ambassador Theater was no longer big enough to seat the crowds eager for help, inspiration and instruction. So the new institute rented the Wilshire Ebell Club for Sunday mornings, a concession never before made by that organization. It seated twelve hundred people. And the people loved Ernest and his message. They attended from near and far, many who lived in Pasadena, Glendale, Hollywood and other cities, drawn both by his eloquence and his ability to prove by actual healings what he taught.

On the platform they found a unique character, one who did not speak in the traditional manner of the clergy but used a phraseology that was obviously original and made no apologies for being himself. He had perfect poise, although he would occasionally jerk the lectern and then line it up like a careful housekeeper. He had power, both of voice and personality. He had systematized his message and presented his philosophy as a whole. There were no gaping holes, no discrepancies in it. This is revealed in the brochure that he wrote and published at that time and that has been but slightly changed through the years, called *What Religious Science Teaches.*

"Here is a man," they said, "who knows and who knows he knows. He does not question his own knowledge." And so secure were they in their belief in him that they could laugh with him when he occasionaly laughed at himself or made fun at the expense of something he had announced the moment before with the greatest solemnity. He was a humorist *par excellence.* No one who heard him either in private or public would dispute it. Sometimes it confused the newcomer or even shocked him; Ernest would sense it and remark upon it. "This is the shock treatment." And both the humor and the "shock" had power.

But most powerful was the sincerity and conviction expressed in what he said. He believed it. He put it into practice. As they listened, they felt that something good was going to happen to them, and the healings attested to the fact that it did.

As soon as the organizational details were over, Ernest began the first class of thirty-five members under the new name of School of Philosophy. He used his own *The Science of Mind* as a textbook. His major effort was to teach them to see the science as a whole. He thought that many students became confused because they knew it only part by part, and some of these parts appeared to contradict each other; so while he taught the textbook line by line, he always referred each statement to the total Principle. Few teachers possess this art, fewer still have the patience to use it. Years later, in a further attempt to establish the total Principle, he gave four lesson-lectures on the subject, as follows: "The Thing," "The Way It Works," "What It Does," "How to Use It." In 1938 he recognized the importance of this summarization and made it the Introduction to the revised textbook. He was patient, direct and witty with students all his life and did not hesitate to begin at the beginning over and over again in his writing and teaching.

It was in this informal but meticulous way that Ernest taught his first class as Dean of the Institute of Religious Science and School of Philosophy in 1926-1927. The course took a whole year, but the work was justified, for from this single class he graduated a number of students who later became members of his staff, and practitioners like Helen Van Slyke, Alberta Smith, Isobel Poulin, and Ivy Crane Shelhamer, whose names are a tradition in the movement because of their efficiency, loving personal influence and ability to prove the principles by "signs following."

*   *   *

The year of 1927 was a very fruitful one, indeed. The new activities had hardly opened up when Deacon Lem Brunson also proposed the publication of a magazine. He offered to finance two thousand copies, which would sell for twenty-five cents each but actually cost the same amount to print. So the institute went forward with the proposition and took subscriptions at $2.50 a year, a price that held for the next fifteen years. I have here a brief personal recollection in Ernest's words, "Lem Brunson put many thousands into the magazine; it is difficult to get a new magazine on the market. Now, of course, a hundred thousand or so copies go to subscribers all over the world and can be had at the newsstands of America and many foreign countries but at that time it took faith." It was first called *The Religious Science Magazine* but was soon changed to *Science of Mind* magazine, a title that was to endure to the present day. The first issue in October, 1927, asserted that it was "A Magazine of Christian Philosophy" and contained a statement of *"What We Believe."*

The first issue of the magazine contained only thirty-two pages but was astonishingly complete. It made mention of the Men's Club, which had already been organized and also of Every Woman's Club, which had thirty-five members at that time. There was an announcement of a "Complete Course" in the Science of Mind, which was to begin in January of 1928. Small as it was, the magazine contained a Junior Department and also stressed a Department of Healing under the leadership of Augusta Rundel. Lem Brunson and J. Farrell MacDonald, a prominent actor in the moving picture industry and a gifted writer, were listed as directors of the institute, and there was a list of eight regular practitioners.

There were numerous fine articles by various people, including Ernest, but the "heart" of the magazine, then as now, was in the series of Meditations offering one specific meditation for each day of the month. My brother loved to tell of a time many years later when a nationally known advertising executive, whose wife had experienced a healing through Ernest's help, wanted to streamline the *Science of Mind* magazine for even wider appeal and distribution. Meetings were held in the evenings in Ernest's living room. New formats were discussed, great innovations and deletions were proposed in the sweeping Madison Avenue tradition. Finally, there was some discussion of altering the Daily Meditations.

At this point Mother, then nearing her ninetieth birthday, who had been knitting quietly and listening, arose and announced that it was time for her to retire, "But I'm sure you won't mind a comment before I go." Her eyes, bright blue as ever, twinkled. "It's a very good idea to throw out the old bath water," she said, "but when you throw out the bath water, be sure you don't throw out the baby."

"There were," Ernest chuckled, "some changes made that night, but we didn't touch the Meditations."

Two articles from the very early issues are of particular interest. In the December issue of 1927, the practice of featuring an article by a front cover display was begun, this time the title was "Finding the Christ," by Ernest S. Holmes. In the revised edition of the textbook nine years later, a chapter of this same title enlarged on this theme and, together with fifty-five pages, "From the Teachings of Jesus," showed the Christian orientation of Ernest's teachings and his reverence for Jesus, "The man [who] became a living embodiment of the Christ." All his life Ernest "searched the Scriptures" and drew light and inspiration from the Old as well as the New Testament.

The second article of interest, in the second issue of the magazine, was entitled "The ABC's of the Ph.D.'s." It was signed H. G. Foster. For three years, H. G. Foster continued to contribute, but her signature changed to H. Foster Holmes; and she represented not only one of the greatest joys but one of the greatest changes in the expanding manifestation of my brother's life. For good things were happening in the personal life of Ernest Holmes as well as his professional life—and inseparable from it.

He was rebuilding and landscaping a lovely new home where he was to live for nineteen years and which became famous to his hundreds of friends and followers as "The Hill."

And he had met Hazel Gillan Foster, niece of his faithful friend Gussie Rundel and widowed daughter of Aunt Annie Gillan, whose cottage in Venice he had rented years before for his first "Home of Healing."

The three and one-half-acre property that he and our brother Guy bought from an early movie star, Louise Glaum, included a gentle sloping hill covered with palms, pine, fir and eucalyptus, overlooking a wide flowered meadow in Palms, then a small four-cornered town only a few miles southwest of the rapidly expanding suburb, Beverly Hills. Here, under Guy's supervision, the existing hilltop house was remodeled for Ernest and Mother and Father, with a new house beside it for Guy and his family. Later a cottage was built in the meadow at the foot of the hill for Guy's son, Lawrence, and his wife. It was, indeed, a "family estate," and Ernest was delighted with it.

He was even more delighted with his ripening friendship with the elegant and lovely Hazel Foster, although he certainly did not know while he was creating "The Hill" that he would bring her there as his wife or that she would become an outstanding example of his teaching, his personal practitioner and an inseparable and inspirational part of his life and work.

Hazel was born in California. Both her mother Annie and her Aunt Gussie were prominent in the clubwoman's world, much more interested in club-and-culture than society; although Hazel herself, as young Mrs. Ross Foster, had been somewhat forced into the social life but never cared about it at all.

As a girl she soon gave promise of a magnificent voice. Her father and mother—she was an only child—sent her to Paris, where she studied with one of the De Reskes. Soon it was apparent that the voice was operatic in power and scope, and for a time she was trained for this career. She herself aban-

doned it. When a friend once asked her why, she said, "Singing on the stage in an opera house would be only part of the
career of an opera singer. The rest of the life was something
I found I did not want. I didn't want to be 'an opera singer.'
I love and am grateful to those who are. But it didn't fit with
my own wishes for a way of life. A public career wasn't for
me." There was no hesitation about this. It was an instant
and clean-cut decision; she never looked back. And she gave
up singing altogether, since she said that, unless she had the
time and the wish to practice and keep at her best, she didn't
want to do it at all. But her love of music and her understanding of it were a never-failing source of joy to her all her life
long.

This was also one of the things that gave her an understanding of professional people—and made her the friend
and stay and help of so many of them.

She had been married before she met Ernest Holmes, to a
brilliant and wealthy young man named Ross Foster, but was
left a widow when still very young. Her father had died, and
at that time she and her mother built what was really the first
luxury apartment house in Los Angeles—on Vermont Avenue
only a few blocks from the Ambassador Hotel. It was a most
charming spreading duplex affair with gardens and lawns,
done in adobe style. Here at one time or another lived many
of the early motion picture greats—D. W. Griffith—the brilliant and tragic Mabel Normand, first great comedy star—
Jack Pickford and his bride, the Follies beauty Olive Thomas
—and Jack's sister Mary Pickford used to visit them and became a friend and admirer of Hazel's.

Most of what I know of Hazel in the days before she met
my brother has come to me from another admirer of hers, a
famous writer who was a fellow Californian and her fast and
close friend throughout Hazel's life. In a letter to me recalling those early days, Adela Rogers St. Johns wrote:

Her manner with these theater people—there was also Jack
Barrymore at a downtown theater and many others—was one of

receiving them into her home. They adored her. Olive Thomas once said that Hazel was the only good woman she'd ever known who understood the temptations of those who were struggling. She had, Ollie said, true loving charity for all. And Mabel Normand told me that she thought if anyone could have "saved" her it was "my Hazel."

There was a quality about her then, and always, that was hard to define. Years later one of my sons came closest to a definition when he gave her a nickname—a loving nickname that stuck. He called her Madame Buddha.

I think the key to the name, and to Hazel Holmes was—no no, not the key—the most notable word for her was *fearlessness*. This was a truly fearless woman. This was part of what came to be her imperturbability. Her unastonishability. This was different from serenity somehow—*that* she also had. But nothing astonished her at the same time that she reacted to it with warmth, with instant encouragment, with enormous faith.

She was then and always beautifully dressed. She used to say that she had learned the value of clothes in Paris. Her hair, which she never cut, was what was then called auburn—a rich red-brown. And her eyes were dark—with the most striking black eyebrows and lashes.

Her religion at that time was really a seeking. She had never found exactly the religion she wanted. But she was always searching and was a woman of prayer.

When she met Ernest Holmes—she still hadn't found exactly the teaching she wanted.

They met at her mother's, with Aunt Gussie in attendance, shortly after Hazel completed a tour of Europe. She began attending Ernest's lectures at the Ambassador, and soon he took to dropping by her charming apartment, where she discussed his teachings with him, quietly but with deep perception; and he discovered that it was a pleasant thing after lecturing to drive her home, and relax in the big living room and think together.

Summer came, and he invited her to go with him to visit some of his friends who had a cottage on a High Sierra lake. I have Ernest's reminiscence of the occasion.

It was hot [he said]. There are hotter places than California inland valleys on a summer's day, I am told, but they are spoken of softly by everyone except the profane. Of course, I know the language but I put it to a different use. At any rate, I had a big old Studebaker, a seven-passenger used car—and there we were in the rolling country near Bishop on the way to June Lake, when pop! there went a tire. I got out and began the damp, unequal struggle—I never was mechanically minded, and in those days you had to pry the flat tire off and force the spare tire on by main strength—with Hazel calling back in cool, encouraging tones. Finally I got the tire on and the car going and we rolled along for an hour, when pop! another tire blew out! This time I had no spare but fortunately the former owner had left cement and patches under the seat and I had something to work with. By the time I got through it was two o'clock in the morning. It was too dark for Hazel to see me, although she was wide awake for she urged me to crawl into the back seat and sleep a while. It wasn't possible until I had lifted out lugs of fresh tomatoes, lettuce and other fruits and vegetables we were taking to our hosts. I slept that night like a wayside lizard, but I looked more like a tramp when we arrived. We were met with much merriment because, no matter how I looked, Hazel had proved herself—well, Hazel! After a day of desert heat, and a night of desert cold, her face and clothing sifted over with fine desert sand, she still wore her imperturbable smile, her high hat had not budged from its proper angle and her gloves were, miraculously, still as white as a newborn lamb.

If this was typical of Hazel, Ernest's next sentence was quite as typical of him. "And so," said my brother, "knowing her better, we became engaged and we were married in October, 1927, and she came to live with us at The Hill."

This was exactly seven months after the institute had opened it doors, and the very same month in which the *Science of Mind* magazine was first published.

Ernest had found a woman whom he could love, body, mind and soul. Hazel had found not only a man she could love but the religion she was seeking, and she became Ernest's most radiant and devoted student as well as his wife.

Thus it was, as 1927 drew to a close, that Mr. and Mrs. Ernest Holmes at Christmastime looked forward to an even wider and more varied expression of the one Life.

And so it was.

II

❧

Open at the Top

ERNEST HOLMES never stopped learning—and he never stopped growing.

If he was opposed to anything, it was to the concept that Infinite Truth could be caught in a mold—crystallized, formalized, finalized; or that it could come through or become the exclusive property of only a special person or group of persons. His conviction that each individual life is an expression of the one Infinite Life, the one Infinite Truth, gave him a boundless faith in the unlimited possibility of every man, and in the potential evolution and expansion of individual and collective consciousness in infinite form and variety. Thus he looked for it and welcomed it wherever he found it and recommended that the Institute of Religious Science and School of Philosophy and its students do likewise.

If this freedom was too sudden and startling for the few, if they stumbled back into yesterday's well-charted, known limitations or hastily sought the sheltering embrace of orthodox authority or fell by the wayside half-blinded by the vastness of the new horizons—there were the many and the faithful who welcomed it and were strong enough to walk in the light.

If this open-minded commitment to growth and change

presented problems in iron-clad organization, it also afforded the greatest opportunity for an expanding movement that would not become obsolete, that could meet the ever-shifting challenges of the world consciousness and be forever current, forever relevant and dynamic in each new today.

For himself, Ernest could not have done otherwise had he wished—for to him growth and change were coexistent with the wider expression here and now of the undeviating Principle of Infinite Life, Truth, Love and Action to which he was consistent all his life.

This was nowhere more apparent than in his teachings, writings and conduct during the early years of the institute, and he made a statement shortly after its founding that to him represented the vitality and dynamics that alone could sustain his ideal.

This statement, which is to follow, was made under these circumstances: Soon after establishing *Science of Mind* magazine, Willett L. Hardin, Ph.D., a scientist, became closely associated with Ernest, and in the spring of the following year, they decided to begin the publication of a new magazine under Dr. Hardin's editorship, which would be called *Quarterly Journal of Science, Religion, and Philosophy*. Dr. Hardin had formed a great admiration for Ernest and the institute, and in the first issue he related that he had been lecturing at the institute for six months and had never found even in universities a greater interest in science and philosophy. He quoted the opinion of noted authorities on the necessity of a rapprochement between religion and science and set himself to the task of cooperating with Ernest and others in bringing this about.

Ernest, in his first article in the *Quarterly* recapitulated the principles of Religious Science and said that we accept the aid of science and that Religious Science is a complement of medical science in an effort to heal.

He asserted: "God, the universal life force and intelligent energy running through everything, is an Intelligent Presence pervading all space; a beginningless and endless Eternity of eternities; a self-existent Cause; a perfect Unit, a complete Wholeness.

"Religious Science [is] shorn of dogmatism, freed from superstition, and *open at the top* for greater illumination, unbound and free."

His last address at Asilomar in 1959 contains the exact words, *"open at the top,"* and he attempted to forever cut away the ground beneath the feet of any and all teachers who would make the message of today the infallible bible of tomorrow.

Ernest was, and expected his students to be, "open at the top," and the *Journal* reflected this stand.

In the autumn of 1930, Ernest and Milton Sills, former Fellow of philosophy at the University, of Chicago, later a noted motion-picture star, became associate editors of the *Journal.* Dr. Hardin was world-affairs interpreter. Among new contributors was James A. B. Scherer, formerly president of the California Institute of Technology, and there was a report of conversations between several of these scholars on the general theme: "Is there a conscious Intelligence in the universe that responds to man's approach?"

Later Dr. Hardin became editor of *Science of Mind* magazine, and the management of both publications was assumed by Lem Brunson until the institute turned the *Journal* over to the University of Southern California, which continued to publish it for some years.

It is quite obvious, in rereading those early published dialogues, that Ernest himself had no doubts about "a conscious Intelligence in the universe that responds to man's approach," and that he delighted in such "conversations" because, as he said, they tended to clear the mind. He and Milton Sills who, with his beautiful actress-wife, Doris Kenyon, had become close friends of Ernest and Hazel, held long discussions on philosophy at about this time. Later, in 1932, after Dr. Sills' death, these were published in a slim volume entitled *Values* which has since become a collector's item.

These dialogues were all reminiscent of Ernest's and my

early "library discussions" in the parsonage in Venice, and our later questing exchanges with Dr. Ameen Fareed on psychiatry, and with Rabbi Ernest R. Trattner on the cabala, and represented a type of learning that my brother practiced throughout his life.

Ernest's openness, his enthusiasm, his keenness of mind and warmth of spirit, drew to him and to the institute a caliber of men and women whose depth and breadth of thought enriched all.

Rabbi Ernest Trattner, who had come from New York to take over a synagogue, City Temple, near the institute head-quarters, contributed frequent articles to *Science of Mind* magazine, one of which in particular on "Spinoza, Prince of Philosophers," impressed Ernest. Dr. Trattner also lectured at the institute on "Knowing Your Bible Intelligently," which began a pleasant association that lasted many years, and there was an exchange of Sabbath services between him and Ernest.

Dr. John Godfrey Hill, a professor at the University of Southern California, also became a visiting lecturer at the institute and spoke on World Religions, and Dr. Ameen Fareed, psychiatrist, gave a series of lectures on psychology and continued to speak for many years and write for the magazine. In May of 1932 there was an article in the magazine by the world renowned Judge Ben Lindsay, dealing with the "Institute of Human Relations." As founder of the Juvenile and Family Court of Denver, his treatment of youth was significant.

Ernest was slowly drawing to himself a great and permanent following of thinking people of importance and influence in the world of education, arts and industry. Clergymen of all faiths came to hear him, and many of them changed their views because of his influence, while a considerable number of them eventually joined his staff. And many eminent teachers and leaders in the New Thought Movement found a home at the institute. Two of these, the one because of the past, the other because of the future, are outstanding examples.

As early as 1928 the name of Christian D. Larson began to appear in *Science of Mind* magazine and to be a part of the major teaching courses. It was the very same Christian D. Larson whose book *The Ideal Made Real,* nineteen years earlier, had introduced Ernest to the New Philosophy, inspired him to go forward in learning and practicing the art of mental treatment and encouraged him to expand beyond physical healing to the "control of conditions."

Now Christian D. Larson was on the permanent staff of the institute in Los Angeles of which Ernest was the founder —and it is not difficult to realize the joy the association brought to my brother nor the benefit derived by the students; nor the significance of his joining in the really remarkable healing of "conditions" done by Religious Science practitioners when the dark historic days following the stock market crash of 1929 let through the institute doors a deluge of needy people, broken not only financially but in health, hope and spirit.

There was also Robert H. Bitzer, who came on at Ernest's invitation from Boston, where they had met at the very successful church founded by Julia Seton, which Dr. Bitzer then conducted.

Clarence Mayer was another prominent New Thought pioneer who was associated with the work of the institute, while W. L. Barth and Clinton Wunder exemplified outstanding clergymen attracted by the wider freedom and new horizons of Religious Science.

There were able younger men, too, and this profoundly pleased Ernest, now known as Dean. In 1928 Reginald Armor, protégé of Ernest ever since my brother had been his Scout leader, contributed his first article to the magazine, presaging a long, valuable and faithful relationship with the institute. And four years later young Donald Fareed, Dr. Ameen Fareed's son, conducted a magazine department on the "Activities of the Junior Church," in which he thanked Dr. Holmes for increased interest and help.

But while these many people, young and old, contributed their varied facets to the teachings and writings of *Science of Mind* magazine and the classwork at the Institute of Religious Science and School of Philosophy and while he welcomed and learned from them all and continued to synthesize or fuse these facets of truth, Ernest Holmes himself throughout life emphasized *healing,* affirming that this was the lifeblood of the movement. Thus, techniques of *treatment* by which this could be accomplished—in increased understanding of the Principle or Law and awareness of the Presence— were among the subjects central to his own teaching, writing and practice. Again and again he reiterated this theme in fresh words, with great variety, but with undeviating fidelity.

Hence, in a lesson on "Principles and Practice of Religious Science," which appeared in the January 1929 issue of the *Science of Mind* magazine, we find Ernest dealing with "Treatment—What, Why and How." He compared auto-suggestion, psychoanalysis, applied psychology, including visualization, concentration and orthodox prayer with the principles and methods of Religious Science and gave instructions on the practice of realizing the Presence and the Power of God. He urged the recognition of the One and Only God and an effort to form a consciousness of complete and perfect union. He impressed his readers with the need to develop desire, attention and conviction, the greatest being conviction, and declared that Religious Science gives more conviction than others and a wider comprehension.

Religious Science treatments tend to expand consciousness [he wrote]. A treatment, then, is for the purpose of changing one's own consciousness, not to change the attitude of God. The power is already there. Treatment is to get a consciousness of Truth as regards a particular problem. Consciousness of Truth directs the Life Force toward *good.* The One Power, God or Life, is the power to produce that good. What we term demonstration is the essential outcome or manifest result.

One important point to note here [he continued], is that while we call consciousness the directive factor yet the real director is of course the Self which caused the treatment and the consciousness. Another point is that all methods of treatment make use of this same Power, but not recognizing it as Infinite, necessarily limit their results to the degree of their consciousness of it.

Conscious as he always was of the "semantic problem," he recognized that this was "jargon" to those unacquainted with applied metaphysics, but he made no compromise. It was Truth, and throughout his life he remained true to his own understanding and the high level of his utterances.

Two years later in a Sunday lecture at the Ebell Club, he was saying the same thing in a different way. "Some psychologists will tell us that the apparent answer to prayer is the result of a subjective release in our minds when we pray and I believe in a certain sense they are right. Just as I believe that the Confessional in the Catholic Church should never have been taken out of the Protestant Church, because it provides a release of the burdens of the soul."

He concluded by giving his own mode (technique but not rote formula) of treatment:

Quiet the mind and definitely state that faith and understanding are present. Mentally state and spiritually feel that a conscious and constructive Presence pervades all life. Affirm that the Spirit wills to respond and that It does respond. Sit quietly and believe. Now state your desire as simply as possible, using only such words as have a real meaning to you. Never try to use other people's thought. You are alone with Cause, see to it that no denial of this thought enters your mind. As simply as you can, create a definite acceptance in the mind that you are being guided into paths of peace and abundance. Feel a response in your thought, feel that what you state is the truth about yourself. *Affirm that you accept and believe and receive.*

Along with "treatment," and his insistence on being "open at the top," there was another theme that ran through

Ernest's teachings throughout his life. This was his firm conviction of "immortality" as being concomitant with an awareness of the One Life.

It occupied the foreground of his mind in 1932, first, because of a surprising conversation with Judge Lindsay, and then because of the sudden loss of both Lem Brunson and our father; and he set these events down in his own words. Describing the conversation with the Judge he wrote:

Judge Ben Lindsay who organized the first Juvenile Court in America was a close personal friend of ours. As a matter of fact, Hazel and I persuaded him to run for the Superior Court in Los Angeles County after he moved here from Denver.

The first time I met him was at a Sunday morning service held in the Ambassador Hotel Theater. As always, the place was crowded and when I left the stage and went behind the curtain, there sat a little man on a wastepaper basket. He introduced himself to me.

As time went on we became very close friends and visited back and forth with him and his wife, Henrietta. One day he asked me to go with him to Santa Barbara to spend the evening with a psychologist who had been retained by the Rockefeller Foundation to write a book on the domestic relations situation, and Judge Lindsay wanted me to explain our system of thought to this doctor and see what the conference would lead to.

I was very much amused when we met Dr. Hamilton because his first remarks were that although he had written books on domestic relations, he considered Judge Lindsay knew more about the subject than anyone else living.

But to get back to our little trip to Santa Barbara. Ben and I were sitting in the rear seat of the automobile and in the course of our conversation, I casually mentioned something about immortality, and he looked at me with a startled expression and said, "Why, Ernest, you don't believe in immortality, do you?" and I answered, "Yes, Ben, of course I do, everyone does. Don't you?"

His answer was strange but interesting. He said, "My God, I hope it isn't true."

This was quite a challenge but I said, "Ben, be quiet a few

moments and let me see if I can figure out why a man with your intelligence and generosity of spirit, a man whose legal decisions have been written into the jurisprudence of many countries, would make such a remark."

I said, "You know self-preservation is the first law of life." And then I said, "Did you know, Ben, it is impossible for a person to conceive of himself as not being? In the first place, go back in time and imagination and you will witness your own birth, as though you were separate from that birth, observing that event. Go ahead in your imagination to the time when you shall separate yourself from your physical body, and imagine yourself at your own funeral. You will be standing there, and in so doing you will be independent of your body lying in the casket. It is impossible to think of yourself as not being.

"But," I added, "there is some deep emotional reason why you feel you do not believe in immortality. Let's be quiet for a few moments and see if we can *feel* it."

The answer seemed definite enough to me. We know that when we unconsciously look forward to more pain than pleasure, we equally unconsciously begin to sever ourselves from this physical body. We want to get away from the liability of life; the death urge becomes very strong and the escape mechanism works to produce the change.

Now Ben had been through a most trying ordeal in Denver and had almost come to feel his entire life's work had been without appreciation, although he could not have felt it was without recognition. His intelligence knew he had had plenty of recognition but his emotions were so frustrated by certain phases of political intrigue that surrounded him, that he merely sought an escape through unconscious but not literal or intentional soul-suicide.

How little we realize the motivations that give rise to chains of thought! and we certainly are more or less hypnotized from the cradle to the grave by the unconscious mechanisms of the mind.

On the other hand the death of Lem Brunson seemed to him a demonstration of a mind set free of these unconscious mechanisms.

I came home from my trip to Santa Barbara with Ben Lindsay on a Wednesday or Thursday morning. I had no knowledge that the Deacon was ill but the minute I sat down in my office I knew something was wrong with him, and without phoning I rushed out and drove to his home in Bel Air. His wife met me at the door. She greeted me in the usual friendly way and took me to his room. While we were all talking, he gave me a pleasant glance, drew a long breath and passed away. That was all, as simple as that. He believed what he believed and the fear of death never passed across his mind.

The same [Ernest added] was true of my father, who loved life. At eighty-six, if he could escape the eagle eyes of Mother and Guy, he would still attempt "a man's work" at The Hill, and on his last day managed to wheel the trunk of a palm tree up our long drive—and died with a smile on his face and a joke on his lips.

Ernest felt the personal loss keenly, but a brochure that he published a few months later called "Fore-Gleams of Eternal Life" was both a tribute to these two men who had meant so much to him and to his unshakable conviction of their ongoing beyond his present sight—and there was no break in his own work, nor in his growing, for it was in this same year that he met Dr. Ralph T. Flewelling and "went back to school" again.

By 1931 the influence of Ernest and the institute was spreading ever more rapidly. In the graduating class of that year there was a person of more than normal interest to the Dean—his wife Hazel, who soon took up her practitioner work in the office next to his own; and Sunday services were transferred from the Ebell Theater to the larger Sala de Oro in the Biltmore Hotel downtown.

Throughout 1932 not only his popularity but activities connected with his own teaching, writing and practice continued to increase, and the casual observer might have thought that this was a life fulfilled to the bursting point.

At this exact point Ernest decided to delve more deeply

into the wider aspects of philosophy. He had been interested in a rather narrow field in connection with the general tenets of Religious Science as a transcendental philosophy of idealism, but he was unacquainted with the academic approach and the correlation with other major philosophies and their historic origin.

His wider interest came about through his meeting with Dr. Ralph T. Flewelling, director and founder of the School of Philosophy at the University of Southern California. This great scholar not only possessed a number of doctorates but had been a pastor of churches in and around Boston in his earlier years. Each month a lecture was given by students or visitors, some of them from abroad, in his university classroom, and everybody joined in informal discussion. Among them was a professor from the University of London by the name of H. Weldon Karl. Ernest was so impressed with these meetings, that—after rejecting Flewelling's suggestion that he take classwork—he proposed himself as a "private pupil," and the professor accepted him!

I doubt that Dr. Flewelling, or any other teacher ever had such a student. The first time Ernest visited Dr. Flewelling, he was shown a stack of books of philosophy and was told, "We will begin with Thales and Anaxagoras." It is interesting that the professor selected two early *physical science* philosophers to point out to a modern idealist and metaphysician. "He was working from the ground up," Ernest once remarked, "but I had no intention of reading all those books; I told him so and he said, 'I thought you wanted to study philosophy.' "

"Do you know what these fellows meant?" Ernest asked him.

"I hope so."

"Then tell me what they *meant*, not what they said. I'm not going to teach philosophy but if you have studied it all your life, they told you something you believe. What is it?"

Ernest afterward told me, "He thought that was peculiar, and then he asked me, 'Why is it so few people come to public lectures on philosophy? You have just heard a lecture by Dr. F——— of Johannesburg, the greatest authority on Platonism in the world. Why is there so little interest?' "

"I myself didn't understand Dr. F———" Ernest replied, "neither does the public. Why don't you philosophers tell what you know *in plain language?* We may not know very much at the Religious Science Institute, but after I learn what you know, I am confident that I can tell it in language everybody understands."

Dr. Flewelling was so impressed by this that he not only taught Ernest privately but gave many lectures at the institute, where he became very popular.

I have in my possession an offhand summary of those private lessons as Ernest evaluated them.

The study of academic philosophy has very little to do with the application of spiritual principles to the problems of everyday living. It isn't that way at all. What we do derive is a rational explanation of the nature of the world as a spiritual reality. Pythagoras, Plato and Plotinus, for example, gave support to the belief that we live in a mental universe—a system of ideas— and this provides a foundation for our teaching which holds that you can change conditions by changing ideas.

I found [Ernest continued], that classical philosophy is like our own except more cumbersome, abstract and confusing.

[He paused and laughed.] A pretty kettle of fish! I had flattered myself that I could compound confusion with anybody until I listened to some of the university lecturers. How happy I was to find one of them who could talk our language—Dr. Flewelling! Even though our personal "philosophies" differed in details, we had enough in common to make it desirable to have him lecture for us.

Aside from the complexities of argumentation [he continued], I found the following principles in the Greek philosophies: there is One Absolute Cause and only One: man has a divine nature; everything in this world is a reproduction of a spiritual or divine pattern, which they said is "over yonder" but is really *"within"* at the center of everything; that everything is motion and number at varying rates of vibration; and that all creation is the result of the self-contemplation of the Creator. Sometimes they call "It" God, or Absolute Spirit or Reality. Finally, I found that they taught evolution, the law of correspondences and the survival of the soul or immortality.

Here Ernest paused to point out that Einstein and Eddington had recently agreed that we live in a metaphysical world and modern physics treats of the universe more as a shadow cast by an invisible substance than as a physical structure.

He had benefited, he felt, from a more intimate and scholarly acquaintance with Aristotle, Socrates, Pythagoras, Plato, Plotinus, Spinoza, Immanuel Kant, Bishop Berkeley, Hegel, Swedenborg; and with the mystics Boehme, Eckhart and the rest. And in later times Ernest tells us that he did, indeed, read all the books suggested by Dr. Flewelling. But Plotinus was perhaps the philosopher from whom Ernest most frequently quoted, probably because he was an exponent of the *archetypal idea* or the *theory of patterns*.

Throughout life the concept of "pattern" continued to be strong in Ernest's mind. He believed that Creative Mind contains the perfect pattern of all things.

He had long since interpreted those figures his breath had produced on the icy windowpanes in our childhood days in Maine as infinitesimal representations of patterns held in the Cosmic Mind, and announced that everything has its own spiritual pattern. He had synthesized Swedenborg's so-called "law of correspondence" with the object of treatment—to create or release the inherent pattern of perfection so that it shall find its correspondence in the body; and he had recognized that it was possible to realize truth on the level of First Cause, that when the ascent is made from thought to Cause, the attention is no longer confined to things, forms or thoughts but is directed to the realization of the perfect "patterns" from which all things are derived.

Looking back over his unfoldment, it is astonishing and heartening to find such thoughts evolving in so definite a manner so early in Ernest's life, for they were original to him then.

After he had seen that the ancients, like Pythagoras and Plato, had presented this teaching in the form of prototypes, we can understand why he was so strongly attracted toward the Neo-Platonist or Neo-Pythagorean Plotinus in these later years.

Dr. Flewelling not only found in Ernest a warm friend and a most entertaining "pupil" but a keen mind and spiritual depth that he much valued. Ernest lectured under his auspices at the university, and many of his personal ideas found reflection in *The Personalist,* an international review of philosophy, religion and literature that the professor founded and of which he was editor for forty years.

Ernest's ability to view even philosophical principles with humor particularly intrigued the professor and is well illustrated in the case of Ernest's appearance before the class in philosophy at the university. Although he was not lecturing on pantheism as such, he was challenged as he often was by the students on this ground, and he made the following reply: "I venture to say that you could stir up more debate between yourselves over *what pantheism really is* than you could over *my* so-called pantheism. You need to settle on a definition before you issue the challenge. But let me give a simple answer. I believe that all that is is God, but I do not believe that it is all there is of God."

Everybody had a good laugh, and I question whether either then or in succeeding years any of them ever came any closer to the final answer except by the inner experience of the self.

Fusion, synthesis, the hope that little by little we can cross over the illusory divisions that he tried to bridge with his humor, were among his constant interests. Not long before he left this world and launched into infinity to explore and confirm these principles, Ernest, lamenting the divisions that semantics and exclusivity create, said to me, "Give them time, and physicists and metaphysicists will use the same textbook."

The year of 1934 was to be another year of change—and greater fulfillment.

Ernest's Sunday services once more outgrew their confines and were moved from the Biltmore Hotel to the Wiltern Theater on Wilshire at Western. The place seated about twenty-three hundred people; but the auditorium was crowded from the beginning, and this continued over a period of years.

It was in August of 1934 that the great adventure was undertaken, or at least proposed, the notice of it being made public for the first time. Under the title of "Announcement," the magazine published a featured page that said, "To meet a need which has now become pressing, for adequate headquarters, its school and other activities, the Institute of Religious Science announces its plan to create a fund which, when it becomes adequate will be used for the purchase of a piece of property and the final erection of a building." Within eight months a sufficient sum had been donated for a new headquarters.

And it was also in August of 1934 that the streams of our lives, Ernest's and mine, once more flowed together for a spell of pleasant refreshment. After a number of most rewarding years at the Church of the Healing Christ, in New York City, I had resigned my pastorate to return to my greater love, the lecture platform, and one of my happiest assignments was to fulfill Ernest's request that I speak for him at the Wiltern during that summer month so that he and Hazel could go on vacation.

In spite of vacation and the summer heat, the auditorium was crowded by the third lecture, and four hundred more were standing at the last meeting. It was very pleasant to all of us.

And on the return of Dr. and Mrs. Ernest Holmes, Katharine and I found ourselves once again enveloped by the love of Ernest, the family man, and caught up in the warmth and charm of his "home" life as it was lived on "The Hill."

For the two could not be separated. The teacher, the teaching and the man himself were one.

III

⟡

The Man Himself

WHAT ERNEST HOLMES *was* spoke for his teaching; he himself was so in tune with it that no static confused the listening ear.

He not only knew the Principle and the Presence, but understood how It manifested as the individual Self; and this self-knowing produced a most unusual and vivid personality who lived to the full the myriad facets of this Thing called Life.

Ernest not only believed in the *goodness* of life; he believed in the *wholeness* of its experience and expression.

Nowhere was this more apparent than in his "personal profile," which etched itself on the memory of those who knew him as a permanent witness to the validity of his steadfast spiritual convictions.

Inseparable from the dedication of Dr. Holmes, philosopher, teacher, lecturer, writer, practitioner, was Ernest the human being; Ernest the delightful humorist, the skillful cook, the dilettante gardener; Ernest the staunch family man, the adoring husband, the warm, generous friend who knew love and laughter and suffered and rose above loneliness and grief and hurt. And the person who never let anyone forget for an instant this inevitable coexistence was Ernest Holmes himself.

When work on this biography commenced two years before his death, it was to prevent such a separation; when he entrusted me with the writing, he expressed definite ideas on the subject. "I have a premonition," he said, "that after I go someone will write my life story. And with it comes the awful possibility of a posthumous halo. I don't wear one here; I don't expect to hereafter. And I'd like to make sure I'm not beatified, glorified, deified—or," he grinned, "vilified."

If such a record were set down, he wanted it to stand, as he himself stood, on the truth. Thus in March of 1958, Ernest began a series of interviews with Elaine St. Johns (Adela's daughter) a close friend and a professional writer, that were designed to furnish an outline of his life and teachings to aid in this work. The questions and answers were taped and several hundred pages transcribed. Over and over on these tapes, he insisted on debunking any myths about himself, and when he turned them over to me, he again expressed his confidence that "you will let me stand as I am."

"Including your golf score?" I demanded.

He nodded.

"And your automobile driving," I persisted, "and your personal financial accounting system?"

"As I am," he said emphatically, "golf score and all."

The golf score was our private joke.

I doubt if anybody actually knew Ernest's attitude toward exercise. I myself thought him to be physically indolent, because he took no part in sports. He had played half a game of golf with me in the 1930's and had walked away from it, and I thought he disliked the exercise and the heat of Griffith Park. Later I discovered he felt it a waste of time. There were far more interesting things to do than chasing an inflated pill. Sitting and thinking was one of them. "Walking is not the best exercise for a metaphysician," he said. "You're working at the wrong end."

When a student asked him what form of exercise he took,

he raised his forefinger above his head and wiggled it. "How else do you exercise?" he was asked. Ernest raised both forefingers and repeated the wiggle.

As for driving an automobile, whether our first Model A Ford or the second-hand Studebaker with the explosive tires in which he courted Hazel or the series of handsome Oldsmobiles the dean drove to and from the institute or his final Cadillac, my brother always drove a car as though it were some kind of beast that had a mind of its own. He held one foot on the gas and one on the brake and played no favorites. The car would weave along, and he would arrive at his destination by a series of minor miracles. All the while he would look as pleased and as innocent as a seraph driving from a higher plane. Which he may, or may not, have been. But it was certainly a first-class demonstration of Presence—perhaps in the sense of an angel on his shoulder—or somewhere in the vicinity.

As for his personal financial accounting system, it certainly demonstrated a principle unique to Ernest—having nothing to do with his demonstration of abundant supply.

Ernest had a clear and acute sense of the true nature of supply, and from the day he received his first "metaphysical money," the five-dollar gold piece at Mrs. Reeseburg's library for his lecture on Troward, he had steadily demonstrated his principle in increasing financial abundance until, at the time of his passing, he had amassed, besides a valuable collection of objets d'art, a considerable fortune.

His native intelligence, coupled with that shrewd capacity for Yankee trading, which he showed in his teens as a collector in Bethel, Maine, never deserted him, and he made his money separately from his salary through his writings and investments, his income from the church being enough only for his personal living. His salary from the church never exceeded ten thousand dollars a year from 1927 to his death. He never asked for more and, in fact, discouraged any discussion of an increase. Nor did he believe in the "expense account" system of accrual. He and Hazel entertained church groups liberally in their home throughout the years, but since it was their "pleasure," Ernest always refused to charge it to the organization as a business expense.

But his personal relationship with these dollars only changed in form from the days when he kept the collection money, uncounted, in a shoebox or suitcase in the closet and invited the family to help themselves.

In his later years he carried a very large cash bank account, something like twenty-five thousand dollars in his commercial account. The treasurer of the institute often commented that, because he did not also use a savings account, Ernest was losing the interest on his money, but he seemed to enjoy the freedom he felt it afforded. His method of keeping his checking account both amused and concerned his advisers. He *did* keep check stubs, and at times recorded his withdrawals. But sooner or later he would be in a hurry and forget to set down the amount of a check or deposit, and from then on until the next bank statement reached him, he would be in a haze. Seldom did his records and the bank statement agree, but he cheerfully accepted the bank's total and used it for a new starting point. He was asked why he did not check the bank's statement. "They *could* make a mistake, you know, Ernest."

"They wouldn't dare," Ernest affirmed. "It's their business to be right. Besides, I never got far in arithmetic. I learned to add, but I don't know how to subtract."

And perhaps this *was* the metaphysical law that drew supply to him in such abundance. He repeatedly taught that, with an Infinity of Good available, it was up to the individual how much he drew from It. "Why," he would ask, "go to the Infinite Source with a teaspoon when you could just as easily use a dipper or a pail?"

He believed in the law of increase, that all good things are "added unto us" if we approach the Kingdom of All-Good with this confidence. He was totally unafraid to give, to let his money circulate, because he did *not* believe in a law of *decrease,* that good could be subtracted from us.

If the institute was the center of his public life, "The Hill" was equally the center of his family life—and Ernest was a family man.

He and Hazel lived together on "The Hill" for eighteen years, from 1927, when they were married, until 1945, when they sold it to Adela Rogers St. Johns; and here they created both a home and a way of life that were altogether beautiful and quite unique.

The property itself was unusual, with the two rambling, one-story houses on the crest of the hill joined by a broad flagstone terrace roofed over with shakes and heavy beams, all entwined with variegated ivy. The terrace faced a broad level half-moon of lawn, ending abruptly at a six-foot stone retaining wall that dropped down to a large circular drive. The path to the drive was shaded by a lacy pepper tree, and the drive circle was surrounded by deodars, the "divine tree" in Sanskrit, which closely resesmbled the cedars of Lebanon and stood almost as tall as they do in their native mountains of India. Somewhere between the pepper and the deodars was a very businesslike barbecue and shaded picnic area, and on the far side of the circle was the cottage and wide expanse of meadow ending in a whitewashed fence, a dirt track and an aged brown barn. On either side of the houses, the hill fell away rather sharply, and to the north a long line of eucalyptus marched single file from house to meadow's end, separating it from adjoining property, while on the other, a small forest of pine and fir concealed the road below.

The building, the terrace and rock work, the barbecue and eventually additional paths and driveways, were the inspired work of brother Guy, with the help of his son, and Guy supervised and was responsible for the maintenance of the entire place.

By the time Katharine and I arrived in 1934, Hazel's gentle but firm influence was everywhere apparent. When we bought a home in Santa Monica as a headquarters to meet increasingly heavy demand for my correspondence courses, we were frequent guests at "The Hill," and between Hazel and Katharine there was not only affection but sympatico.

I remember Katharine reporting to me that Hazel, while loving beautiful things and always making the interior of their home both comfortable and elegant, detested housework—and "made a metaphysical demonstration" that this would not be her part of their life and work. She once said that she had been able to make a demonstration for *no dust* —and for *order*—and this was one thing all people should establish in their own minds—the Kingdom of Heaven that is within you is *orderly*. So she did actual treatment work that her house should be run in orderly fashion. And it always was. There was always the right person to love to do the housework for Ernest and Hazel. Ernest, still a really fine cook, loved to do it. When they had guests he used to like to make old-fashioned New England dinners. I never saw a man who could barbecue better than Ernest—and Hazel always let him do it. Whether she *could* or could *not* cook, I do not know. But that she *did* not, of this I have ample evidence.

At the time we were there most frequently, they had a Filipino cook, Max by name, a combination housekeeper-cook and a chauffeur for Hazel and Mother. Max prepared delicious dishes under Ernest's skillful eye, for Ernest all his life delighted in giving directions or in actually creating special dishes for the pleasure of the friends who often dined with them. And once again Hazel delighted to stand aside and admire his skill.

And while Hazel had made as distinct and exquisite an impact on the gardens at "The Hill" as she had on the house, she never actually cared for turning the earth. Occasionally Ernest liked to putter around with the potted plants that adorned the terrace, and Hazel gave him some help—but more advice.

She was fond of exotic plants, succulents, birds of paradise, and these grew in profusion around the two houses and the borders of the lawn. At Christmastime "Hazel's poinsettias," massive scarlet blooms on six-foot talks, along the south wall, were a conversation piece. Her hibiscus made most colorful floral arrangements, while her beloved cactus was planted in the center of the circular drive.

All in all, it was a truly remarkable display.

The social life open to Dr. and Mrs. Holmes was wide and varied. They dined out frequently, attended the opera, the Hollywood Bowl, important openings and motion-picture premiers, took their place at outstanding civic events—and Ernest enjoyed it all. It was part of the rich tapestry woven by life. But better still he liked to gather his friends into the serene circle of his home, to break homemade bread and such other delicacies as he could devise, to sit before a roaring fire, and to depend for entertainment on *conversation*.

My lasting memories of being entertained on "The Hill" are not of the picnics and formal parties. They are of the warm, intimate evenings that Ernest himself loved best.

With the charming addition of Hazel and Katharine, our bachelor "library discussions" of old had become "drawing-room dialogues."

While Ernest himself never felt the urge for world travel, he delighted in armchair exploration, whether via the printed page or an eyewitness account, which put living flesh on literary skeletons and abstract thoughts.

I remember one particular evening he and I were discussing the tremendous impact of Thomas Troward on his great friend and "pupil," the Archdeacon of Westminster, Basil Wilberforce, who was also the chaplain of the British House of Commons. We had agreed that the Archdeacon had not only admitted publicly in his sermons his debt to Troward, but that through their relationship there had been an historic unity between the Church and the New and Practical Metaphysics; for through Canon Wilberforce, a famous preacher and writer, Troward's teachings were voiced in historic Westminstser Abbey of the Church of England as well as in his books, such as *Spiritual Consciousness*.

244 ERNEST HOLMES, HIS LIFE AND TIMES

We were picking the bones of the relationship on the intellectual level—concluding that their essential difference lay in the fact that Canon Wilberforce wanted the form of metaphysical thinking as the keynote of the Church itself rather than a separate movement or cult, while Judge Troward loved the freedom of his association with the "Higher Thought Center"—when Katharine spoke.

"I met the Archdeacon once," she said, "I blush to remember it."

Ernest almost pounced at her. "How and where?" he demanded.

"I was in London," she said, "and went to the cathedral one Sunday morning. I didn't know the clergyman who spoke, but as he went on I could recognize many phrases and arguments I had read in books by Basil Wilberforce like *Why Does Not God Stop the War?* or *Seeing the Unseen,* and I thought—'this man is a shameless plagiarist.'

"After the service the clergyman shook hands with the parishioners as they passed out through the great arch. I was so upset that I quite forgot my manners, and when he took my hand, I, well, I stammered, 'How c-c-could you? Y-y-you, a priest, a m-m-minster—to steal a sermon without giving c-c-credit to a great man?'

"He looked at me in utter bewilderment. 'What do you mean?' he asked.

"I thought he was pretending ignorance; and I got quite angry, and my voice rang loud and clear. 'You know perfectly well what I mean. You're a plagiarist! You stole most of your sermon from Archdeacon Wilberforce.'

"His response was a shout of laughter—he had a laugh as big as the cathedral—that caused everyone to turn and stare, and completely unsettled me.

"'*I'm* Wilberforce,' he chuckled. 'Bless you, my dear, I've only been stealing from myself. . . . And just where do you come from?'

"'The United States,' I said in a very subdued voice.

"'I never was so flattered in my life. Am I so well known

there?' He thought a moment. 'I want you to have tea with me. Can you come on Wednesday afternoon?'

"I could and I did. I rang a bell at the gate to Dean's Yard and was met by a footman in pantaloons, long stockings and buckled shoes. He took me into the garden, where Canon Wilberforce greeted me, and we drank tea and talked about America for nearly two hours."

"And about Troward?" Ernest demanded.

"And about Troward," my wife nodded. "And about Frederick L. Rawson and his *Life Understood*. I remember his saying that Rawson was so *absolute*, he'd told him he did not believe it at all necessary to think of the person for whom you were praying or treating. All that was necessary, Rawson said, was to realize God. Canon Wilberforce was amused by Rawson's criticizing him personally for saying God *in us* instead of we are *in God*."

Ernest was amused, too, and concluded this charming excursion to Westminster Abbey and the garden at 20 Dean's Court by focusing it on an aspect of truth.

"Both must be right," he said "the sponge is in the sea but the sea is in the sponge."

But the chief thing that arrested my attention that night as we sat before the fire was the manner in which Ernest was as "open" and receptive to the ideas and opinions of his own family, or his students, or to young people, as to his friends among scientists and scholars.

There was only one exception—and that was to anyone who filled their conversation with negative reflections on the listener. He spoke flatly. "I never like to talk with people who keep saying, 'Do you follow me?' or 'Do you get me?' or 'Do you understand what I mean?' " He grimaced. "I was talking with a man recently who kept saying, 'Do you follow me?' and after he had repeated it for about the third time, I said, 'Mister, I not only follow you but I am about three blocks down the road waiting for you to catch up. Please hurry!' "

Yet I have heard him seek the views of his youthful niece Josephine and of Albert Einstein on the same subject on the same day. Like all teachers of metaphysics, during his life-time he had had to face the problem of evil in a world at war, but he continued to affirm that good is the ultimate power and peace, man's rightful condition and destiny. He was pacific but not a pacifist.

At lunch on "The Hill" one day, when this was very much on his mind, I heard Ernest say, "You know, I firmly believe that permanent world peace is not an illusion but a potential possibility and an evolutionary imperative, and that science will *aid* in that evolution." Then he turned deliberately to his niece, by far the youngest person at the table. "What do you think of that, Jo?" he asked. And he listened thoughtfully and carefully to her affirmative response and reasoning.

That night he and Albert Einstein had an opportunity to exchange ideas when they sat side by side at a dinner given by Dr. Robert A. Millikan at Caltech for the purpose of dis-cussing science and abstract laws. Again Ernest voiced his premise and heard from Dr. Einstein many illustrations of principles, not the least of which was an affirmation that sci-ence is "truth" and ultimately "good" will vindicate itself.

"So you see," he told us the next day, "Dr. Einstein agrees with Josephine." Nor did it appear incongruous to him to af-firm this meeting of the minds between a learned scientist and his young relative, since the opinion of both was based on metaphysical principles.

For if it is impossible to disassociate the eminent dean of the Institute of Religious Science from Ernest, the family man of "The Hill," it was equally impossible for him to dis-associate his regard for individual family members and their home life from the activities of the Institute of Religious Science.

Several times a week Mother accompanied Ernest to head-quarters and was much in demand as a successful practitioner. She loved her "practice" at the institute, but not content with that alone, she undertook all kinds of social-service activities, assisting in the Goodwill organization and the Red Cross, and afterward forming the Institute Sewing Circle, a service club that among other things gave 185,000 renovated garments to the poor. As late as 1960 the Los Angeles County General Hospital through its president, issued a certificate of recognition for voluntary service, to the "Mother Holmes Welfare Group."

Nellie Walsh Heflin assisted Mother by driving her around in the car, and they, with Gussie Rundel, formed a triumvirate—among the first listed practitioners at the Carondelet Headquarters. The trio believed in social parties for the needy, and as one man phrased it, they "served religion in the head and chicken and roast pork on the piano."

Our first cousin Idella Chadwick became a practitioner and remained at the institute for nearly a quarter of a century, conducting many meditation meetings, contributing to the monthly magazine meditations as well.

Our brother Jerome, when he retired from the active Congregational missionary ministry, became a member of Ernest's staff for three years and lectured and taught at the institute. He also did a radio show, and some of his broadcasts were published in book form. While Guy, besides managing "The Hill," took over as superintendent of the headquarters buildings. Later on Guy's son Lawrence assumed the same duties.

Guy's daughter Josephine was for years an indispensable part of the family of co-workers. She was a brilliant and beautiful girl, and Ernest both loved and leaned on her. He persuaded her to learn stenographic work, and she became his righthand woman. She rode with him to headquarters every day, took dictation in shorthand, later transcribing it.

For some years she edited *Science of Mind* Magazine and when Ernest went on the radio, Josephine took over the Monday meetings. Her talks were afterward edited by Maude Lathem and published in a book titled *How To Get The Most Out of Life*.

Even after her marriage, her work at the institute continued—the name Josephine Holmes Curtis appeared on the monthly meditations, and as a teacher on the major course until she left to join her husband in their own business.

I know of no clearer demonstration of the influence of a prophet than that he is accepted in his own household. Nor a clearer demonstration of Ernest's true regard for his family than that they were a highly valued part of his public work.

Although he worked intensively most of the time, had neither the time nor urge for world travel and found most of his relaxation in life on "The Hill," he did enjoy an occasional trip. With Hazel at his side, he would drive to Palm Springs, to San Diego or to "destination unknown." They both particularly loved San Francisco, that gleaming city of our early triumphs, where they usually stopped at the Fairmont Hotel, high on top of one of the city's hills and commanding a breathtaking view of the bay. Nor did they always travel alone. One year they took a party to the Huntington Hotel, engaged a complete suite, and Ernest insisted on doing the cooking for all of them.

Occasionally, too, they drove or flew to the eastern seaboard, where they were met by members of the Ernest DuPont family, who had become interested in Ernest and his teachings through an experience of physical healing. One year they sailed with the DuPonts on their yacht along the eastern coast and to Montreal.

Ernest always came back from these trips refreshed and enthusiastic, for these, too, he considered a part of that rich tapestry of life. And in these, as with social and civic events, cooking and conversation, he participated with great zest. But his true enjoyment in all these *forms* of diversion came from one basic thread that was both warp and woof for the fabric upon which the design was wrought—and that thread was contact with other individualizations of the one Life.

Here again there is truly no way to separate the man himself—to depict Dr. Holmes at work and Ernest at play. His work was *for* people, and his recreation *was* people. If a "hobby" is, as Mr. Webster asserts, "an engrossing topic, plan, etc. to which one constantly reverts; also, an occupation or interest to which one gives his spare time," then whether at work or play Ernest was enjoying his single hobby.

His hobby was *people*. He loved them. Whether they appeared to others as rich or poor, sick or sinful, family, friend, flock or "foe," Ernest loved them all. To him they were beautiful. It was the sercet, I believe, of his healing work. It was the secret, I am sure, of his personal popularity. And he had a particular affinity for the young of the species.

It has been said that Ernest and Hazel Holmes had no children. This is a half-truth. Although in the physical sense their marriage was, as the genealogists put it, without issue and while they never legally adopted nor presumed to take the place of any natural parents, yet in the spiritual sense the young folk who claimed kinship with them and benefited in so many ways, materially as well as spiritually, are too numerous to mention. And Hazel's nickname for her husband was "Papa"!

This invisible family was large, loving, loyal—and the arrival of these blessed events spanned almost half a century.

The first occurred in 1913 when young Reg Armor turned up in Ernest's Scout troop in Venice. The length and depth of that relationship endured nearly fifty years during Ernest's lifetime. Not only was the office of Reginald C. Armor just down the hall from Dr. Holmes' at the institute, but the home of Reg and his pretty wife Elsie and their boy and two little girls was just across the hedge from Ernest's and Hazel's house on "The Hill."

The last was in 1950 when Director Bob Vignola brought a young relative, Bill Lynn, to dine with the Holmeses one evening. Although a college student, the young man was shy, but his quick smile and good looks made a pleasant impression on Ernest and Hazel. In fact, my sister-in-law laid aside the "reserve" for which she was noted more quickly than usual, not only inviting him to return but once calling him "son."

Bill has recalled for me the very first dinner he had in their home. They had moved from "The Hill" by this time, but the food in the new mansion was still of Ernest's devising. "We sat down to cornbread, pan-fried pork, baked beans and applesauce, and all those 'little extras,' for which Ernest's tables were always famous," Bill said. Somewhat overawed by Ernest as "a famous person" he was surprised at his informality. Ernest appeared at table in a colorful sport shirt, open at the neck, wearing loafer shoes, so jovial in manner that young Bill was not only put at ease, he was charmed.

During ensuing months Ernest and Hazel entertained Bill from time to time and eventually set aside one of their guest rooms as his weekend home while he was attending college. In the summer of 1951 they invited him to be their guest on an automobile tour into the Pacific Northwest. It was an exciting experience for the young man, as he had been working his way through college for three years, including summers. They picked him up at the fraternity house, Ernest in his sport shirt and ball cap, and Hazel in a tailored suit, a veiled hat and white gloves.

Bill's report of this trip is a delightful glimpse of my brother and his wife "off duty." They started, Bill wrote me, without an itinerary, no hotel reservations except for those made the night before; "loafing along," . . . "no plan to get somewhere but only to enjoy where they were."

One thing I learned on this trip [Lynn writes] was what it means to let go. Time and again I was amazed by their ability to enjoy life. I was sure there would be messages waiting when we checked into a hotel, but no! Ernest explained: "No one knows where we are except ourselves, and the only thing they do know is the general direction in which we are traveling. No one will call, no one will write, no one will know exactly when we shall be home. I learned long ago that I'm not indispensable."

To the best of my knowledge neither of them gave a second

thought to business while on vacation, except that each Sunday
Ernest would slip away somewhere for an hour and treat for those
who were delivering their Sunday sermons.

There were times when they embraced an entire family,
as they did with the children and grandchildren of Adela
Rogers St. Johns.

IV

❧

Ernest and the "Philosophy of Doing"

BY SPRING of 1935 Ernest and the institute Board of Trustees had settled upon the present headquarters at 3251 West Sixth Street in Los Angeles.

The building had been the work-and-display shop of interior decorators. It had been lavishly designed, and the interior architecture still charms the visitor; occasionally an entire class of architects comes to view the long hallway with its glassed ceiling, its raised floor and grilled wall at the far end. There was a great deal of renovating to be done in the new building, including the removal of an elevator, the fusing of small rooms into larger ones for offices and classrooms, and the development of a meditation room on the first floor, with Alumni Hall above it.

The walls of the long hallway were hung with rare paintings, and later in 1948 a large portrait of Ernest by Ferdinand Earle was added. The entrance foyer was carpeted in crimson velvet set off by rare tapestries given by the widow of Milton Sills and a huge Flemish piece of priceless value donated by the Ernest DuPonts.

Ernest chose the large room done in Italian style at the rear of the building and added to it a huge Italian hand-carved desk and fine paintings given by admirers through the years.

Next door was a beautiful little room that became Hazel's, and Augusta Rundel settled herself in a small room near the entrance. The wide hallway gave on a series of rooms for working practitioners.

From his windows Ernest could look out at drooping willow trees leaning over a running brook that spilled over in the spring and formed a marshland. Today the brook has disappeared, the marsh has been filled and serves as a huge parking place for the institute and a great skyscraper stands across the street. But when the move was made the new headquarters was set in its natural landscape.

It was now the tenth year of the annual course, and there was a further expansion of the curriculum. To the studies in philosophy, religion, psychology and metaphysics were added lessons in human relations, creative thinking and even a survey of the field of psychic phenomena and parapsychology.

The dean was also concentrating on a completely revised and enlarged edition of *The Science of Mind* textbook, working on editorial revisions in collaboration with Maude Allison Lathem. This expanded edition, published in 1938, stood the test of time and teaching. Ernest never felt the need to revise it again.

Wide readership of both the textbook and the magazine, the successful pioneer healing work by institute-trained practitioners and visiting lecturers, as well as the growing personal influence and reputation of Dr. Holmes himself at this point brought about another expansion in the "body" of the movement.

There had been so many requests from groups all over the country asking that a chapter of the institute might be established and a leader sent to them, that such a step seemed necessary, and in September, 1938, the Board of Trustees authorized such chapters.

It was stated that "Up to now there has been no medium through which [these groups] could experience or express the consciousness of identity with one another, or share the feeling of like beliefs and manner of living. . . . Now it is possible not only to believe but also to belong.

"Extensions will be known as 'Chapters of the Institute of Religious Science.' Each Chapter will be an autonomous body under the rules and regulations of the parent Institute."

The statement of policy continued: "A Central Chapter will be formed in conjunction with Headquarters. The Parent Institute will continue as it has been with the great responsibility added of training the many new workers needed, preparing and supplying literature and administering the organization and conduct of the work through the local chapters."

A plan for the establishment of adequate funds for the work was divided into five parts: a fund to provide land and buildings for the central chapter; an extension fund for organizing and administering the new chapters; an educational fund for assisting the training of leaders, particularly the younger generation; a literature fund; and finally an endowment fund, the income to be used for designated purposes.

It was agreed that the new edition of *The Science of Mind* should be used as a universal textbook. By this method it was planned to bring organized study into other communities and as soon as practical to prepare and send out practitioners and teachers qualified to teach and to carry on a local work.

There were some such teachers already at hand, and in October of 1938, Ernest inducted Robert H. Bitzer, who was to become one of the most outstanding men in the field, into Sunday services at the Hollywood-Roosevelt Hotel and opened another chapter in Pasadena. Shortly, several other such groups were organized and established, one of them being in San Diego under the ministry of Harold E. Gerard and another at El Ray Theater on Wilshire Boulevard, Los Angeles, led by Ivy Crane Shelhamer. By the end of 1939 there were five chapters in Los Angeles, eight in other California cities and five "affiliated organizations."

Maude Lathem had become editor of the magazine, freeing

Josephine Holmes Curtis to join with Jerome Holmes, Reginald Armor and the whole institute staff to assist Ernest Holmes in preparing a vital new type of teaching—home study. When the teaching by mail, entitled "Extension Course," became a reality in 1939, each lesson was based upon specific references to the textbook. The obvious object was not only to protect the Religious Science message itself from change or corruption, but also to assure the growth of a collective mind or soul of the institution.

As expansion of all the activities of the institute took place rapidly, the time had now arrived for a more efficient formula of administration. A pressing need was felt to exercise some authority over the contents of the message being put out by various leaders.

Furthermore, students who had taken the major courses had begun to advertise as practitioners, and it was apparent that more specific clinical training courses should be given before qualification. This was called "Practitioner's Clinic" at first but is now known as "Practitioner Training Course." No one could practice under the name of Religious Science who had not been graduated and qualified. This regulation not only provided assurance of retaining the purity of the message but also protected the practitioner himself from making mistakes that could come under the surveillance of the law. Consequently there has never been a lawsuit over malpractice in all these years.

But some concern was still felt over consistency in leadership.

Up until then the new ministers had relied, as had Ernest himself, on other metaphysical organizations for ordination, although the state charter had granted the Religious Science Institute the right to perform this function. Now in 1939 changes were made not only in certifying practitioners and teachers, but for the first time the institute provided ordination for Religious Science ministers.

All of this Dr. Holmes accepted with cooperation. Ernest's attitude toward the "organization" was always more paternal than that of founder or dean of an institution. He enjoyed seeing the family grow; he trusted and prayed that it would be happy and healthy, he gave to it whatever he had; but the organization, *per se,* was not his department. The caliber of the board of trustees was impressive, presided over by a well-known businessman, W. W. Haughey, and numbering among others the Honorable Lewis Howell Smith; and Ernest gratefully permitted it to function. His responsibilities, beyond loving the whole "family," he took to be distinctly twofold.

One was *teaching.*

We find Ernest continuously engaged in lecturing, writing and conducting classwork personally at the institute, with his emphasis, as always, on treatment, while broadening the scope of education by adding in 1940 such specialists as Dr. Frederick P. Woellner, professor of education at UCLA; Dr. Frederick W. Bailes; Dr. Carl S. Knopf, dean of the School of Religion, Donald Eitzen, Assistant Professor of Pastoral Theology, and Dr. Hans von Koerber, Professor of Asiatic Studies, all of University of Southern California; and Dr. Paul Popenoe, director of the Institute of Family Relations, Los Angeles.

The other was *healing.*

If healing was, as Ernest maintained, the lifeblood of the Religious Science movement, then Ernest himself and his wife Hazel were the heart that worked steadily to keep the lifeblood flowing. Ernest never deviated from his "philosophy of *doing"*—How do you practice? What results do you get? What are you *doing* with your theories?—and Hazel was his staunchest disciple.

In 1940 Ernest began reporting actual cases of healing, telling exactly what was said and done. In one instance he described the healing of an alcoholic whom he had known socially in Los Angeles. While Ernest and Reginald Armor were stopping briefly in a San Francisco hotel, they received a call from another room, and it proved to be Ernest's alcoholic acquaintance—asking for help. Ernest did not know then or later how the man knew of his presence, but he and Reg went to see him.

The man was too intoxicated to stand, so they put him to bed and, when he slept, returned to their room, where they treated him throughout the evening maintaining in Ernest's words:

"This man is conscious that he is pure spirit. He is poised and at peace within himself. There is nothing in him that craves alcohol. He is not seeking to escape from anything. He meets every issue of life without fear. There is nothing to run away from, nothing to avoid. At all times he has a sense of well-being, of happiness, of security and of expression. There is no memory of having received any pleasure or benefit from alcohol. The spirit within him is satisfied. It is radiant. It never seeks to escape from itself. It exists in its own sense of adequacy. It exists in joy, in freedom and in peace."

They "worked" alternately for hours. At length they felt that he was free and healed. This proved true. He was not only completely sober in the morning, but Ernest kept watch on this case for the next ten years, and the man never drank again.

He delighted in the challenge of experiments where results could be checked and was never opposed to working with the medical profession. During one summer he worked with some Religious Science ministers on a project at a Southern California mental institution. One of the staff directors, a personal friend and admirer of Dr. Holmes, provided Ernest with a list of names volunteered by inmates and their families for specific spiritual help. These names were distributed among Ernest and his group, who individually undertook specific daily treatment work. They met together at head-quarters every few weeks, and reports from staff doctors indicated excellent results. Some patients, where the medical prognosis had been poor, had shown marked improvement. Others had left the institution far ahead of the medically predicted date.

At about this time Ernest also began meeting with a small group at the institute each Tuesday at noon, and this practice continued for over a decade. A roll call of members was made each meeting by Myrtle Keith, the school registrar, and a guard was always kept at the door to prevent intrusion, while Ernest sat on the small stage and "thought aloud." It was indeed a spontaneous affair, and any individual in the group was permitted to break in on him at any time. They were familiarly known as "Ernest's Angels." Unusual cases were often discussed, especially in dealing with patients who had not yet responded to treatment.

It is indeed unfortunate that no recordings were made of these intimate teachings, and I am able to recover only some reminiscences of them in a conversation with Elaine St. Johns in 1958.

His emphasis on healing he would say was to help them see behind Principle to the Presence and the relationship between the two. He affirmed, "We must be careful to realize that we do not believe in the *Divine* Mind and the *human* mind as such; we do not believe in the conscious and the subconscious mind, as such; or conscious and superconscious, as such; but [we believe] merely in different levels or activities of consciousness. Otherwise by the time you had all these spread out and broken up, you would have so many minds it would make you dizzy."

Ernest's Angels were an audience of advanced understanding, and able to grasp his rejection of a personal subconscious mind, and his emphasis on Presence as distinct from Principle—he later spoke of "The Presence and the Power as a dual unity"—was designed to awaken a state of consciousness beyond the intellect, a feeling or responsiveness that meets the soul at every point of contact. It transcends Troward's definition of personality as comprised of the power of initiative, choice and purpose or the Jewish saying that "verily, the Law is a Person."

It was Ernest's own insight developed out of a life in constant contact with the souls of men and the Soul of the universe. Thus he could reach the minds and hearts of his hearers by means of the spiritual being or *persona,* beyond the limitation of words, and teach them to look to the Being of Beings whose name has never been pronounced but who responds to each in the terms of his personal need. Presence responds to you, he said, in a heart-to-heart contact as the key of one instrument responds to the key of another when they are both in tune. No cry of a bird escapes the ear of the Eternal.

This, he believed, was the foundation for spiritual healing.

Ernest did not reject psychological concepts when they described the modus operandi of Spirit. As he stated again in the introduction to the textbook *The Science of Mind* in 1938, there is *The Thing Itself, The Way It Works, What It Does* and *How to Use It.* He looked upon psychology as a mode of explaining the *processes,* while firmly holding that the *process* should never be confused with *causation.*

It is particularly important to note here that while for the next five years a great deal of attention was paid at the institute to psychology in its various forms, Ernest never lost his central theme.

The thing that distinguishes spiritual mind treatment from ordinary psychological methods is that in it the practitioner does not treat physical or objective conditions, but he also does not emphasize conditions in the psychic or subjective world. The starting point of every spiritual treatment, and the foundation on which it should be built, is that we are surrounded by an unconditioned and absolute First Cause—Mind, Spirit or God—and that the Energy and Intelligence which act upon our thought can do so in entire independence of any existing circumstance whatever.

He restated it as the Healing Christ:

The Christ is not a person and Christ is, in a sense, more than a principle. Jesus, the Christ, means Jesus, the man anointed, illumined, the man who has comprehended spiritual things and come to understand the spiritual nature of the universe in which he lived. So Christ is the universal possibility of all men, the possibility of the Divine Influx of the Universal Mind into the individual soul. . . . The Healing Christ is a Divine Presence, immediately with us and needs but to be admitted. . . . We must think of the Healing Christ as that Principle which operates through us constructively rather than destructively. . . . Therefore the Healing Christ is not afraid. . . . The spiritual man is not afraid of birth, he is not afraid of experience, he is not afraid of death. . . . The Healing Christ comes with peace, with poise, with assurance . . . with compassion, with sympathy, with understanding. . . . The Healing Christ is, of course, the power in the modern metaphysical movement which we seek to use for healing purposes. . . . Every man has the power which God has imparted to all men through that Divine incarnation, which is the emanation of the Universal into and through the individual. . . . The Healing Christ comes to each one of us as we embody the ideals of that Christ.

During World War II, besides their constant personal treatment work, Ernest and Hazel Holmes donated 45,000 paperbound copies of his book *This Thing Called Life* to the armed forces.

Among the many letters received from the soldiers in appreciation was one from a boy in the South Seas who wrote that his troop possessed only two copies, and since everybody wanted to read one of them, they had pasted the books page by page on boards where all men who were off duty could read them.

During the Korean War, immediately after breakfast Ernest would retire to his room or drive to the office and spend some time treating for the peace and protection of all life. Hazel would do the same, and they sent literature and messages to the area of conflict. The effectiveness of their specific work where it was requested by members of their large "family" and "flock" came in innumerable individual testimonials.

It was remarkable to many that Hazel Foster Holmes, with her background of professional training, her public poise, her outstanding appearance, never made a speech, gave a lecture or taught a class during the many years in which she worked almost daily in her charming office at the Institute of Religious Science.

Her friend Adela once asked her about this. "Hazel said," Mrs. St. Johns wrote me, "that she thought a *practitioner* was different from anyone else. To *practice,* as she saw it, was to stay basically, deep down, always in a state which would be *ready* to meet any claim or emergency on the phone at any time. She felt that actual *practice,* as she understood this, demanded quiet, dedication, and removal from the scene of the difficulty, whatever it was. She was aware that personality can be a great factor for the preacher or teacher. But personality and personal emotion was detrimental to the practitioner.

"Hazel wanted to be a true, dedicated practitioner. Nothing else. And she became one of the truly, truly great ones."

Hazel drew her own kind of people—people from the movies, artists, musicians; she was coauthor as a practitioner with many authors, and she was part of the work of such stars as Doris Kenyon and Milton Sills and many others. She was also Ernest's practitioner—consultant—and other self. The strong core of his work.

Her telephone responses were famous; in a way they are the thing best remembered about her by the hundreds who called her for help in the last years after she gave up her office at the institute. It didn't matter what was told her— and some of her friends and patients called about extraordinary things! She had a great fondness for offbeat, out of the ordinary problems. She sought to prove that spiritual treatment was to be used and was effective in every situation, condition, problem and difficulty of life.

At one moment of one day a guest in her home recalls that she was helping—the word she herself used—an important board meeting of a big industry in Detroit, a football game in Multnomah Stadium in Portland, Oregon and a

threatened divorce in a family where there were children—
a case that was on the front pages of the newspapers.

"To hear her voice," one of her patients told me, "was *at
once* to contact a serene confidence, an active faith. Always
up, never *down.* Never hurried. And, again, quite ready
imperturbably to meet anything. She had a habit when anyone gave a name of saying, 'Is this my friend John?' Or 'Is this
my Helen?' Or whatever the name, or even, 'Is this my new
friend Mr. Smith?' As though the call was a joyous surprise—
or as though she was there to *cope.* Come down to it that
phrase pinpoints Hazel Holmes—she gave everyone an immediate sense that *now* she—and therefore—they—could cope
with whatever it was."

A woman who lived on the outskirts of a big city and
therefore did not have modern plumbing facilities once
called her frantically to say that while her cesspool was being
cleaned the man had fallen in and a wall collapsed on him.
There seemed no way to get him out, and everyone had gone
quite mad with terror. Hazel Holmes said in an instant tone
of authority, "You are trying to tell me *you* have discovered
a place where God is *not?* No, no. There is no such place of
corruption or danger anywhere in His universe. Remember
Benjamin. Remember his brothers threw him into a deep pit,
intending him to die there. He was rescued. Go at once and
demand of the Power and Presence of God a rescue squad.
Call the fire department. Go at once." And hung up. Actually,
a few moments later the son of the house, who had run out
to the street, came back with a builder's truck that had been
passing and on which there were ladders, and the man was
rescued. But Hazel wasn't content with this. She wanted
plumbing. Less than a month later, the city included this
home in the extension of the civic system. This may seem a
strange example, but there are so many people in this nation
of farmers, slum dwellers, ranchers, people in small towns
who have strange problems! Hazel's major idea was to cope
with them all.

In one early taped conversation Elaine St. Johns said to

Ernest: "Hazel has achieved the greatest degree of detachment I have ever seen. She is loving, she cares; you have no sense of coldness, but you feel she knows how to separate herself from the scene and stand aloof from the troubles and problems presented to her."

Ernest, agreeing, commented on the ease, the simplicity of her treatment work. She had a method that was spontaneous, direct. She did not "work" with long declarations of principle, nor read or repeat inspirational passages to approach the Presence. She was there. She stayed there, and then, as Ernest expressed it, "She just does it. She accepts that there is a law involved but she just puts it to work."

He seemingly digressed, at this point, with a story about Hazel's mother, Aunt Annie, at a time when Mrs. Gillan was living with them on "The Hill." "Hazel's mother," he said, "was a beautiful and talented woman. Among her talents was the remarkable capacity of clairvoyance. It had nothing to do with forecasting the future, but she could 'see' what was going on at a distance, like the famous Cayce." It interested Ernest, because she one day "saw" Aunt Carrie, with whom he had lived in Boston and, after describing her accurately, remarked that she was visiting in Seattle, Washington, which afterward proved to be true. Aunt Carrie was in the act of eating a piece of pie. Someone at the table had questioned if a second piece might not be too much for her, and she replied, "When I see a piece of pie I do not consult my digestion but my appetite." This amused both Ernest and Aunt Annie and later proved equally true.

But the point Ernest made was that Hazel, while she never used it apart from her practice, possessed this talent in the same way as had Quimby, who was able to penetrate to cause and thus avoid the sidetrack that is called diagnosis. No matter what description the patient gave of the malady or the condition, Hazel knew directly what was wrong, not what *appeared* to be wrong.

Ernest commented, "Psychosomatic medicine follows a similar law. The psychiatrist tells you to separate the neurosis from the neurotic and says 'it is the neurosis talking and not the neurotic.' Hazel was able to make this separation and believed and knew that the treatment has nothing to do with the *opinion* of the thing or person she was working for nor his opinion of himself nor the opinion of others. Whether the opinion is true or false is not the important factor. The truth of the matter is the only thing of importance. Hazel declared the truth. This is the real meaning of the Law of Mind in action."

And knowing it, made Hazel Holmes a successful practitioner and the beloved disciple in Ernest Holmes' "philosophy of doing."

The expansion of the work of the institute was going on rapidly. In February, 1943, there were eighteen groups or chapters besides the parent institution, and twenty practitioners were at work at headquarters. In July twenty-nine activities were listed and noted teachers, among them Christian D. Larson, Frederick W. Bailes, Carmelita Trowbridge, Lucille Graham, Helen Van Slyke, and Clarence O. Flint.

Despite the rapid growth of chapters in the field, the major concern of the institute remained education. Thus in September of 1944 the major course was greatly expanded and became the most complete in the history of metaphysical movements. Six distinguished professors from the universities of Southern California were added to the regular faculty of the institute, and the course required thirty-six weeks divided into four quarters. Classes in Streamlined Public Speaking were added, as well as Bible Studies, Comparative Religions, Idealistic Philosophy and the interpretation and application from the point of view of Science of Mind.

In September of 1946 there was an announcement of a National College of Religious Science, which offered a study course for Certification as Bachelor of Religious Science. It was outlined as having been "prescribed by the Board of Trustees and by the Education Department for training in leadership in a field of everyday living and [also] the professional field of the ministry."

The subjects included the Metaphysics of the Bible, Leadership Development, Homiletics, Class Teaching, Ancient and Modern Philosophy, Public Speaking, Applied Psychology and Comparative Religions, which covered over two hundred class hours.

There was an advance announcement also of the second and third years of post-graduate study issuing certificates as Master and Doctor of Religious Science as projected for 1947–1948.

The list of teachers was impressive, including not only the university professors, but two college presidents, a rabbi, and a Paulist priest.

To facilitate this work, Dr. Lowrey Fendrich was called in, with the title of dean. Formerly the minister in a large Presbyterian church in Washington, D.C., Dr. Fendrich was a recognized scholar.

In 1943 the Women's Club of the Institute of Religious Science was formed. Its object was to further all activities of the institute, and there were 621 charter members, with Mabel Kinney as president. This club has carried on enormous social, literary and civic as well as spiritual activities.

In 1948 the Board of Trustees authorized an "Expansion Department for the purpose of cooperation, faith and prayer to bring the benefits of Religious Science to the World."

This mild phrase was to result in both triumph and tragedy for the movement as a whole.

V

⌒⌒⌒

Gains and Losses

IN JANUARY of 1949, the twenty-second major course of study and practitioner training was inaugurated. It embraced three terms of lectures with approximately thirty-six hours of lesson time each. The class instruction included Philosophy and Religion, Philosophy and Psychology and Psychosomatic Medicine to be followed by several hours of clinical training for those who wished to become practitioners. In addition to this there was also a leadership training course for those who wished to go into the ministry or become teachers of Religious Science.

And in the same month, Ernest, after much consultation with the various outstanding leaders, joined the Expansion Department in proposing to the Annual Conference of Religious Science Chapters and Churches, then loosely held together by their personal loyalty to himself, a new form of organization to be called *International Association of Religious Science Churches,* or IARSC, designed to "work with the *Institute of Religious Science* and every Chapter will be represented in this Conference by its leaders and authorized delegates."

To further the closeness of relationship between the two bodies, the parent organization would change its mode of election of the board of trustees. Hitherto the board had been an autocracy, a self-perpetuating body, filling the vacancies as they occurred, but under the new design, the churches would elect seven members to the headquarters board.

In April Ernest wrote of it as "A Spiritual Democracy," and affirmed his belief that

this document is patterned after the Constitution of the United States and is probably the most nearly unique instrument ever used by a religious body. It provides for autonomous government by each church while tying all together in one unified effort. It creates, maintains and perpetuates one Institute as a teaching order having outlets of teaching chapters in all local churches.

The most outstanding and unique idea embodied in the new Constitution is that it permits the free function of a limitless number of churches throughout the world, while at the same time maintaining a definite integrity in the teaching of the Science of Mind which is to be given through the churches. It is truly democratic, truly cooperative, and at the same time unified in its authority through a representative council elected by the Convention of Churches in annual session.

I wish to congratulate the Committee, the leaders and the delegates of this Convention. I deeply and sincerely believe that this marks the beginning of one of the greatest religious movements of the ages.

In that same year Anna Columbia Heath Holmes died, aged ninety-nine.

Two years earlier her son Ernest had written an article about her, entitled "Zest for Living," explaining what Religious Science had meant to her for the thirty-one years in which she had known its teaching and emphasizing that the secret of her life was enthusiasm, which still possessed her at the age of ninety-seven. It continued to sustain her until the day she died.

She had moved with Ernest and Hazel from "The Hill" into the new home on Norton Avenue at the end of World

War II. In her ninety-fifth year she had been present at a dinner given for her youngest son at the Ambassador Hotel, where some six hundred people, including those most prominent in the city, came to honor him. There she heard Professor Frederick P. Woellner laud Ernest Holmes and the work of the institute, and Superior Judge William R. McKay pay tribute to Ernest's good work in behalf of the Domestic Relations Court. Later she read the messages of congratulation that poured in from the mayor; the attorney general; Rufus von Kleinsmid, president of the University of Southern California; and other notables.

She had come a far way from the spinning wheel and the thoughts and dreams she had had as she worked by lamplight those long evenings in Lincoln, Maine.

She had seen six of her eight sons become teachers, three become ministers, two win a Phi Beta Kappa key, one become a home missionary and one a foreign missionary in Japan, and two of them achieve a listing in *Who's Who in America*, and *Who's Who Among American Writers*.

In her ninety-eighth year she went for a visit to the home of her son Jerome and his wife Jennie in Los Angeles, happily continuing her activities in knitting, tatting, sewing and reading, making ready for the Christmas season, her bureau drawers loaded with handsome homemade gifts. And it was from Jerome's house that she left us.

She was tired at the end and lay at length on her bed for a few days, resting for her new journey. Then I received a wire from Ernest, saying, "Mother passed quietly away last night in her sleep. Do not come; she is with you there, too."

They laid her body away, covering her with a blanket of orchids. She looked young, they said.

Ernest's wire reached me in Connecticut, and I, too, knew Mother was with me there, for my wife, my lovely Katharine, was gravely ill; and I welcomed the sense of Mother's companionship that came to me then.

We had lived in the east, Katharine and I, for some years now, wonderful, happy, productive years.

It was here, while I was on a lecture tour in 1948, that Katharine fell ill. And it was here, in the fall of 1949, that she, too, started on her new journey.

In 1950 the silver anniversary of the college was celebrated. In the last ten years of that period there had been 794 students, of whom 59 had become licensed teachers, 93 had been ordained. Dr. Fletcher A. Harding was called from the Riverside Church to become director of education. Conditions were reviewed for earning the recognition of Bachelor of Religious Science, it now included 120 hours of class instruction divided into five units of 24 hours each. It was stipulated that a licensed teacher and practitioner must possess a master of Religious Science certificate and also one year of supervised training. And it was in this same year that the institute began a new kind of study under the title of Leadership Course. It was widely publicized and offered training under eminent authorities in the field of metaphysics. Its aim was to train practitioners and former graduates of the institute for active ministry in Religious Science. It provided twelve weeks of intensive study.

Broadcasts of Ernest's radio messages, the program "This Thing Called Life," were extended to cover the entire West Coast, with plans to expand to reach nine of the western states.

There was an important new personality in an office adjoining Ernest's at headquarters, William H. D. Hornaday, who was later to play an outstanding part in the institute as minister, teacher and member of the Board of Trustees.

Son of a Methodist minister and a Quaker mother, Bill Hornaday had attended Whittier College where he became the debating partner of Richard Nixon, who was later to become President. His heart was in spiritual matters, and he found an advanced teacher in Ernest. He studied in class and with my brother personally. Ernest had recognized his talents after having brought him in for a radio address and soon persuaded him to become a practitioner and teacher and to conduct the radio program for the institute.

There were other important new faces in the movement during those years. Norman P. VanValkenburgh, a well-known businessman from Pasadena, California and a devoted friend of Ernest's, was now president of the Board of Trustees.

In 1953 Willis H. Kinnear became editor-in-chief of *Science of Mind* magazine, and a greater range and diversity of subject matter appeared on its pages—and new names on its authors' list. The shifting winds were blowing in the new direction of the spiritual implications of the physical sciences as well as psychology. Gustaf Strömberg, a former member of the staff at Wilson Observatory, a great personal friend of the Holmeses, whose name is to be associated with Einstein, Eddington, Moulton and others wrote the book *The Soul Of the Universe*, and contributed to the magazine frequently.

Arthur E. Compton, authority on atomic power, wrote on "Science and the Supernatural," and Ernest reviewed J. B. Rhine's book on *The Reach of the Mind*. Articles of similar character appear under such titles as "Universal Energy," and a review of *Weeds* by Dr. Carver. And Omar Fareed, M.D., wrote "A Doctor's Diagnosis—Do Your Emotions Show?" which dealt with the psychosomatic factor in skin diseases.

This trend was balanced by new emphasis on truth through poetry and articles by Don Blanding, the "Vagabond of Verse," which poured through the magazine in a stream for some ten years.

Later a new field was explored in dealing with "Salesmanship, The Laws of Business Success," by Frederick A. Sykes; "Mind and Faith" by Thomas J. Watson, with an encomium by the editor stressing the author's leadership and guidance of the IBM with high ideals and concern for humanity.

Philosophers continued to hold their particular interest for the Religious Science students, and the name Sir

Sarvepalli Radhakrishnan, vice-president of India, formerly professor of Eastern religion and ethics at Oxford, and an outstanding thinker, appeared as a contributor to the magazine, while Frederick Mayer, professor of philosophy at the University of Redlands conducted a regular feature called "The Philosopher's Corner."

Meanwhile Ernest Holmes continued doing the things he had done for four decades—teaching, experimenting, healing. And to him the three were one.

His first public experience in teaching had been in 1916 at Mrs. Reeseburg's metaphysical library before thirteen people. His last was a sermon in the magnificent Founder's Church of Religious Science before a huge congregation in 1960. Between those two he taught hundreds and thousands in a variety of places and a variety of ways. Some of his words were recorded by tape or shorthand and incorporated in books or preserved as lesson-lectures.

In the year of 1954 Ernest's belief in spiritual democracy was tried—and not found wanting.

With growth had come new problems in administration, and in December of 1953, the Board of Trustees, partially because of requirements of a religious institution in the handling of its assets, changed the name of the parent organization from the Institute of Religious Science to the Church of Religious Science,* naming field organizations as affiliated churches. This would bring the field organization into the parent Church as the Department of Affiliated Churches. This necessitated a new organizational design which was presented, with the founder's approval, to the annual meeting of churches in January of 1954. To the surprise and disappointment of Ernest and the board, the reorganization proposal met with some vigorous opposition, and a division of the churches occurred.

Though deeply hurt, Ernest never spoke an unkind word of, nor offered a rebuke to the dissident leaders. They all

---

* In January 1967, the Church again changed its corporate name to United Church of Religious Science.

continued to serve the same *principles,* to teach from his *The Science of Mind* textbook, to practice the same faith—and he continued to love them. In the deep places of his heart, *there* he did not accept division, never stopped working and praying for harmony, for his principle was that Spirit is *one,* Its mainfestation is Perfection, and what blesses one, blesses all. There were now, it appeared, two flocks and some scattered sheep. But they continued to look to one shepherd, and he continued to pray for them all.

It was in the fall of 1954 that Ernest and Hazel moved into the stately home on Sixth Street and Lorraine Boulevard which had been acquired by the church.

Hazel had recently retired from the little room at the institute where she had worked for years. She did not give up her practice, but she had more time to spend now on the graceful house and her gracious hospitality. It was in her sitting room that she now did her healing work, and here she used to wait in the afternoon listening for Ernest's step; or coming to the head of the stairs standing on the balcony overlooking the foyer, she would call to their wonderful and devoted housekeeper, "Lena, has Papa come home yet?"

Over the garage there was an apartment occupied by Reuben Webb, who assisted Ernest with his driving and gardening and helped Hazel in the house. He was so inspired by the new mansion that when he appeared one morning to drive Dr. Holmes to church, he was dressed in a new cutaway coat, striped trousers, top hat and gloves. Ernest took one look and then ordered Webb into the back seat while he himself took the wheel and drove them both sedately to the Beverly Hills Theater, where he was to speak—Ernest fore and Webb aft of the Cadillac!

On the main floor Hazel and Ernest arranged their antique furniture and collection of works of art and added new pieces from time to time. Ernest poured out his heart upon the entire place, outside and in, like a lover, not only spreading gravel and renewing the lawn outside, but rearranging the works of art indoors in more favorable light or location. He cared most for Italian and Chinese pieces. They owned several priceless statues of Kwan Yin. And it was in these surroundings that they entertained guests ranging from one to several hundred. I remember being present one afternoon when there were three hundred people at lunch, gathered either in the spacious dining room or on the terrace, and on one evening when they gave a reception dinner to 150 guests in honor of the governor of the state, Goodwin J. Knight.

Despite the lovely new home and the joy he and Hazel had in it, the next few years were not an easy time for Ernest. He had now been hard at work during the lifetime of an average generation; he was sixty-seven years of age, and until the flock scattered, he had been looking forward to a transference of the burden to younger shoulders. But now he felt impelled to add to it, and he went out into the field with missionary zeal, speaking at established churches, opening up new "fellowships" (embryonic churches), helping in breaking of grounds for new edifices and speaking at their dedication. The work bore fruit. In a period of five years, the number of church buildings owned by the local congregations jumped from 5 per cent to 62 per cent.

In all of this he was abetted by the missionary zeal of Dr. Hornaday. There were two other men who gave him needed assistance at this crucial time: the Reverend Barclay Johnson, and the Reverend Mark Carpenter. And in June of 1956 Ernest shifted one activity to the shoulders of a younger man. He asked Dr. Gene Emmet Clark to take over his Sunday lectures at the Beverly Theater.

One of the things that always greatly encouraged my brother was the capacity and willingness of these younger men to step in with their enthusiasm and energy—to enlarge the "body" of the movement again and again.

But Ernest Holmes had not retired.

He continued to be guest speaker in Religious Science pulpits from coast to coast, to dedicate churches, to attend the Asilomar Conferences and to teach at the institute. There was a growing desire among the affiliated churches for a founder's church, to be built next door to the institute, and Ernest, perhaps remembering Mother's wistful longing for *both* the Spirit and the form, was exploring the idea. But placing his Sunday service in the capable hands of another did afford Hazel and Ernest more freedom and flexibility, more time for their home and friends, to travel and enjoy each other.

For eleven months, they did just that.

And then, on May 21, 1957, Hazel Holmes died.

Two nights before, Hazel's oldest friend, her beloved Adela, visited them.

"After dinner," she wrote me, "Ernest had to go back to the institute and give a lecture—I talked with Hazel for a time. She was very gay. We'd enjoyed our dinner immensely. I left early the next morning—and Hazel came to the top of the stairs overlooking the foyer, and said goodbye. I never saw her more at ease."

When Ernest returned from the institute two evenings later, there was no Hazel on the balcony, no cheerful greeting. Surprised, Ernest mounted the winding stairs, and found her in her own suite.

She had gone as Hazel would have wished to go—swiftly, with dignity and ease.

VI

The Lonely Years

DURING THE remainder of 1957 Ernest continued to confront his deep grief.

To Lucille Graham, an old friend and fine practitioner, he admitted, "I have always thought myself prepared for anything but I never thought it would be like this."

He told me two years later that he felt he had overcome it. He had gone into Arizona alone, driving his car, meeting with God on the highway and taking account of himself. He came back calm and quiet; but he was not a Stoic, he was a man in love for many years, and he remained lonely for Hazel through the brief remaining time. I flew down from Oakland for an occasional weekend and to go on a jaunt with him.

"Let others carry on," he'd say. "Let's take a trip." And away we would go into the mountains, to enjoy lunch in a log cabin inn or to Palm Springs for a few days or to drive across the desert along the highway overlooking the Salton Sea. "Dead but still alive," he observed. He was far from morbid, but he was unusually quiet; he showed me great affection, talking of our families, and especially Mother, Hazel and Katharine. "Do you wish to go?" I asked once, but he fell silent for a long time and then changed the subject.

In his daily life Ernest attempted to carry on as before. He

275

went out in the evening from time to time. He asked friends in. He went to the institute daily. He sat on the front steps at noon to get the sun in his face. He lectured, he wrote, although he told me that he had said everything he had to say, most of it many times. But it brought him into contact with people; and on Sunday afternoon a group of intimates usually dropped in after church.

Yes, Ernest was surrounded by good friends, but the "other half of himself" had gone on ahead—and, while he personally was detained by business, he never stopped actively missing Hazel.

There is every evidence that Ernest began his preparations in 1958 for the closing of his ministry. Both the internal evidence of his teaching and the direct confirmations of his friends prove it. Three things remained to be done:

To complete the building of a sanctuary.

To finish an epic poem that he had conceived as a synthesis, in one volume, of "questions which all thoughtful men have asked, answered by the wisdom of the ages."

And, insofar as he was able, to clarify, unify and protect the Science of Mind teaching. Because he firmly believed that, unless destroyed inwardly, Religious Science was the greatest spiritual impulsion in the modern world.

The sanctuary was to be called Founder's Church.

The board of trustees had made the decision to erect a great modern church building on the grounds of the extensive institute holdings at Sixth and New Hampshire Streets, where once was the willow tree, the running brook and the marsh.

Ernest had given the matter prayerful thought. There were beautiful Religious Science churches now throughout the nation. The institute had none. Services for its congregation still packed the Wiltern Theater to hear Dr. William Hornaday, but, said Dr. Hornaday to Dr. Ernest, "Think of our need for a place to work socially. Apart from Sunday services, we need a chapel, a dining room, kitchen, Sunday school facilities. At present we add people on Sunday only to subtract them on Monday."

Ernest thought. He hesitated. He thought again. . . . He yielded. "I am tempted to a wider service, and we can meet the challenge," he said.

Later he told me he had recalled not only Mother's views on having a church, but a sign I told him of having seen in England. Over the sanctuary door there was chiseled in stone, "This is the gate of Heaven," but beneath it was a hand-lettered sign, "Please go around the other way."

"I've come to the conclusion that the sanctuary door should be there, and be *open*. We'll make sure the Presence is inside," he said. "I avoided the word *religious* and the word *church,* until I came to realize that the world is more interested in the spiritual than the mental. It yearns for a religious faith and an experience with God. Psychiatric terminology and idealistic philosophy are useful in their place but Science of Mind is a doorway to the Real and the Eternal."

His personal interest fired the enthusiasm of the Board of Trustees. A building committee was appointed, headed by Paul Graham, a successful industrialist, who declared to the church, "Now we will work together, pray together, plan together."

Caught up in the determination to realize this bigger "body" for the Idea, Ernest visualized many of the details. Prior to the ground-breaking ceremonies he could be seen spreading out newspapers on the site to demonstrate the placement of various parts of the church, the choir loft, the pastor's study, the organ to be named after Hazel, and the walled gardens around the building. "What we raise here will be beautiful"; he affirmed, "it will bless people of all faiths just to see the building."

Ernest lectured several times at the Wiltern Theater services in 1958 and 1959 expressing his pleasure in the prospect of "a magnificent symbol of our spiritual convictions; a thing of beauty forever—an adequate edifice for our Sunday worship and midweek activities."

Building the sanctuary had begun.

The epic poem was to be called *The Voice Celestial*.

It was in the spring of 1958 that Ernest, recalling that several volumes of my own verse had received popular and critical acclaim, telephoned and wrote me in regard to some polishing of such parts of the epic as he had already written and expanding it.

In the months after Hazel's passing, he found some outlet for his emotions in writing verse, which was later to be incorporated in the work. In April there was a two-page spread of his poem, "Eternal Days," in *Science of Mind* magazine. It was written for his own comfort as well as to assure his followers. In it he said that "no man need to prepare to meet his God. He is with Him each day and every hour of the day. . . . Death loses its sting when we realize the eternity of our own being."

It was at this time that Ernest also wrote his part of the chapter on "Life and Death" that appears in *The Voice Celestial*.

When he sent me the material, I found his thoughts stimulating but somehow incomplete. Ernest's writing had been more in the nature of poetical essays under special headings, but I conceived of making them chapters, putting them in dialogue form, adding my own lyrics and a second section to the book containing the biographies of the ancient teachers from whom our synthesis was derived. Ernest had already written the songs that we would ascribe to them.

The change in concept to a trialog and a progressive treatment in a semifictional form was such an innovation that I was somewhat apprehensive when the time came to show the work to Ernest at Asilomar that summer of 1958. We sat in the living room of his suite in Tide Inn Cottage, side by side on the divan, and he read it aloud. It was a thrilling experience for me, and he was elated. This was a meeting of our minds at the level of our highest understanding, he said, and "the ripened fruits of our joint lives and thoughts."

I explained to him how I proposed to expand the work to make it a progressive epic and that it would reach a considerable volume. He urged me to go ahead, assuring me of his constant cooperation. My correspondence with him over the next two years shows his unabated enthusiasm, and I flew to Los Angeles from time to time to work in his home. Or we took a short trip, or he came to San Francisco to work with me. Before its completion he assured everyone that *The Voice Celestial* would live long past all our other works.

The polishing he had requested would have required only a few weeks.

Now he had embraced a new and wider concept, and the work took us more than two years. But he believed in it so firmly he was determined to see it through.

Ernest Holmes never showed the slightest interest in the perpetuation of his own name through the future of the Church of Religious Science. So far as fame was concerned, he often expressed the opinion that "all philosophies would be rolled up as a scroll and numbered among the things that used to be." And regarding the philosopher, he humorously referred to the temporary nature of fame by saying, "Stick your finger in a pail of water, take it out again and see how permanent an impression you have left." He was consistent to the last, for he would not allow the public to know the place of his burial so there could be no possibility of making it a shrine.

His concern for the future was strictly in regard to the preservation of the purity of the message. Unlike the Hebrew prophets who forecast only what would happen *unless,* Ernest forecast what would happen *if.* The prophets said in effect: "Unless you change, the nation will perish." Ernest said, "If you keep the purity of the truth, the future is secure."

He believed in the universal truth to which he had dedicated his life—and in these closing years, he welcomed the

evidence that missionary work by younger men was emphasizing the universality and continuing to stimulate his
"flock."

Dr. Hornaday had been invited to Switzerland to study
privately with Carl Jung; he spent time with Albert Schweit-
zer in Lambaréne, Africa; he had an audience with His Holiness, Pope John XXIII. He had also brought to Ernest's home
His Holiness Jagatguru Shankaracharya, spiritual head of
millions in India and of a monastic order a thousand years
old. It was not easy to conceive of the latter as the supreme
pontiff of a hundred million followers as he sat in his white
robe in the great drawing room in Ernest's home with a hood
drawn over his head—a physically weak and fragile figure indeed, but with a purpose indomitable—the awakening of the
world-conscience in the interest of universal peace.

Ernest the shepherd felt an increased urgency to clarify,
unify and protect the message—to lift his flock to his highest
understanding of Truth—before he left them. To this task,
at the Asilomar conferences of 1958 and 1959, in the lovely
campground by the rolling Pacific, he addressed himself.

He dealt specifically and directly with three subjects—mysticism, the religion of the future, and the new literature.

During those two summers there was a wistfulness about
Ernest as he came and went on the campgrounds, a man who
walked alone in this templelike grove with its soft carpet of
pine needles, its pillars of pine and its lofty canopy of green.
He sought solitude on the shore beyond the wall of sand
dunes, dressed informally in the oversize lounging jacket that
was his favorite attire at the retreat. Sometimes admirers
would search him out to snap a picture or secure an auto-
graph. He welcomed them kindly, complied with their request and turned his face again toward the sea. Was he thinking the long, long thoughts of youth or the longer thoughts
of age and eternity? I do not know. Sometimes his mind went
back to Hazel, and then he would respond with unconscious
warmth to the slightest affection bestowed on him by those
he met on the paths. "I lean on love," he said.

By leaning on Love, he was made strong. His words at Asilomar were of unusual power.

There is little doubt that Ernest was impelled to deal with *mysticism* at this time both from an inner compulsion to put the capstone on his ministry and because he had been pondering the words of Carl Jung. When Dr. Hornaday returned from Switzerland, he brought Ernest a message from Dr. Jung. "You tell that man that no religion can be a success without a great degree of mysticism in it."

Ernest himself was a mystic, although long wary of the word *per se,* since it tends to be grossly misunderstood by the Western world; but if we accept the commonly inscribed basic definitions—"union with God," "intuition of the Divine," "realization of the Eternal," "the belief that direct knowledge of God, of spiritual truth, is attainable through immediate intuition or insight"—then Ernest's assertion of a "divine immanence within a divine transcendence," is an affirmation for mysticism.

Ernest's mysticism had shone through the curtain but had not been fully developed until this time, for his primary interest was not introspection; he had noted that he was dealing with intangibles, subjective states and principles, which, as in all religions, are mystical in and of themselves and stressed that "what we call the human is merely the way in which we use the Divine." He spoke of the many forms of consciousness described by William James, supporting the principle that we can "be aware" on an entirely different plane of existence than the one in which most of the world functions.

Through the years he had repeatedly stated that Emma Curtis Hopkins, with whom he had studied in the early days in New York, and Meister Johannes Eckhart, the fourteenth-century Dominican monk, were in his opinion the greatest of all the writing mystics. He highly esteemed the works of Evelyn Underhill and felt that she had made a more comprehensive study of mysticism than any other writer, but he saw no evidence that she herself had experienced cosmic consciousness. He thought that the exact reverse was true of Rufus Jones, who had been unable to articulate what he had experienced. Ernest had also read Dr. Richard M. Bucke's *Cosmic Consciousness,* but had not been impressed with Bucke's one and only personal experience, which seemed more poetic than convincing. Although highly esteeming Emerson and Troward, he found no evidence that either of them had experienced this highest mystical state.

He did make the attempt to describe it in *The Voice Celestial,* which Ernest considered in essence a treatise on mysticism.

This is the way he described the experience:

> Like tides from an invisible ocean of life
> Bringing messages from the shore of time,
> Eternity presses upon us.
> It belongs to the present moment;
> Occasionally a door opens,
> Eternity enters and brings the light,
> Messages from the unknown mystery of being,
> Ranges of consciousness unlimited. . . .
> And on and on to the Great Heart that breathes
> In rhythmic lovingness in everything!
> O heart of Christ, O heart of God, O light.

Ernest tried to differentiate between mysticism and cosmic consciousness; the first being easily experienced, he felt; the second, very rarely if at all.

For five days at Asilomar he dealt with mysticism. It was also crystal clear that the objective of his teaching was not to encourage a dramatic "experience," but a constant awareness of Presence. He cautioned once more against "losing the Presence in the practice of the Principle—in the metaphysical field where they practice the Principle without the Presence, something freezes up."

Ernest's teaching, he said, was in essential harmony with that of Meister Eckhart, who held the position that the physical universe does not exist apart from God, and Ernest affirmed that "our religion is a mystical religion but it is not a religion away from earth; it is a religion where the grass grows, a religion that no longer separates the physical, mental and spiritual, but finds action and reaction and actor one and the same thing, and here and now. . . . This state of the mystical concept cannot be delivered by ignorance nor comprehended by the religious fanatic who believes in the ultimate destruction of a human soul."

Ernest correlated Eckhart with Plotinus because both of them incorporated the philosophy of idealism with the mystical; he considered that Plotinus' concept of *man* as a microcosm who embraces the qualities of all orders of creation provides a rational explanation of "the radiation of all things from God and their ultimate return to Him, the first emanation being the *Nous* or 'the Thing in Itself.' "

Readers of the textbook *The Science of Mind* will recognize this phrase as the title of the first chapter, a phrase that Ernest found also in Kant and in later years in *The Life Divine* by Sri Aurobindo. Ernest applied this principle to practical healing when he quoted from Plotinus, "I do not argue, I contemplate, and as I contemplate, I let fall the seeds of thought into the mirror of mind, which then becomes the mirror of matter."

Again and again he emphasized that we subsist both physically and psychologically on the fact of existence itself— "existence is the biggest word in our language"—"there is a world which was not made, did not make itself and just is and continues forever—but active."

His object was to bring the listener into conscious unity with the One, saying, "It is the perception of this—the spiritual awareness of the reality of things—that gives power to our work because all the words in the world without meaning won't do anything—we would just be talking to ourselves."

Thus the objective of the lecture series on mysticism was to generate the *mystical apprehension of reality* and arouse the emotions attendant upon it. It was not an appeal to the emotions themselves but an awakening, an awareness, which would result in *doing* as well as *being*.

Ernest made it clear that each soul must enter the door of truth by himself—it is "the flight of the alone to the Alone," he quoted from Plotinus. "Inner experience and religion *per se* are not the same." It is impossible to really explain God to anybody. He still remains the mystery. Prayer can be defined, but only those who pray can know where they have gone and what they found. Nor are we under the compulsive will of God, since each of us individualizes his own concept of himself in relation to God. This enables us to understand the meaning of evil and sin, which are experiences fabricated by misconception or the reverse use of the law. "The law can produce bondage as well as freedom and appears to have so much latitude that it creates for us what we call hell because of false interpretation, and we are more or less hypnotized from the cradle to the grave."

He attempted to release the student from the hypnosis of limiting God to Principle. God is Person, and Principle is the way Person works. He said, "It is valuable to differentiate between psychic states which result from tapping the individual or the collective unconscious or field of memory, and the mystical in which by intuition and illumination you contact the eternally real."

He felt that in the common experiences of every day there was opportunity to realize the mystical and he recalled his first introduction to the individualized consciousness of God in the life of a tree when he was a boy in Maine. He went on to say that the birth of a child or even a litter of kittens opens some door to the mystical. There was nothing "difficult" or "weird" about it, yet because of different goals and states of awareness, some feel it, some do not.

He quoted from *The Life Divine* by Sri Aurobindo, whose one thousand pages he had read three times, his own copy of which he presented to me later, asking me to read it. There are innumerable underscored passages, but I found that Ernest had already uttered the same principles years before.

While an admirer of Aurobindo, Ernest warned against a too easy acceptance of his principle that "the gnostic being" (the man who has arrived at the apex of knowledge of the mysteries of being) needs no standards of virtue because "all becomes a self-flow of spiritual nature." While he considered it to be as true as St. Augustine's principle, "love God and do what you please," he was concerned lest the average individual make false interpretation of it, and he took a stand against a self-established rule of conduct that lowered the standard of ethics and morality, probably the greatest danger of the emancipated life. He laid stress upon the fact that the future of the church depends on the moral example of its teachers and leaders as much as upon their teaching.

Ernest concluded with a quotation from Browning, "I spoke as I saw . . . of God's work—all's love, yet all's law," and he began his meditation on that note:

Deep within our souls shines an eternal light that envelops everything we contact, heals and blesses everything we touch and brings life for death and joy in a song—Eternal Spirit within us, Blessed Life and Infinite Peace—everything that denies this, we deny; everything that affirms the Living Presence, we announce; and all the past—whatever we believe it may have been—and every negation is wiped out and there is no past. "Behold, I make all things new!"

Infinite Beauty, Harmony and Rhythm in which everything fits together in form—O Beauty that is in our own souls—and the depth of that infinite Peace in which all action takes place without moving, where everything is effortless: We abide in Thy love that merges with our own and flows through us as stream with stream to find a higher level through self-action—to Thee we surrender; not to some abstract love of God which has no meaning to the soul, but to the warm pulsating rhythm of feet upon the pavement; and the horses' hooves; and the roots of the grass; and the song of the lark; and the wild power and surging strength of the waves; the freshness of the wind and the dew and the rain in our faces; and the warm embrace of each other.

This is all we know about it, but if there is back of it more of love, we welcome that by whose eternity and in whose immensity we have an equal share in all that is. O Infinite Beauty, rapture beyond vision, we accept all that is delivered to us and even as we accept it, we give it back in joy to Thee. O High and Lofty One who inhabits eternity and still finds a dwelling place in our own mind and heart and soul, Thou art all.

In a sermon given just before the summer conference, Ernest said: "We are a melting pot of people who are seeking a new spiritual freedom without losing the old values. Dr. Flewellyn, Professor of Philosophy at the University of Southern California, told me that he considered we are conducting the greatest spiritual experiment since the dawn of Christianity."

In a single series at Asilomar he spoke of the future of the Church twelve times, but little of it had to do with material growth and physical expansion. It would be contingent on the preservation and expansion of the fundamental principles already known.

Certain basic principles would never change, he affirmed. The identity of immanence with transcendence is the over-all fact of Religious Science thought, and when this immanence is established in the race mind, a new civilization will bloom in fullness.

Conscious identity with God enables a man to act like a god and demonstrate the fulfillment of his hopes and dreams.

The survival of an organization or its physical structure and churches is not at issue. It is the survival and activation of the final truth that God is in man manifesting Himself to the world. This concept is, he said, as yet beyond the grasp of humanity as a whole. With Bucke, he believed that if all the great masters who have appeared in history were to be assembled at the same time and place, they could be contained in a single room. Nonetheless, we are heir to their revelations, and it is a distinct function of Religious Science to make them known to the ages. "We start with the proposition that *God is,* God is what I am; God may not be what I appear to be, but what I really am must be God or I wouldn't be. Instead of fighting with critical theology, let us so live that the truth will be evident to all."

The presence of the "divine spark" in everything was the heart and soul of Ernest's message.

For me [he said] to live is God. What I seek is to help the world break out of the superstitions of the ages. The individual mind which we often speak of as *human* is so encased in the collective thought of the ages, its superstitions, its dread of the unknown, its fear of it, its uncertainty about it, its irrational emotionalism over it, that it has, out of nothing, created a preposterous God. . . .

Now this is why I say the religion of the future—I don't know what it will be like; but I know of a lot of things that won't be there—hell will be cooled off, the devil (so-called) will go out of business, and— [He trailed into silence, then smiled.] I think I killed him off long ago. But certain scare-evangelists keep trying to dig him up again. This too shall pass out of all religions. It will cure millions—it will dehypnotize them. The absence of God and the devil will clean up the unconscious so that fear of the unknown will also disappear. This will heal body and soul, and sickness will pass away forever.

Basically the various schools of psychoanalytical thought are all in agreement that the center or core of every neurosis involves four things: rejection, guilt, anxiety and insecurity. We shall find this true of traditional Christianity, for the common denominator of their theologies today, whether Anglican, Protestant or Catholic, is the problem of sin, redemption and immortality. The universal hunger is for a life beyond this life in which we will find happiness and peace because we are free from guilt and self-condemnation.

Now from our viewpoint, which might be called spiritual psychosomatic medicine, we hold that realization and union with God will automatically remove the feeling of rejection, and consequent anxiety. When the soul experiences such a union, it is freed from the necessity of protracted analysis. Results are immediate.

How can this be brought about? That is what our classes and our textbook are designed to show.

Let us see what immediate good one can derive from the knowledge that the whole problem of sin and salvation is summarized and solved in the realization of the Divine Union. You know exactly what you are after. There is no mixup and uncertainty. There is no need for a go-between. There is no question that God can and will help you.

Did this mean that he was against psychiatry, doctors, nurses—orthodox ministers?

"No!" he stated. "I believe that the modern or the coming religion will throw a bridge across the river that separates the various modes of healing until the final consciousness is reached which will heal by spiritual mind treatment alone. The early metaphysicians opposed such cooperation not from superstition but from concern lest the patient lose faith in spiritual healing. I myself have always worked with doctors when asked."

What about ministers?

There are so many kinds it would be hard to answer. We can confidently say that the average modern clergyman is far ahead of the pews. On the other hand, there are many who say in effect, "Believe me or go to the devil." Of one thing you may be sure, even those who are sympathetic with our technique cannot follow it fully. We teach that belief in the universal Christ is necessary; for the healing power is in the *indwelling* Christ.

Superstitions like belief in hell, purgatory and a personal devil will have passed away. . . . The religion of the future in my estimation will not be exactly like the modern metaphysical movements including our own at the present time. Nor need we expect more emphasis on the attainment of health or material possessions. We are not selling a better soap or a new perfume; but we do seek a higher consciousness, putting the kingdom of God first. There will be a greater effort on the part of all forms of religion to realize the incarnation of God in human life, that is the recognition of individual immanence in universal transcendence.

The issue will not be directly moral or ethical, but we shall have acquired a higher consciousness of the virtue of goodness out of the lessons learned from the fruits of badness; pain having taught us the better way. Goodness will be found to be its own reward, and there will be justice without judgment. By the same token there will be less condemnation of others from the simple fact that such condemnation arises out of unconscious self-condemnation. . . .

Just the same [he added] you will suffer condemnation unless you remove the cause. Religious Science makes more demand on character than any other system.

It also demanded, he said, an evolving expression of truth in the form of literature.

A great literature is necessary to make our work universal. Two things may stand in the way—the arrogance of ignorance and psychic confusion. Our danger is from having things grow up around us that have nothing to do with us. If so, I would want to come back and haunt you.

We ought to develop so well that a great literature will grow up around our work, making it more universal. But I hope it won't be a repetition of the few things I have said. We do not want a lot of echoes. When I was a boy we used to yell into an empty rain barrel to hear the echo, but we never learned anything from it. . . . If I pass on tonight they can take everything I ever wrote and toss it into the ashes—it is going to be thrown there someday, anyway—but two things will remain, and only two which go with them; there is a Presence and a Power in the universe which constitute dual unity of action and reaction—and the polarity from which all things come.

While calling for a new and better literature, he recognized the danger involved.

Let it not be an arrogant claim to special revelation [he said], a stupid projection of the ego. Keep the body of truth pure and clean and strip off the embalming shrouds of a petty conformity while at the same time reverencing the emergence of new and higher truths. Bring immanence into focus and with Eckhart realize that God never leaves—He is always at hand. If this be known and practiced, we shall not wander too far into the fields of speculation. Time and consecration will eventually feed the roots of the tree with the substance of its own truth.

This is very important to me—the last word has not been said—others are not to go on my revelation—I am no prophet, I have no personal revelations and if I had I would distrust them, because they might be hallucinations; and I don't trust in self-styled prophets. But never let our movement get into that static position intellectually that shows a dearth of spiritual growth where you suppose everything has been said. Remember this, you teachers and preachers—*there is nothing in our movement that restricts anybody, nothing ties you down; to think otherwise is stupidity. Moreover there is nothing in our movement that is trying to promote anybody.* Our movement is democratic. I no longer hesitate to say these things, because I do not care what happens so far as I am personally concerned. If it becomes a movement—grand; if it doesn't, it doesn't belong to history—I comment now impersonally—this is true.

We are the most independent spiritual organization the world has ever known, as I view it. Now let us live up to our independence; let's not take a power and a privilege or a liberty to destroy freedom or spiritual insight—which would destroy that which we are trying to do; and let us see if it is possible that we are a thing of destiny. If so, the tide of evolution will have cast up on the shores of time *that* which will take root of itself.

Let no new bondage grow out of a greater freedom.

Let the evolution be the freeing of the mind from restrictions in growth.

Let it be without confusion, but *let us have the hope and belief that somewhere in the spiritual evolution of the human race there might arrive, or has arrived or can arrive a group of people in the spiritual field who will have enough intelligence, respect and admiration for each other to cooperate in a spirit of freedom in this endeavor—and trust God to do the rest.*

As I listened something stirred in my memory. Where had I heard concepts similar to Ernest's statement regarding immanence and transcendence? Presently I experienced a partial recall. It had to do with my studies in theology forty years before. It was a paragraph from a book by Dr. William Newton Clarke, Professor of Christian Theology for Colgate University. The following is the passage: "This thought of the immanence of the transcendent God is a magnificent conception that is destined powerfully to influence religion, theology, science and common life. It is at once so vast and so new an idea as scarcely to have begun its work. . . . By this thought, religion will be freshly inspired, theology will be transfigured, and science will become a spiritual worship."

VII

◊

Ernest's Farewell

THE YEAR OF 1959 was a year of closing doors, not for the church but for Ernest himself. To the casual observer he appeared to be following the usual routine. As a matter of fact, he was in the process of transferring the burden. The reorganization of the board was completed, so that final decisions were in its control. It is true that many problems were still referred to him, large and small, and he interested himself in the details of the rapidly materializing Founder's Church. I remember a small debate arose over the question of placing a cross at the apex of the rotunda to represent Christian ecclesiasticism, but Ernest rejected it on the grounds that a cross and a crucifix are too easily identified in the popular mind; but when they placed a cupola in the same place, Ernest objected to that as well, saying that it made the church look like a barn with an air vent for the hay.

He met daily with the controller over various aspects of the church building and frequently conferred with Dr. Hornaday, to whom Ernest had transferred most of the burden of his pastoral activities. It was a heavy assignment, because the nondenominational character of the Church attracts thousands of people who come to Los Angeles. These things done, Ernest was not only freed from these duties and routine meetings but felt that he had now provided what safeguards he could for the future of the Church.

Some days now he simply withdrew to his office at headquarters and sat for hours in silent meditation.

When the church building was nearing completion and long afterward, Ernest would quietly enter the sanctuary every day and sit in the same seat and meditate and pray for a long time.

The consciousness of love enveloped the whole building enterprise, and I recall one of Dr. Hornaday's own meditations, in which he said, "Our church shall forever reflect the understanding of Truth which reveals paths of harmony, love and security and guides our footsteps. Let us love each other as we have never loved before."

Love was a word that was much with Ernest in these closing months.

The annual convention of the Religious Science Churches was held in January. Most of the ministers attended the sessions, and the churches were represented by duly appointed delegates. There was a great banquet at the Ambassador Hotel. Ernest spoke to them very simply, defining the Religious Science Church as "a state of inner awareness. It is not," he said, "just a teacher, although this is good; it is not an eloquent preacher, although this is good. We do not know that God is peace unless we also are at peace. Our motto is that to know is to do and to do is to know. Jesus proved this not by his brilliant speech but by his life. He loved!"

He said that "self-existence is the biggest word," and affirmed that "we must conceive of that which never was born. It isn't even self-cause (since it never was caused); it always was, is, and is to be. . . . All we know of God is the practice of His presence. . . . Probably God is love—this we believe—but we do not know it just because the Bible says so. We know it only if our arms are around somebody."

To a young student who stopped him in the hall at the institute, bewailing his lack of progress, he said, with a chuckle, "You're on an eternal journey, you know, my son; as time goes on you will reach different summits of the mountain you are climbing and looking back will see how far you have really gone. The awakening soul must not despise its sums in addition because it cannot extract the cube root. Meanwhile you can resort to the highest healing power—love."

At that time he was doing continual treatment work in his home, keeping to the broader aspects—completion of Founder's Church, that it have a healing consciousness, that the life of the movement, as a whole, grow and expand in harmony and unity, that *The Voice Celestial* embody our vision for it.

He was constantly interested in our "library discussions," which centered now around *The Voice Celestial*.

Three topics with which we dealt stand out particularly in my memory—sin, symbology and patterns. The first because Ernest was definitely against it, even as a word. The second because he had been over a half a century puzzling it out. The third because it was so important to him that his last letter to me, written a week before he died, was on that subject.

Ernest deplored the word *sin* because he felt it denoted a congenital state of mind and emotion. He cautioned me against the use of the word in *The Voice Celestial*.

But with my orthodox theological training, I "sneaked" it in. I had the Farer say, "What you call error, some call sin," and after that I got away with it five times.

"Why," he asked, "do you want to use it? I have always taught that there is no sin but ignorance, following the belief of Emerson."

"A rose by any other name could smell as sweet and sin by any other name is still sin," I said.

"My object is to avoid the sense of dualism—a universe of good *and* evil. I would define sin as 'missing the mark.' "

"In recent years you have adopted a good deal of theory and terminology of psychiatry—" I began. "You are attempting to remove guilt feelings as the source of disease. Is that not an acknowledgment of sin?"

He looked at me sharply. "Define *guilt*. Aren't you confusing it with sin?"

"It's the feeling you have because you have sinned."

"That may be the theologian's definition, but it would be better to explain it that the primary nature of man is goodness and that he is punishing himself because he feels he ought to know and do better. In fact, his guilt may often be due to misconceptions. What he really wants to do is to get back to his goodness."

"The criminal knows he has done an evil deed and—"

"Often confesses his crime because he wants to get back to the original goodness he instinctively feels," Ernest interrupted. "To me this is one of the most significant proofs of the basic goodness of the soul and that all men possess the divine spark. Man feels guilt when he departs from the fundamental goodness. Therefore guilt is evidence of an inherent perfection—an instinctive urge of the soul."

He said, thoughtfully, "The 'sin and salvation' of Christian theology, the 'renunciation' of Buddhism, the 'masochism or need of self-punishment' of psychology, and the theory of reincarnation are all derived from an unconscious sense of guilt and the rejection that the mind (soul) has for itself. But reincarnation is too long a way around; hell as punishment portrays either a helpless or vindictive God; the renunciation and final complete denial of the self as an ego—all of these are a part of self-rejection or an unconscious sense of the need to be punished. Man was born to purity, and his self-punishment is an instinctive effort to return to the Father's house."

"I do not see how a sense of guilt can absolve them. Do they finally arrive at a point where they feel they have punished themselves enough? Is hell the terminal?" I asked.

"Jesus introduced the remedy. He healed body and soul by forgiveness. That is one of the reasons why I believe in the confessional of the churches—they help to remove the cause of guilt—even though I do not agree with their terminology.

"The *healing* of ignorance . . . not the threat of punishment is what makes it possible for a man to 'sin no more,' " he continued. "The answer to guilt is Grace."

"The divine influence acting in the heart?" I asked.

"Grace is the ever-present Pattern of Perfection," Ernest said.

The word *pattern* appears twenty-five times in *The Voice Celestial*.

Ernest believed that "design and pattern exist in everything, and as a result of treatment a definite objective manifestation will exactly correspond to the prayer," and recalled that "Plato held that there is a divine pattern for everything 'here' and that 'things' are copies of what eternally exists 'over there.' It is interesting that modern science has returned to this view. Physics has become metaphysical and is dealing with the physical universe more in the nature of a shadow cast by an invisible substance. How closely modern science confirms Moses, who was told to 'make all things according to the pattern showed to thee in the mount.' "

"Dr. Gustaf Strömberg," I said, "seems to take the position in his book *The Soul of the Universe* that there are electromagnetic fields, which create the patterns of all living organisms, and he looks upon these patterns as molds which originate in the cosmos."

"No earthly father!" Ernest reaffirmed. "Man and animal are like Elijah who came out of nowhere and returned into glory." He paused. "If they originate in heaven, they will eventually be restored to the bosom of the Father," he concluded.

It was apparent to me that this meant to him another link in the chain of evidence in favor of the survival of personality, a support to his conviction of immortality—if the pattern was never born, it could never die.

He felt, too, that symbols had value *only* if related to the essence or pattern that they represent. "Beyond this," he

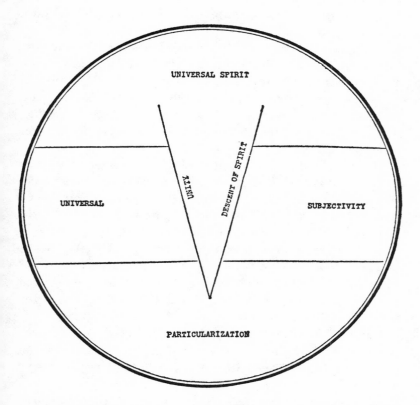

*This chart shows, first, the Universal Spirit; then the Universal
Soul or Subjectivity, which is the medium of all thought, power
and action; then the particularization or manifestation of Spirit.*

*The point drawn down through the center symbolizes the de-
scent of Spirit into matter, or form. It is necessary that Spirit be
manifested in order to express Itself. The word Unity on the
descending line shows that all come from the One. Man reenacts
the whole Universal Life, and his nature is identical with Spirit.
What is true of the Whole is true of any one of Its undivided
parts. Man comes to a point of individualization in the Whole
and is subject to the Law of the Whole.*

said, "symbols may appear to give importance to the relative, to give reality to 'things' apart from mental-spiritual substance or causation."

The value of a symbol, Ernest thought, lay in its interpretation, and he spent his life in clarifying the patterns of the Eternal in which he had absolute faith. He was not opposed to symbols but cautioned as to their use and meaning, and he made popular, through use in his textbook, the following, which represented to him the descent of Spirit into matter or as matter.

Since his teens, Ernest had studied symbology with great interest—and concluded that architecture, art and poetry were tools whereby symbols could be used to refer the mind back to *The Thing Itself,* to the perfect pattern latent in Spirit.

Relative to architecture, he said, "We are building a round church to symbolize that our arms embrace the whole world. . . . the essence is universality. The pattern oneness." He had, over the years, collected 102 different symbols that could be associated with *Truth,* such as scales, which represent justice; the lyre (music); lamp of knowledge (man, spirit and mind). As symbolic art these were entered into a design to be painted in a many colored mural on the choir wall of Founder's Church and titled "The Wisdom of the Ages."

In September of 1959 we took a jaunt into the desert. On our return to Los Angeles, we carefully reviewed our finished manuscript of *The Voice Celestial* and it was sent to the publisher. One-third of his task was done.

Discussions were resumed about this biography before I returned home, and in October he wrote to me in Oakland that all was going well with the church building. The cornerstone had been placed inside the church on Sunday, October 18, with hundreds of people in attendance and short speeches by Ernest and others. To a bronze box they entrusted messages to the Church of the year 2059, one message by Ernest, another by Dr. Hornaday and a third by the Board of Trustees, the keynote of which was the conviction that the philosophy of Religious Science would in the next hundred years find an acceptance in the hearts of men and that the age-old yoke of fear, superstition and dogma would have disappeared.

Ernest himself, as he wrote me, had done all he could through his life and teaching to clarify, unify and protect it. He had prayed that a group had arrived in spiritual evolution who had enough love for each other to cooperate in a spirit of freedom in this endeavor. He trusted God to do the rest.

Thus, insofar as he was able, he had finished another task. Two-thirds of the work was done.

In November I flew down, at his request, and we continued our discussions on the biography. I was distressed to find him looking thin and worn and spoke to him about exercise. He looked at me absent-mindedly and made no reply. Our conversations came to an end several weeks later. He embraced me warmly as I left. I never saw him again.

I was at home in Oakland for the Christmas season, and as I read my brother's message in *Science of Mind* magazine, I was moved by his frequent references to Christmas and the message of Jesus affirming that the Great Teacher demonstrated to us that man can exercise creative power when he realizes that the very purpose of his life is to express the nature of the Divine. "Just as Jesus recognized that he was one with the Father, so must we. It is the birth of such an awareness which we should let happen to us at this Christmastime."

I had no premonition then, but looking back I have wondered sometimes how far across the border Ernest was looking when he wrote

At this Christmastime you and I should look across the new horizon. . . . God's Love always embraces us, His Wisdom is always within us, and His Joy is ours to share. Just as surely as tomorrow shall come and the sun shall rise again across the darkness of the horizon and spill its beauty and warmth to awaken the valleys into fertility, so shall this be a new day in each of our lives, bringing us into a greater joy of living because of a greater consciousness of the Almighty within our own souls.

On December 27, 1959, Dr. Hornaday officiated at the last service to be given at the Wiltern Theater. His subject was "Behold, I Make All Things New," and in a letter to me dated the last day of that year, my brother wrote, "We are opening the new church on Sunday so have been very busy. It is beautiful and we are very happy about it."

And so the great day came. The church was dedicated. It was January 3, 1960.

There were ceremonies throughout the day, beginning at eight-thirty, with Dr. Reginald Armor officiating in a Meditation Hour, a regular feature of the church, and followed at nine-thirty and again at eleven-thirty with identical services, except that Dr. William Hornaday gave the address at the first service and Dr. Ernest Holmes at the second. There were two great bouquets of chrysanthemums on the platform, but they dimmed under the carefully modulated lights from the director's and recorder's booth, until the speaker and the pulpit were visible in dramatic simplicity.

At four o'clock that afternoon there was a final ceremony very dear to the heart of the founder. Dr. Mabel Kinney made the presentation speech of the Hazel Holmes Memorial Organ and then, with the voices of the cathedral choir under the direction of Edward Novis winging in song, George Goulding struck the opening chords.

And Ernest Holmes, listening to the glory of the music, knew that his work was done.

He gave his last sermon in Founder's Church on February 21.

At Eastertime, on April 7, 1960, he went to join his wife.

I flew to Los Angeles two days later to be present at the funeral services in Founder's Church.

During the day over five thousand people paid their respects to Ernest, filing quietly in and out of the church.

Nearly two thousand crowded into the service, and another thousand heard it by public address system in other rooms.

There was a great outpouring of Ernest's friends. Forty of us relatives had gathered in the minister's study and were ushered to the front seats in the sanctuary. The loft facing the congregation was filled with the vested choir and great masses of floral designs were stretched across the platform. Dr. Hornaday stood on one side and Dr. Armor on the other.

When Dr. Hornaday rose to speak, his words were simple and from the heart. He confined himself largely to the teachings of the founder and the Bible. He emphasized Ernest's confidence in immortality, and said, "Just one year ago Ernest wrote, 'Man is born of eternal day, not because he wills or wishes it, not because he labors or strives toward it, not because he earns it as a reward, but simply because Spirit has breathed life into him and the Spirit which has breathed life into him cannot take it away!' "

Dr. Hornaday continued: "The great movement of Religious Science—with its ministers, its teachers, its practitioners, its thousands of members—stands today as a living memorial to the insight, love, givingness, faith and conviction of this great, great man."

He closed on the note my brother would have wished, by reading Ernest's poem of hope and joy:

> They are not dead.
> Those we have fondled to our breast
> Have found sweet peace and quiet rest;
> They live and move among the bless'd.
>
> They are not dead.
> Beyond earth's slowly setting sun
> Another life has just begun;
> Another course of action run.
>
> They are not dead.
> Beyond earth's storms and mists and rain
> Beyond all sorrow, fear and pain
> New life, new joy, shall spring again.

They are not dead.
They have but found new songs to sing,
New life and laughter there to bring
To love's eternal spring.

Index